General editor
Peter
Herriot

New
Essential
Psychology

Attitudes
and
Decisions

J. Richard Eiser and *J. van der Pligt*

Attitudes and Decisions

WITHDRAWN

Routledge

London and New York

First published in 1988 by
Routledge
11 New Fetter Lane, London EC4P 4EE
29 West 35th Street, New York NY 10001

© 1988 J. Richard Eiser and J. van der Pligt

Printed in Great Britain by
The Guernsey Press Co. Ltd., Guernsey, Channel Islands

British Library Cataloguing in Publication Data
Eiser, J. Richard (John Richard), 1945–
    Attitudes and decisions.—(New essential
psychology).
    1. Attitudes – Sociological perspectives
I. Title   II. Pligt, J. van der (Joop)
III. Series
303.3'8

Library of Congress Cataloging in Publication Data
Eiser, J. Richard.
    Attitudes and decisions/J. Richard Eiser and J. van der Pligt.
    p. cm.—(New essential psychology)
    1. Attitude (Psychology) 2. Decision-making. I. Pligt, J. van
der (Joop) II. Title. III. Series.
    BF327.E36 1988
    153.8'3—dc19

ISBN 0-415-01112-4

Contents

Preface

This book is an attempt to bring together two areas of psychological research that have often been considered rather separately. The concept of attitude has long been a central part of social psychological theories. Many would argue that it is the *most* important concept in social psychology; nor can it be ignored by other social sciences. Depending on the orientation of particular authors, attitudes have been viewed as a kind of motive, a reflection of underlying values and/or personality traits, learned reactions to stimuli and/or variables that intervene between a stimulus and a response, subjective evaluations, self-descriptions, predictors of behaviour or enduring cognitive structures. In our view, progress in attitude theory now depends on regarding attitudes within a broader context. Attitudes do not exist in splendid isolation within the heads of individuals. They are expressed in action and in interaction with other people. They are communicated through symbols, the meaning of which depends on specific contexts and cultural assumptions that *other* people share. They are not mere meditative reflections on the world, but a way of planning our interaction *with* the world. In short, attitudes are both a social product and an intrinsic part of social action.

The study of decision-making has traditionally been approached from rather different standpoints. Again, decision-making is not a purely psychological concept. But, within other social sciences, economics, rather than sociology or political science, has been where decision-making has been afforded most attention. Within psychology, decision-making has mostly been regarded as a form of cognition. Even so, theories of decision-making have tended to owe less to broader trends within cognitive psychology than to mathematical models, often borrowed from or shared with other disciplines such as economics and statistics. Such models typically describe optimal choices on the basis of more or less uncertain estimates of particular outcomes. More recently, a number of observations have made the study of decision-making more authentically psychological. First, it has been repeatedly shown that we do not handle probabilistic information in the way that these statistical models say we should, but instead base our choices on rules and strategies derived from past experience with similar problems. Learning and memory are therefore crucial to the process of decision-making. Second, we deal with information differently if it relates to something that we care strongly about or value. So attitudes and motives are crucial too. Third, human decision-making is not just a one-off or all-for-nothing business. Although we are affected by the consequences of our decisions, we may still be able to revise our decisions in the light of such consequences. Thus the process of decision-making involves interaction with, and feedback from, the environment. Since the environment includes other people who are also decision-makers, it is a *social* process, depending on communication with others and the interpretations we make of others' thoughts and behaviour.

All this points to a convergence between the two broad areas of attitudes and decisions. In exploring this convergence, however, another dichotomy needs to be questioned. This is the distinction between so-called 'theoretical' and 'applied' research in social psychology. One point that is missed by those who cherish this distinction is that many of the 'theoretical' or 'basic' issues of present-day social psychology are the 'applied' issues of not so long ago. Work on prejudice and intergroup discrimination is a prime example. The fact that we have *theories* of prejudice and discrimination does not make such work any less applied or applicable – rather the contrary. Good applied research should also be theoretical. By the same token, however, good theories – in our discipline at least – should not be mere ethereal abstractions. They should relate to the concerns of real people, living in real time and in real places. If they do not, their explanations will be implausible and their predictions inaccurate. 'Applied' research, for us, is just research that attends to this context of people, time and place. Such work can and does contribute at least as much to the development of theory as the deep thoughts of any purist.

Attention to the real context of people's attitudes and decisions brings out another important point, and one that may partly serve as a protection against the criticism that such research is too 'individualistic'. Not all decisions and attitudes are free, either in the sense of being freely expressed, or in the sense of being freely acquired. The time and place and social groups to which we belong constrain not only what we do, but also what we feel and think, and what we *can*, or believe we can, do. Our attitudes and decisions influence how we behave, but rarely, if ever, are our actions or decisions unrestricted by the environment in which we live.

The view of social psychology expressed in this book is one that we have developed over a long period of collaboration. It also reflects the influence of many other colleagues' insight and advice, which we acknowledge with gratitude. More directly, we wish to record our thanks to Martin Böcker, Karin George, Marian Gowen and Catherine Mullins for their help with the preparation of the manuscript.

1

The language of attitudes

What are attitudes?

Many definitions of attitude have been offered, but there is one paradox with which they all must deal: on the one hand, we talk about our attitudes as though they were something personal or private 'inside our heads' but, on the other hand, *when* we talk about our attitudes, we expect other people to understand us and even to agree with us. The reason for this is that an attitude is not just some vague kind of mood or sensation, but a form of experience that (a) *refers* to specific objects, events, people or issues, and (b) is primarily *evaluative*. We *express* our attitudes by describing the *objects* of our experience in evaluative terms. An attitude is not just a 'good feeling' or a 'bad feeling', but a feeling that something really *is* good or bad or whatever. We do not typically treat our attitude as 'just a matter of opinion'. We regard our attitude as 'the truth', at least until someone can introduce new facts or arguments to change our mind.

What happens when people disagree? Sometimes the

consequences of attitudinal disagreement can be very serious indeed. People may kill each other, or start wars because of disagreements that, when all is said and done, are attitudinal. Friendships and family ties may be broken off, and others left unformed, for the same reason. But above all there will be argument, debate, talk – sometimes bitter, sometimes good-humoured, but talk nonetheless – with each side trying to convince the other (or any uncommitted bystander) that their interpretation of events, their view of the world, is the correct one.

The very fact that people disagree with one another is in itself a challenge for theories of attitude formation and change. Our interpretation of the world about us is *selective*. Indeed, so immense is the amount of information to which we potentially have access that it could not be anything else. Selectivity involves paying more attention to some pieces of information and less, or none at all, to others. If we never did the equivalent of saying 'enough is enough', if we were never satisfied with less than complete knowledge of the circumstances surrounding any event we had to interpret, we could never come to a decision, and hence we could never *act* in any purposeful way.

The term 'bias' is often used by psychologists to refer to this kind of selectivity, but without necessarily any pejorative connotations. Whether selectivity is fair or unfair is something that needs to be judged, if at all, according to other criteria. These may include the plausible relevance of information attended to or ignored, whether irrelevant characteristics of the source of the information affect the attention it receives, and whether the decisions produce welcome or unwelcome consequences. Selectivity as such, however, is inevitable. Here, though, we come across what we believe to be a widespread, though not inevitable, aspect of human nature. People typically have poor insight into the extent to which, and the ways in which, their interpretations of events are selective. Instead, they experience their own view of the world as the only reality – the truth, the whole truth and nothing but the truth. Hence they may find it difficult to understand, still less to accept, the views of the world held by others with whom they disagree.

Whatever people's reluctance to understand or accept alternative points of view, however, they cannot always just ignore the fact that others can disagree with them. For many, it is not just *freedom* of thought that is at stake, but whether their thoughts are right or wrong – whether, in short, they have a grasp on reality. Thinking 'wrong' thoughts can have very serious consequences indeed, and we are not very far away historically from the burning of heretics at the stake. Nor, in our own age, can political or religious dissenters feel secure from death, torture or intimidation. If totalitarian societies allow for only one definition of reality, and are prepared to enforce this definition by brute force, more democratic societies may still impose constraints on the range of permissible dissent, and the manner in which it may be expressed.

As at a societal, so at a personal, level there will be differences in degree of tolerance for alternative points of view. But even so, there is a difference between 'tolerating' dissent from one's own opinion, and accepting that others' views are no less valid than one's own. Once we express our feelings and interpretations in the form of statements about objects, people, or events in the real world, we are claiming a special relationship with reality – a correspondence between what we feel to be and what really is. However, since these same objects, people or events can be parts of *other* people's consciousness, and these other people are making their own claims on reality too, whenever we make such statements, we run the risk of being contradicted. Even against a background of societal and interpersonal tolerance, we may need to be able to defend and explain our attitudes, if only to secure the tolerance of others. This we do primarily through language. It is for this reason that language lies at the very core, not merely of attitude research, but of attitudinal experience.

Attitude measurement

Because language is so important to attitudinal experience and expression, it is only natural that most techniques for measuring attitudes rely heavily on verbal material in the form of interviews or questionnaires. The real point at issue is how people's answers to questions can be converted to a numerical score. The advantage of numerical scores is that one can then compare different people's attitudes with one another, or the attitudes of a single person in different contexts or at different times. The

3

disadvantage of numerical scores is the risk of reducing something that may be rich and complex to a single index that then assumes an importance out of all proportion to its meaning. Much the same kind of concern surrounds other forms of psychological measurement, such as intelligence testing. Just knowing that 'Mary has an IQ of 128' tells us nothing about the relative balance of different intellectual skills and abilities that contribute to her overall score.

Numbers and measurements by themselves are innocent. Everything depends on what assumptions are made in their interpretation, and the purposes of prediction or classification for which they are used. The predominant assumption in attitude measurement is that people differ from each other in terms of their positions along some dimension or dimensions. Although there are a number of techniques of multidimensional scaling of attitudes, by far the most common form of attitude measurement involves differentiating between people along a single dimension according to how favourable or unfavourable, or pro or anti, they are towards some specific issue. This approach acknowledges the potential complexity of attitudes, but, on pragmatic grounds, defines *in advance* what object or issue is to be the focus of the attitudinal inquiry, and what aspect of people's attitudes towards that object or issue is of concern to the researcher (Thurstone, 1928).

From this point of view, what attitude measurement attempts to do – and *all* that it attempts to do – is to provide, in quantitative terms, an answer to the question 'How much does this person approve or disapprove of this object or issue?' Such simplicity is bought at a price, and the price is a degree of self-restraint over the inferences one allows oneself to draw from the fact that someone has a particular attitude score on a particular issue. Even so, it is a price worth paying for access to one of the most practical of all psychological techniques. Here, then, is a quick guide to two techniques aimed at quantifying simply how pro or anti a person is on some specific issue.

Thurstone's 'method of equal-appearing intervals' (Thurstone, 1928) involves constructing a set of statements (or 'items') that range from expressions of extremely anti to extremely pro viewpoints on an issue, ideally with all intermediate positions between the extremes being evenly represented. Each item

4

attitude-scale construction requires judges to rate the degree of expressed favourability towards the issue of the statements from which the final scale is constructed. These ratings provide the data from which the scale values of the different statements are calculated. Thurstone's assumption was that these scale values should not be systematically affected by judges' own attitudes on the issue. In other words, pro and anti judges should rate the expressed favourability of the statements in the same way.

Hovland and Sherif (1952) took an established scale of attitudes 'toward the social position of the Negro' (Hinckley, 1932) and had the statements rated for favourability by different groups of judges, who were black, or were white with either anti-black, 'average' or pro-black attitudes. The main finding was that black and pro-black white judges rated many more of the items as expressing moderately or extremely anti-black positions. This effect is usually termed *contrast*, in that it appears to take the form of judges contrasting, or 'pushing away', their ratings of the items, towards the end of the scale opposed to their own opinions. A secondary finding was that a few of the items, particularly those close to the favourable extreme, were *assimilated*, or 'pulled towards' judges' own positions, i.e. judged as more extremely pro by pro-black (and black) judges.

Sherif and Hovland (1961) went on to develop their 'assimilation-contrast' model of attitudinal judgment. This states that when we judge other people's attitudes on some issue, we use our own position as an 'anchor' or comparison standard. When we hear or read a statement close to our own position (and of the kind we ourselves would agree with) we 'assimilate' it, i.e. rate it as more pro if we are pro, and more anti if we are anti. However, if the statement is beyond the range of positions we would accept, we 'contrast' it, i.e. rate it as more anti if we are pro, and more pro if we are anti. It follows from this that people whose own attitudes are more extreme (whether pro or anti) should give more extreme or 'polarized' ratings of a set of statements at *both* ends of the anti/pro dimension.

There followed a number of studies (Sellitz, Edrich and Cook, 1965; Upshaw, 1962, 1965; Zavalloni and Cook, 1965), using the same issue of attitudes towards black people, all conducted in the United States. These confirmed the Hovland and Sherif (1952) findings, and addressed a number of methodological and

7

theoretical issues. According to Upshaw (1962, 1965), the way any statement is rated will depend on where it falls within the judge's 'perspective', a term used by Upshaw to refer to the *range* of positions a person takes into account when making judgments. From this point of view, what is critical is how the judge defines or fixes the end-points of the judgment scale in relation to the end-points of his or her 'perspective'. It is as though the judge first decides what kind of position to call 'extremely anti' and what kind of position to call 'extremely pro', and then assigns ratings to the individual statements depending on how near they are to either of these end-points. If different judges (or groups of judges) *mean* something different by labels like 'extremely pro', then they will use the rating scale differently. According to Upshaw, someone whose own position is extremely pro will have a perspective that extends further in the pro direction than will a more anti person, and so will be likely to rate statements as closer to the anti extreme of the scale. Similarly, someone who has a very wide perspective will tend to see more items as close to the neutral point, whereas someone who has a very narrow perspective will see more of the same set of items as close to the extremes, and hence will give more polarized ratings. Upshaw, however, has generally not been particularly concerned to predict what factors lead judges to adopt wider or narrower perspectives (see Upshaw and Ostrom, 1984, for a recent account of perspective theory).

It may seem a rather trivial conclusion to say that people give different judgments because they are using language differently, but in fact it is very important. Differences in linguistic usage can reflect profound social and historical changes. If we go back to the Hovland and Sherif (1952) data, we can observe items that were regarded as moderately or extremely favourable by judges in the earlier study by Hinckley (1932), being viewed by pro-black (but not anti-black) judges as definitely anti-black. Two clearly segregationist and/or racist statements that come into this category are the following: 'The Negro should have the advantage of all social benefits of the white man but be limited to his own race in the practice thereof' and 'Although the Negro is rather inferior mentally, he has a fuller and deeper religious life than the white man, and thus has an emphatic claim upon our social approval'. At the same time, the anti

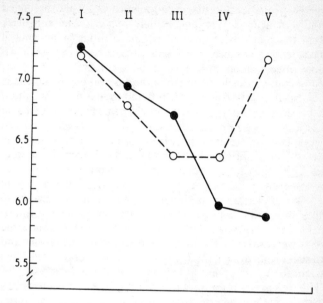

Figure 1.1 Relationship between judges' attitudes and polarization (mean differences between ratings of favourable and unfavourable items)

●——● relationship observed by Zavalloni and Cook (1965); ○----○ approximate form of relationship predicted by Sherif and Hovland (1961). Attitude groups: I, Black students, actively involved; II, Pro-black white students, actively involved; III Pro-black white students, not actively involved; IV Anti-black white students, not actively involved; V Anti-black white students, actively involved.

(reprinted with permission from J. R. Eiser. *Social Psychology: Attitudes, Cognition and Social Behaviour*, p. 151, Cambridge University Press, 1986.)

The main purpose of the Eiser (1971) study was to demonstrate that categorization (or 'accentuation') effects could occur in the judgment of attitude statements. Judges had to rate 64 statements about the non-medical use of drugs in terms of a scale labelled 'extremely permissive' to 'extremely restrictive'. In the control condition these were presented as statements 'drawn from newspapers', whereas in the experimental condition the 32 more pro-drug items were all attributed to one newspaper, and the 32 more anti-drug items to another (judges were told that fictitious names had been substituted for the real names of two newspapers). As predicted, this manipulation led to an accentuation of judged differences between the two halves of the item series, with the pro-drug items being judged more 'permissive' and the anti-drug items more 'restrictive' than in the control condition. Polarization of judgment was also influenced by judges' own attitudes on the issue, but again not exactly as Sherif and Hovland (1961) would have predicted. The most polarized ratings were given by the most pro-drug judges, whereas those with most anti-drug attitudes tended to rate more statements close to the neutral point of the scale.

This raises again the problem of why, in the earlier studies (e.g. Hovland and Sherif, 1952; Sellitz *et al.*, 1965), anti-black judges failed to show the predicted polarization effects shown by pro-black judges. A rather mundane, but eminently plausible, reason might be that anti-black judges are confused by the instructions to rate the anti statements (with which they agree) as 'unfavourable' and the pro statements (which they personally regard unfavourably) as 'favourable'. In other words, some judges might misinterpret the instructions to mean that they had to say whether their *own evaluation* of the statements was 'favourable' or 'unfavourable'. Although such an error might not influence the responses of the pro judges, it could lead to some anti judges using the scale the wrong way round, which could account for the observed effects on the means for the anti group as a whole. Support for this possibility comes from a study by Romer (1983), who checked how well his judges had understood the standard instructions. In fact, many misunderstood them, but when these were excluded, the results were more as predicted by the assimilation-contrast model, with anti judges giving more polarized ratings than neutral judges. The issue used by Romer, however – that of abortion – was different from that in the earlier studies.

An alternative possibility, originally favoured by Eiser (1971; Eiser and Stroebe, 1972), was that the response pattern shown by anti-black judges reflected a reluctance on their part to label the anti-black items with which they agreed as unfavourable towards black people, since this might carry with it the implication that they personally were prejudiced or racist. The effects of judges' attitudes in the Eiser (1971) study might reflect a similar reluctance on the part of anti-drug judges to characterize themselves as restrictive. In more formal terms, it was proposed that judgment of attitude statements depends both on judges' own agreement/disagreement with the statements and the *value connotations of the response language* that judges have to use. If it is assumed that, taking one's sample as a whole, a phrase like 'favourable towards black people' was seen as 'better' or more evaluatively positive, than a phrase like 'unfavourable towards black people', then pro-black judges would be using a response language congruent with their own evaluations of the statements, whereas anti-black judges would not. The same should apply to pro-drug and anti-drug judges if it is assumed that the term 'permissive' generally carried more positive connotations than the term 'restrictive'. Polarization of judgment (in Sherif and Hovland's terms, assimilation-contrast) should therefore depend on whether judges' evaluations of the items are congruent with the value connotations of the response language. If they can apply a 'good' label to the items they think are 'good' and a 'bad' label to the items they think are 'bad', they should polarize; however if they have to apply a 'bad' label to 'good' items, and *vice versa*, they may avoid making extreme discriminations on such a scale.

When it comes to explaining the results of previous studies, this interpretation is *post hoc* and ultimately untestable, since we cannot be sure how subjects would have viewed the response scales presented to them. What *can* be tested is the prediction that deliberate manipulation of the response language should produce differences in polarization of judgment. This prediction has been supported in a series of experiments which have shared the basic feature of providing judges with different kinds of response scales. Some of these are chosen so that the pro end is marked by an evaluatively positive label and the anti end by an evaluatively negative label (P+ scales), and others (A+ scales) are chosen so that the anti end is labelled positively and the pro end negatively.

The consistent finding is one of an interaction between judges' attitudes and the type of response scale: on P+ scales, pros polarize most and antis least, whereas on A+ scales, antis polarize most and pros least. Put differently, judges give most polarized ratings on scales where their 'own end' is the more positively labelled (see Figure 1.2). This has been found on issues such as adolescents' attitudes towards adult authority (Eiser and Mower White, 1974, 1975), risk-taking and avoidance (Eiser, 1976), and drug-use (Eiser and van der Pligt, 1982). For example, in the Eiser and Mower White (1975) study the P+ scales were disobedient–obedient, rude–polite, unhelpful–helpful and uncooperative–cooperative and the A+ scales, bold–timid, adventurous–unadventurous, with-it–old-fashioned and creative–uncreative. A number of other effects due to response language are also observed, in particular due to negatively valued adjectives being seen as applicable to more extreme positions (Eiser and van der Pligt, 1982, 1984a; van der Pligt and Eiser, 1980).

Language and persuasion

Research into the judgment of attitude statements therefore raises the general question of how people choose between alternative modes of attitude expression. When people make more extreme discriminations along a given continuum, this tells us is that they have accepted the response language as an appropriate way of talking about the issue as they see it. If the response language is incompatible with their preferred mode of talking or thinking about the issue, they will avoid using it as a way of expressing their own evaluations (van der Pligt and van Dijk, 1979).

Another way of putting this is that our view of social issues is selective, so that some aspects of the issue are *salient* to us personally whereas other aspects are not. Differences in salience may then be reflected in the kind of language we prefer to use to describe our opinions and those of other people (van der Pligt and Eiser, 1984). People who prefer to talk about the same issue

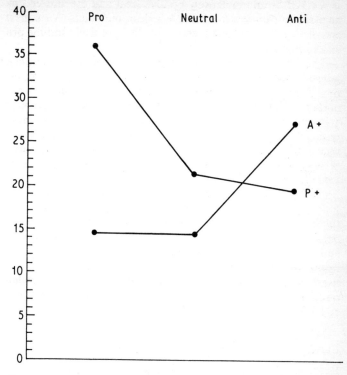

Figure 1.2 Mean item group differences (polarization of judgment) as a function of judges' attitudes (pro, neutral, anti) and value connotations of scales (P+ scales; pro end positive vs. A+ scales anti end positive) (data from Eiser and Mower White, 1975). Ratings of items scored from 0 (anti end) to 100 (pro end)

(reprinted with permission from J. R. Eiser. *Social Psychology: Attitudes, Cognition and Social Behaviour*, p. 162, Cambridge University Press, 1986) in terms of different kinds of language will generally be regarding different aspects of the issue as salient – in other words, as they selectively experience it, it will be a different issue for those on either side.

Consider, for instance, the war between Britain and Argentina over the Falkland (or Malvinas) Islands. Either side's involvement could be portrayed by supporters as 'defending national honour' and by opponents as 'seeking a military distraction from economic problems at home'. The truth or falsehood of either construction of events is not the point at issue here. What is important is that different *evaluations* of the rights and wrongs of what was done go along with different ways of selectively thinking about and *describing* the whole sorry affair.

This relationship between thought and language may operate both ways. We do not only use language to tell others what we think, we use language in order to persuade others to think the same way too. Propaganda, advertising and simple debate share the features of trying to increase the salience, to other people, of particular interpretations of events. This raises the question of whether people may sometimes come to adopt particular attitudes on an issue because of the kind of evaluative language they are led to use. This possibility was investigated in two studies by Eiser and Ross (1977) and Eiser and Pancer (1979).

The study by Eiser and Ross (1977) used the issue of Canadian students' attitudes towards capital punishment. The experiment was introduced to subjects as concerned with 'the psycholinguistic problem of directive semantic search strategies', in other words, with how being provided with words to incorporate in an essay, as opposed to having to search for appropriate words, influenced 'stylistic structure and verbal fluency'. With this rationale, subjects were asked to write a short essay on capital punishment (but without being told to support a pro or anti position) incorporating as many words as possible from a list of 15. In the *pro-bias* condition, they all implied a negative evaluation of capital punishment (e.g. callous, sadistic). Subjects' own attitudes on the issue were then assessed. As predicted, those who had written essays incorporating pro-bias words gave more pro-capital punishment responses on average than those who had used the anti-bias words. Subjects whose initial attitudes (assessed earlier by a more general questionnaire administered in a supposedly unrelated study) were more pro incorporated more of the pro-bias words in their essays than did anti subjects, whereas anti subjects incorporated more of the anti-bias words than did pro subjects.

The Eiser and Pancer (1979) study replicated this design, using the issue of adolescents' attitudes towards adult authority. In this study the word-lists (based on the Eiser and Mower White, 1974, 1975 results) included both evaluatively positive and evaluatively negative words. As before, the pro-bias condition appeared to produce shifts of attitude in a more pro direction, and the anti-bias condition, shifts in a more anti direction (with no attitude change being apparent in a control condition in which no words were provided). However, this experimental effect was short-lived, as shown by the fact that there was no significant difference between the groups when subjects' attitudes were re-assessed one week later.

Although language can be used as an important persuasive tool, one should beware of considering it as all-powerful. In the next chapter we shall describe research that shows that verbally expressed attitudes (and by implication, changes in attitude at a verbal level) are not necessarily translated into overt social action. Even without considering overt behaviour, however, a question remains concerning how persuasive communication produces attitude change.

One of the most influential attempts to answer this question is research on what are termed *cognitive responses to persuasion* (Petty and Cacioppo, 1985). The basic idea is that attitude change is dependent on the thoughts in which people engage when they receive a persuasive communication. Various factors can influence the extent to which people will 'elaborate' in their own minds the information and arguments presented to them, and scrutinize what is said to them as opposed to accepting it at face value.

One such factor is that of subjects' involvement with the issue, that is the extent to which it is personally relevant or important to them. Petty and Cacioppo (1979) had students react to messages proposing changes to regulations at either their own, or another, university. The messages contained either strong arguments (which would stand up to close scrutiny) or weak arguments (against which counter-arguments could easily be thought up).

The strong message was more likely to be accepted under conditions of high than low personal relevance, whereas the reverse was true for the weak message. This is taken to imply that, under conditions of low involvement or perceived relevance, subjects were less likely to think carefully about the information they were given.

From these and similar results, Petty and Cacioppo develop a distinction between what they call 'central' and 'peripheral' routes to persuasion. The 'central' route is said to involve thoughtful weighing-up of the pros and cons of the relevant positions advocated in any message. The picture is one of someone carefully thinking through the information presented and *deciding* what position to take. The 'peripheral' route involves a more simplistic processing of information, and more reflex-like responding to evaluative and/or emotional cues provided by the context. A comparable distinction, between 'systematic' and 'heuristic' processing of persuasive information, has been proposed by Chaiken (1980). The contrast between 'mindful' and 'mindless' behaviour introduced by Langer (1978) is also quite similar.

Language can therefore influence attitudes in more than one way. On the one hand, it is likely to be the medium through which new information is brought to mind, and through which new possibilities are asserted and new arguments are proposed. It can provide a framework for calculation and decision-making, whether of a practical or a moral nature. At the same time, though, language can directly evoke feelings of good and bad, or right and wrong, and hence prompt a selective and potentially one-sided interpretation of reality.

Many philosophers have pointed out that words can fulfil different communication functions at the same time. Nowell-Smith (1956), for instance, distinguishes between the descriptive, evaluative and gerundive meanings of many words in ordinary language. For instance, a word like 'generous' (1) denotes or describes a certain class of action or personal disposition (giving, etc.), (2) implies that this class of action is 'good', and (3) implies that this is the kind of action one *ought* to perform in the appropriate context. Whether or not these different meanings are considered independent of one another, the important point here is that *all three* kinds of meaning are part of the concept of attitude. Attitudes are (1) concerned with *describable* objects and events, (2) *evaluations* of such objects and events, and (3) guides to how one *ought to act* with respect to such objects or events. The structure of attitudes is reflected in the structure of language through which they are expressed.

2

The relationship between attitudes and behaviour

The notion of consistency

One of the most influential ideas in social psychology is the idea that people do not separate their various attitudes into different cognitive compartments, but instead organize their beliefs, feelings and decisions about how to behave into more general structures. The main principle of organization here is assumed to be that of *consistency*, otherwise termed 'cognitive consistency', or 'balance'.

The last term comes from the work of Heider (1946), whose 'balance theory' was the original formulation of this principle. According to Heider, people are motivated to organize their evaluations of objects, people and events into simplified structures that contain the minimum possible sources of instability or contradiction. The best-known aspect of balance theory concerns the relationship of our own attitudes to those we think that other people hold. Do we like people if we think they share our attitudes? And do we change our attitudes so that they are more similar to those of people we like?

Heider's theory rests on a distinction between 'balanced' and 'unbalanced' triads or structures, the former being those where evaluative inconsistency or ambivalence is minimized. In the simplest case, this is said to apply either when you perceive someone you like as agreeing with you, or when you think that someone you dislike disagrees with you. Balanced structures are assumed to be easier to learn and remember, to be more resistant to change, to be more easily predicted on the basis of partial information, and to be experienced as more pleasant. This last assumption in particular reflects the fact that Heider views balance, from a motivational point of view, in essentially 'intra-psychic' terms. That is to say, the need to achieve and preserve 'balance' does *not* arise specifically from the demands of social interaction with other people, but from the intrinsic feeling of 'rightness' or 'good form' inherent in balanced structures. (This has much in common with other concepts derived from Gestalt psychology.)

The notion of balance or consistency was developed by a number of other theorists who introduced various refinements and modifications. According to Newcomb (1968), preference for balance only applies in the context of a positive interpersonal relationship. In other words, you only care if someone else agrees or disagrees with you if you like that other person; you want your friends to agree with you, but you do not care whether people you dislike agree with you or not. Unlike Heider, Newcomb regards preference for balance (in this sense of agreeing-with-friends) as arising from *social* factors facilitating interpersonal communication and attraction (see also Newcomb, 1981).

'Congruity theory' (Osgood and Tannenbaum, 1955), deals specifically with the attitude change produced by learning that a 'source' has evaluated a concept positively or negatively. Unlike the later approach of Petty and Cacioppo (1985), no account is taken of the kind of arguments incorporated in the message. Even so, congruity theory is an attempt to formulate quantitative predictions of the amount of attitude change that will occur following a communication as a function of a person's initial evaluations of both source and concept. Among the interesting features of this approach is the idea that *both* source *and* concept may be evaluated differently after a communication, with the amount of change being inversely related to the extremity of the initial evaluations, that is, the more extremely pro or anti you are at first, the less you are likely to change.

'Affective-cognitive consistency theory' (Rosenberg and Abelson, 1960) is an extension of Heider's work to more complex structures including beliefs about cause and effect (as opposed to approval/disapproval and such like). For instance, this enables one to represent the particular kind of 'inconsistency' (again, more strictly, ambivalence) involved in someone saying that they enjoy smoking, but that they know smoking is likely to damage their health.

More recent theoretical developments include emphasis on other organizing principles in addition to balance as defined by Heider (Insko, 1984), and also on the role of individual differences in cognitive style that may affect people's tolerance of, or even desire for, imbalance and ambivalence. Streufert and Streufert (1978) propose the concept of 'general incongruity adaptation level' (GIAL) to account for the fact that sometimes individuals seem to seek greater uncertainty or complexity (if their GIAL is high) and sometimes less (if it is low). They argue that the motive for balance may depend on both personal and situational factors. This can be represented by thinking of different people having different GIALs in different contexts. For example, some people may be more tolerant than others of their friends holding different political views to their own, but less tolerant of their having different tastes in leisure activities.

The three-component view of attitudes

A good many studies have attempted to relate verbal measures of attitude on the one hand to various forms of social behaviour on the other. Do people who express racist attitudes at a verbal level, for instance, act towards members of other races in ways that display open hostility or discrimination? The answer seems to be, not necessarily. In a widely cited review, Wicker (1969) concluded that only in a minority of studies was any close relationship found between verbally expressed attitudes and overt behaviour. This conclusion, and the literature on which it is based, is clearly very damaging for any approach that treats attitude as a major cause of behaviour, and tries to justify attitude research by claiming that it allows one to make better behavioural predictions.

A number of theoretical approaches allow for a mis-match between attitude and action without taking this as evidence that attitudes are unimportant and attitude research is irrelevant. One of the most important of these is the 'three-component' view of attitudes, proposed by Rosenberg and Hovland (1960). As shown in Figure 2.1, attitude is assigned the status of an intervening variable between 'stimuli' (objects, people and events) and 'responses' of various kinds to these stimuli. An attitude supposedly contains three 'components', defined as 'affect' (concerned with feelings, evaluations and emotions), 'cognition' (concerned with beliefs about whether something is true or false) and 'behaviour' (concerned with intentions and decisions to act). Different qualitative forms of response are associated with each of these three components. It should be noted that verbal responses are *not* treated as a distinct category by themselves, but are split up between the three categories in the same way as other forms of response.

A number of studies based on this model have asked subjects to answer questions about their liking or disliking of an attitude object ('affect'), their beliefs ('cognition') and then compared these measures with each other, and with self-reports of behaviour. Ostrom (1969) conducted such a study using the issue of the Church, whereas Kothandapani (1971) used the issue of contraception. Both concluded that affect, cognition and behaviour were interrelated, although still distinguishable from each other. The debate has since moved to a more sophisticated level with regard to the statistical criteria that are appropriate for distinguishing between sets of intercorrelated items (Breckler, 1984). However, even if we take Ostrom's and Kothandapani's conclusions at face value, we are left with a rather muddling state of affairs whereby any observation of a good match between behaviour and verbally expressed attitudes is taken to show that the different components are interrelated and any observation of a poor match is taken to show that the components are distinct.

This points to the need for research that explores factors that

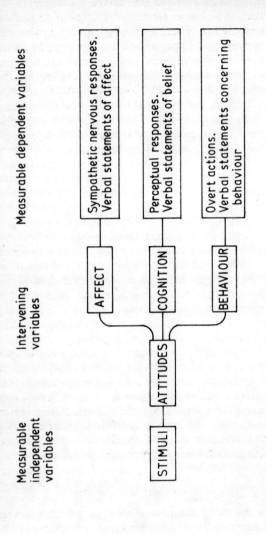

Measurable
independent
variables

Intervening
variables

Measurable dependent variables

STIMULI — ATTITUDES

AFFECT — Sympathetic nervous responses.
Verbal statements of affect

COGNITION — Perceptual responses.
Verbal statements of belief

BEHAVIOUR — Overt actions.
Verbal statements concerning
behaviour

Figure 2.1 The three-component view of attitudes (adapted from Rosenberg and Hovland, 1960)

can make the relationship between the different components higher or lower. Fazio and Zanna (1981) suggest that consistency between behaviour and (the affective component of) attitude is likely to be higher for attitudes acquired through direct, personal experience. Breckler (1984) takes a rather different line, by arguing that some studies may have produced inflated estimates of the associations between affect, cognition and behaviour by relying on self-report measures of the different components, typically without the attitude object being physically present. Breckler points out that this requires subjects to respond not to the object itself, but to its symbolic representation in memory. For this reason, *all* self-report responses, whether supposedly affective, cognitive or behavioural, may be largely mediated by the cognitive system.

Breckler reports two studies in which he obtained measures of affective, cognitive and behavioural measures of attitudes towards snakes. In the first, subjects were actually presented with a live snake. Verbal measures were obtained of all three components, with affect being additionally measured by heart rate, and behaviour by actual approach or avoidance of the snake. The data here suggested that affect, cognition and behaviour were distinct components, though moderately intercorrelated with each other. (The correlations were 0.38 between affect and cognition, 0.50 between affect and behaviour and 0.70 between cognition and behaviour.) The second study followed the same procedure, except that only verbal measures were used, and subjects were only asked to imagine that a live snake was present. Although the three components were still distinguishable statistically, the intercorrelations were far higher and more uniform (ranging from 0.81 to 0.86). In more concrete terms, someone who believed, for instance, that a snake was perfectly harmless might *say* that they wouldn't be afraid of it, and that they would be prepared to pick it up, but if actually confronted with a snake, harmless or not, they might react quite differently.

The prediction of behaviour from attitudes

Although the three-component view of attitudes has guided much research on the relationship between attitudes and behaviour, the problem remains of whether verbal measures of *any* of the three components can be relied upon as predictors of overt action. Fishbein (1967) and Fishbein and Ajzen (1975) have pointed out that, in many of the studies reviewed by Wicker (1969), researchers were using rather general verbal measures of attitude to predict rather specific kinds of behaviour. They argue that the low correlations observed may be due to a mismatch between the levels of generality/specificity in the measures of attitudes and behaviour. When attitude and behaviour are measured at the same level of generality/specificity, the correlations are far higher (Ajzen and Fishbein, 1977).

Central to the Fishbein and Ajzen position is the need to distinguish between attitudes towards some object or person, and attitudes towards some specific *action* to be performed towards that object or person. It is the latter kind of attitude that best predicts behaviour. However, the relationship between attitude and behaviour is still not regarded as a direct one. Behaviour is seen as determined by intention, and intention is a joint product of attitude towards the behaviour and what is termed the 'subjective norm'. This is essentially the summation of beliefs about how other people, whose opinions one values, would regard one's performance or non-performance of the behaviour. The predicted relationships are represented in what Ajzen and Fishbein (1980) refer to as the 'theory of reasoned action' (see Figure 2.2).

This approach has led to successful predictions of behaviour across a range of topic areas, such as smoking (Fishbein, 1982), alcohol use (Budd and Spencer, 1984, 1985), contraception (Davidson and Jaccard, 1975, 1979; Pagel and Davidson, 1984), mothers' choice of bottle or breast-feeding (Manstead, Proffitt and Smart, 1983) and consumer behaviour (Fishbein and Ajzen, 1980). The essential ingredients of this approach are, first, a recognition that the relative importance of attitudinal and normative factors in the determination of intention may vary depending on the context, and, second, a tight specification, within the measures of both attitude and subjective norm, of the precise target and context (when and where) of the behaviour in question. Thus, decisions about contraceptive use, for some people, may be more determined by what they think others may think of their behaviour than by their calculation of personal pay-offs. Also, when it comes to measuring attitudes or subjective norms

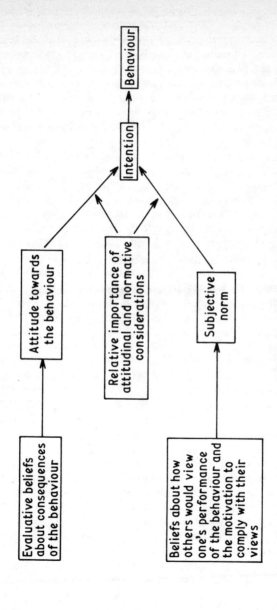

Figure 2.2 The 'theory of reasoned action' (adapted from Ajzen and Fishbein, 1980)

on this issue, the best prediction will not be from some general set of beliefs about, say, 'family planning', but about *oneself* using a *specific* contraceptive method over a *specific* period of time.

Despite its predictive success, the theory of reasoned action has not escaped criticism at both a theoretical and an empirical level. A commonly voiced objection is that the measures of attitude and subjective norm have to be phrased in *so* narrowly specific a manner that they look almost the same as the measure of intention that they predict. The implied allegation is that one is almost ending up with additional measures of intention, rather than of attitudinal or normative factors in any broader sense.

Another problem concerns the dependence of the attitude and subjective norm components on specific individual beliefs. Since the same argument applies to both components, it is simpler to explain this considering how individual beliefs contribute to an overall attitude. In fact, this was also the first step of the model to be developed (Fishbein, 1967). According to the theory of reasoned action, attitude is determined by a limited set of evaluative beliefs that are *salient* to the individual. This takes into account people's limited capacity for attending to different pieces of information at the same time. Although Fishbein and Ajzen (1975) acknowledge that different beliefs may be salient or important for different individuals, in fact they make nothing of this. Instead they recommend a procedure whereby researchers should determine, on any issue, a set of 'modal salient beliefs' that are likely to be seen as important by one's subjects *considered as a whole*. Of course, this is very convenient in that all one's subjects can then be asked the same questions about their beliefs.

The form of the proposed relationship between beliefs and overall attitude (towards an act) is as follows: attitude is the sum of beliefs about the probability of certain consequences happening as a result of the particular act, each multiplied by how good or bad the individual considers each consequence to be. The model is a special case of a more general class of decision theory, termed expectancy-value, or (more specifically) subjective expected utility theory (see Chapter 4). As we shall see, expectancy-value formulae often predict decisions quite well, even though there is reason to doubt that they describe at all realistically the process of decision-making itself.

The nub of the problem is this. How literally is one to take the implication that *before* anyone can decide whether they approve or disapprove of some action or object, they have to search their memory for a set of seven or so salient beliefs, *then* perform a likelihood-by-evaluation multiplication on all these beliefs, and *then* summate the products? In slightly different terms, is the 'theory of reasoned action' merely a catalogue of the kinds of variables one should measure in order to *predict* behaviour, or does it, as its name implies, purport to *explain* how behavioural decisions are made? This question is made more difficult by the ambiguity in the theory over whether individuals are in any sense aware of the mental calculations that supposedly underlie their behavioural decisions.

In fact, the kind of correlational evidence that is taken as support for the theory of reasoned action can be interpreted in different ways. An alternative view put forward by Fazio (1986; Fazio, Powell and Herr, 1983) is that attitude influences behaviour by selectively activating various thoughts stored in memory and hence producing a *selective* perception of the attitude object. In other words, if one already holds a positive attitude towards an object or concept, say 'summer holidays', then this will mean that one is more likely to call to mind positive than negative thoughts or associations (or in Fishbein's terms 'evaluative beliefs'). These associations will then shape one's selective perceptions of what summer holidays are like, which in turn will influence one's decision to go on holiday or not. Thus, according to Fazio, although attitude is dependent on previous positive or negative experiences, it influences, rather than is merely influenced by, the 'evaluative beliefs' a person calls to mind when deciding on a course of action. This is compatible with our argument in Chapter 1 and elsewhere (van der Pligt and Eiser, 1984) that people with different attitudes may see different aspects of an issue as salient. Fishbein and Ajzen (1975) argue that people decide that something is good or bad because of the salient beliefs that they hold. Another possibility is that regarding particular beliefs as more or less salient is a consequence of adopting a particular kind of attitude.

Another criticism of the theory of reasoned action concerns the role of previous behaviour. Fishbein and Ajzen (1975, p. 16) allow for the possibility of behaviour producing feedback that can influence subsequent attitudes and subjective norms, but in other respects their model seems better suited to situations where a person is weighing up the pros and cons of an action for the first time. In very many cases, however, this condition does not apply. The action under consideration will be similar, if not identical, to actions performed many times before. In short, models of the relationship between attitude and behaviour do not simply have to explain 'reasoned action', they have to explain *habit*.

A practical question that has often been asked of social psychologists is whether habitual behaviour can be influenced by persuasive communication. Another way of putting this question is: which is more important in determining people's future behaviour – their attitudes and beliefs, which conceivably can be changed, or their previous behaviour, which cannot? This question has been asked in a variety of contexts, but currently a great deal of attention is being paid by researchers to the kinds of habits that can affect people's health. It is probably no coincidence that 'health behaviours', such as smoking, exercise and diet, provide some of the most widely cited instances of apparent attitude–behaviour discrepancies, as when smokers continue to smoke despite acknowledging the dangers to their health.

Another example is drug-use, which is of special relevance for attitude–behaviour theories in that it is frequently considered to be a class of behaviour that is physically determined, and beyond the reach of persuasive influence. Bentler and Speckart (1979) measured students' attitudes towards, and self-reported use of, three classes of drug: alcohol, marijuana, and 'hard drugs'. The important difference between their study and most previous ones in the field of attitudes and behaviour is that they built a longitudinal element into their design. Subjects gave their ratings on two separate occasions, albeit only separated by two weeks. On each occasion, they reported their attitudes, subjective norms and intentions to use the various drugs over the next two weeks, as well as their actual use of the drugs over the *previous* two weeks. Bentler and Speckart (1979) interpreted their findings in terms of the model shown in Figure 2.3.

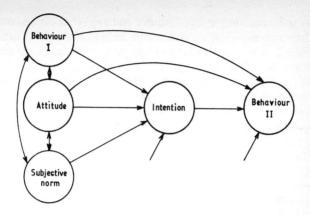

Figure 2.3 A model of the attitude–behaviour relation incorporating previous behaviour (from P. M. Bentler and G. Speckart (1979). 'Models of attitude behavior relations'. *Psychological Review*, 86, 455. Copyright 1979 by the American Psychological Association, reprinted with permission)

The implications of this revised model are that:

(a) Attitudes and subjective norms are correlated with previous behaviour, and no attempt is made to say whether they or the behaviour 'comes first'.

(b) Attitudes can have both an *indirect* influence on behaviour, through influencing intention (as required by the theory of reasoned action), and a *direct* influence, irrespective of intention.

(c) The influence of subjective norms on subsequent behaviour is indirect.

(d) Previous behaviour can influence subsequent behaviour both directly and indirectly.

The different paths in the model may vary in importance from context to context, as Bentler and Speckart observed when comparing their findings for the three types of drug-use. However, contrary to the assumptions of the theory of reasoned action, attitudes and previous behaviour predicted subsequent behaviour *directly* (i.e. over and above any effect mediated by differences in intention) in all three analyses.

It could be argued, even so, that the theory of reasoned action was never intended to apply to behaviours, such as drug-use, which may not be under 'volitional control'. That is to say, part of the way addiction is commonly defined is that addicts cannot help taking drugs, even if they want to stop. As we shall see (in Chapter 5), there may be problems with defining addiction in this way. There are two problems with this counter-argument, however. Firstly, the theory of reasoned action *has* been applied to the prediction of addictive behaviours (Fishbein, 1982; Schlegel, Crawford and Sanborn, 1977) with reasonable success. Secondly, previous behaviour can directly predict subsequent behaviour in the context of habits that do not involve physical dependence. For instance, Fredricks and Dossett (1983) compared the Fishbein and Ajzen (1975) and the Bentler and Speckart (1979) models with respect to the prediction of students' classroom attendance. They found that subsequent attendance was predictable from previous attendance, irrespective of intention. On the other hand, the effect of attitude on subsequent behaviour was mediated by intention, as Fishbein and Ajzen (1975) would predict.

The overall conclusions from these and similar studies seem therefore to be that (a) both attitudes and behaviour need to be measured at more than one point in time, before any generalizations can be drawn regarding whether *changes* in attitude produce *changes* in behaviour or vice versa; (b) the relative importance of different predictors of subsequent behaviour will vary from situation to situation; (c) again depending on the context, intention may or may not play an important mediating role between such predictors and subsequent behaviour; and (d) neither the Fishbein and Ajzen (1975) model nor that of Bentler and Speckart (1979) provide any explicit theory about how either attitudes or behaviours are *acquired*.

Behavioural influences on attitude: cognitive dissonance

As we have seen, much work has been concerned with predicting behaviour from people's attitudes. In addition, it has been common to think of attitudes as causal antecedents of actions – of people behaving in particular ways because of the attitudes they hold. On the other hand, there is considerable research that points in the opposite direction by suggesting that people may change their attitudes to bring them more into line with behavioural decisions that they have already made.

The starting point for such research is Festinger's (1957) *Theory of Cognitive Dissonance*. According to Festinger, any decision between alternative courses of action can give rise to an experience of tension or 'dissonance', which will be stronger the more difficult the decision is to make. This state of tension will remain even *after* a decision has been taken, to the extent that the person has any doubts that the chosen course of action was correct. When this happens, the person will be motivated to engage in various kinds of cognitive restructuring to remove such feelings of tension and uncertainty. Festinger's theory shares a number of assumptions with other cognitive consistency approaches (see Chapter 1), in that the prime example of dissonance is where the cognition that one has chosen to behave in a particular way is *inconsistent* with the cognition that such behaviour is somehow 'bad', or may have 'bad' consequences. Like Heider (1946), Festinger assumes that such inconsistency will be experienced as unpleasant, and that people will be motivated to avoid or modify the thoughts that give rise to it.

Although there are a number of ways in which people may resolve experiences of inconsistency (Abelson, 1959) or cope with decisional conflict (Janis and Mann, 1977), the distinctive feature of cognitive dissonance theory is the idea that *present* attitudes can be changed so as to be made more consistent with *previous* decisions. The experimental paradigm used most widely to test this prediction is that known as 'forced compliance'. Essentially, a forced compliance study involves the experimenter getting subjects to agree to perform a piece of behaviour which in some ways is inconsistent with their pre-existing attitudes. After the subjects have performed this behaviour, or at least have agreed to do so, their relevant attitudes are reassessed (often by another experimenter). Depending on the conditions, what is frequently observed is that subjects report attitudes that are more in line with their previous behaviour.

The classic study of this kind is that by Festinger and Carlsmith (1959). Male students were first tested individually for an hour on a tedious combination of motor performance tasks. Then each student in the experimental conditions was asked by the experimenter to fill in for an absent research assistant, whose task it was, after supposedly participating in the experiment, to tell the next subject (in fact a specially hired female student) how interesting and enjoyable the tasks had been, *and* to be prepared to be 'on call' if needed again in the future. For this, in one condition the subject was offered $1, in the other $20. After then intentionally deceiving the waiting subject, they were interviewed by a *different* experimenter, supposedly conducting a separate evaluation of how interesting, enjoyable, etc., students found the experiments in which they participated.

The result, as predicted by Festinger and Carlsmith, was that subjects reported, in the post-experimental interview, that they had found the tasks significantly more interesting and enjoyable if they had been in the $1 condition than if they had been in the $20 condition or in the control condition where they were not asked to say anything to the next 'subject'. This finding was widely hailed as a 'non-obvious' contradiction of the notion that people should feel more positively about behaviours for which they have been more positively reinforced (e.g. Rosenberg and Abelson, 1960). The explanation, according to dissonance theory, is as follows: the cognition that one has said the tasks were interesting (and has agreed to say so again if needed) is inconsistent with the cognition that they in fact were boring. This inconsistency or dissonance can be resolved in various ways. One way is by looking for other compensations, such as a relatively high rate of pay like $20. This route, however, is closed to those receiving the low rate of $1, but what *is* offered to them is the idea that maybe the tasks were not so boring after all. (It is crucial to note that the experimenter does not ask subjects to 'tell a lie' in so many words. On the contrary, his manner implies that he personally sees the tasks as quite interesting.) These subjects, therefore, reduce dissonance by changing their attitudes to make a better match with their behaviour.

This experiment was followed by a number of studies where subjects were induced to put forward arguments, orally or in written essays, against their own position on some issue. These studies, in general, replicated the so-called 'dissonance' effect of more attitudinal change in the direction of the position advocated during such role-play, under conditions of low rather than high incentive. This 'dissonance effect', however, is dependent on a number of factors. One of the most important of these factors is perceived *freedom of choice*. Linder, Cooper and Jones (1967) led student subjects to write essays in favour of proposed legislation (to which they personally were opposed) which would have banned left-wing speakers from addressing meetings at state-supported institutions in their state of North Carolina. The instructions to the subjects either stressed that the decision whether or not to perform the task was the subjects' own ('free-decision' condition) or simply told them that this was what the task, for which they had volunteered, would involve ('no-choice' condition). The payment offered in each condition was either $0.50 or $2.50. As predicted, subjects in the free-decision condition reported that they were less opposed to the legislation, if offered the lower rather than the higher payment. However, in the 'no-choice' condition, the higher payment produced more attitude change. Linder et al. conclude that dissonance theory only applies under conditions of perceived free choice: dissonance does not arise when people feel they were not free to decide to act in any other way. Frey and Wicklund (1978) have also observed that another effect predicted by dissonance theory – the tendency to search for information supportive rather than non-supportive of a prior decision – is more likely to occur if that decision is perceived as having been freely made.

Closely related to perceived freedom of choice are notions of personal responsibility and the foreseeability of negative consequences (e.g. Cooper and Worchel, 1970). The more we feel personally responsible for, or can foresee, negative consequences of our behaviour, the more we change our attitude to accord with it. For example, in a study by Cooper and Goethals (1974), subjects were induced to write arguments against their own position. When subjects were led to expect that their arguments might be presented to other people (thereby possibly influencing these people in an undesirable direction), they showed greater attitude change (towards the arguments they had invented), even when they were told (after finishing writing) that their arguments would not be used in this way after all. On the other hand, *no* attitude change was found by Goethals, Cooper and Naficy (1979) in a condition where subjects were first told that their counter-attitudinal arguments would remain secret, but then (after the essays were written) were informed that their arguments would be shown to other people after all. This exceptional procedure was used to show that what is important for an aversion of dissonance is that such negative consequences are *unforeseeable*, rather than merely *unforeseen*, at the time that the behavioural decision is made.

These and similar findings have shifted the emphasis in recent dissonance research away from notions of strictly *cognitive* inconsistency towards an interpretation in terms of the more motivational and/or emotional effects of feeling responsible for a bad decision. In short, 'dissonance has precious little to do with inconsistency between cognitions *per se*, but rather with the production of a consequence that is unwanted' (Cooper and Fazio, 1984, p. 234).

Self-perception, impression-management, and arousal

Although Festinger (1957) regarded attitude change as a means of reducing unpleasant experiences of tension and inconsistency, this interpretation has not gone unchallenged. Bem (1965, 1967) proposed a 'self-perception theory', according to which any self-report of attitude is an inference from observation of one's own behaviour and the situation in which it occurs. If the situation contains cues, such as the offer of a large incentive, which imply that we might have behaved in such a way regardless of how we personally felt, we make no inference that our behaviour reflected our true attitudes. However, in the absence of obvious situational pressures, we assume that our attitudes are what our behaviour suggests they are. If we have described something as interesting and enjoyable, then that is how we must have really felt about it.

Bem (1965, 1967) put these ideas to the test in a form of experiment he terms 'interpersonal simulation'. This involves presenting so-called 'observer' subjects with a summary description of the procedure used in some well-known dissonance experiments, telling them of the agreement by a subject to perform the counter-attitudinal act requested by the original experimenter, and then asking them to estimate the original subject's final attitude response. When studies such as that by Festinger and Carlsmith (1959) are simulated in this way, the estimates given by Bem's 'observer' subject seem to match the responses of the original subjects quite closely, and to show the predicted effects of different levels of incentive. When they are told that the subject was offered a high incentive, observers are less likely to assume a match between the subject's behaviour and attitude.

Despite these encouraging early results, self-perception theory has not fulfilled its promise as a general replacement for dissonance theory. At an empirical level, it is in fact far from clear that Bem's observer subjects were using the *same* information as subjects in the original experiments that he attempted to simulate. On the contrary, when observers are given fuller details of the original procedures than supplied by Bem's summaries, their estimates tend to be *more* discrepant from the original subjects' responses (Jones *et al.*, 1968; Piliavin *et al.*, 1969). At a conceptual level, too, it is very difficult to distinguish the hypothesis that people change their self-reports of attitude on the one hand, so that these self-reports correspond more closely to what their behaviour would be taken to imply (self-perception theory), from the alternative hypothesis that they do so in order to feel that they made the correct decision in terms of what they believed and wanted at the time (dissonance theory). Greenwald (1975) goes so far as to argue that there is no experimental procedure that can unambiguously distinguish between these alternative possibilities.

Another interpretation has been that both self-perception and dissonance-reduction processes may be operative, but to different extents in different contexts. Fazio, Zanna and Cooper (1977) argue that dissonance theory may apply when people behave in ways contrary to their initial attitude, whereas self-perception theory may apply better where their behaviour and initial attitude are broadly consistent. Consider, for instance, an experiment by Kiesler, Nisbett and Zanna (1969). They had subjects commit themselves to obtaining signatures from passers-by for a petition against air pollution. The experimental manipulation consisted of cues provided by another 'subject' who agreed to participate immediately before, but in such a way as to emphasize or de-emphasize the relevance of subjects' own attitudes to their behaviour. This was achieved by having the previous 'subject' accept either with the words 'Okay, I wouldn't mind convincing people about something I really believe in' or 'Okay, it would be good to be in a study that really shows something'. Subjects reported their own attitudes as being more strongly anti-pollution after committing themselves to participating in the first than in the second condition.

This last finding raises the more general issue of whether what matters is our *own* inferences about the way we behave, or the inferences we feel that *other* people might draw about us. The term 'impression-management theory' is that given to a general approach relating to people's concern with behaving in such a way that other people will regard them favourably. Tedeschi, Schlenker and Bonoma (1971) argued that the effects of many dissonance manipulations might not reflect genuine cases of 'private' attitude change, but rather an adoption of a public response that protected subjects against the possible accusation that their behaviour was insincere. Thus, subjects might pretend that they really believed in what they had said or done so that it did not appear as though they had let themselves be 'bribed'.

Despite the evidence that impression-management concerns may operate in a variety of contexts (Baumeister, 1982; Tetlock and Manstead, 1985), it is doubtful whether this argument can explain many of the effects of dissonance manipulations. Two considerations point in this direction. First, in many experiments, including that by Festinger and Carlsmith (1959), subjects' final attitudinal responses were elicited by a separate experimenter unaware of their initial attitudes, of their actual behaviour, and of the inducements, if any, offered to them. Second, in many experiments, asserting that one's behaviour was not absolutely contrary to one's true opinion might avert the accusation of venality, but only at the price of admitting to a normatively quite undesirable opinion. Pushing it to its extremes, 'impression-management' in such contexts could amount to saying something like 'How dare you suggest I had to be bribed to say what I said. I really *am* a fascist'! As a result of these and other difficulties, impression-management theorists (e.g. Schlenker, 1982; Tedeschi and Rosenfeld, 1981) no longer tend to claim that changes in attitude responses are a mere pretence. Instead, much attitude change is seen as an attempt to avoid social anxiety and embarrassment, or to protect positive views of one's own identity. According to this view, the roots of the 'tension' hypothesized by Festinger (1957) may lie in people's *social* concerns with how others might evaluate them, and how they should evaluate themselves.

Another way of looking at such findings is that people may well experience a state of unpleasant tension if they feel they have acted inconsistently with their beliefs, or rather, following Cooper and Fazio's (1984) argument, if they feel they have made a free decision which has had bad consequences. Croyle and Cooper (1983) found evidence of more persistent elevation of physiological arousal (as measured by spontaneous electro-dermal activity) among subjects who wrote a counter-attitudinal essay under high-choice as opposed to low-choice instructions, or who wrote an essay consistent with their own opinions. However, feelings of unpleasant tension may also be produced by factors less directly related to the notion of cognitive disson-ance, and such tension or arousal may be confused with the feelings people may have if they believe they have made a bad decision. According to such an interpretation, attitude change in such experiments should depend both on the amount of arousal, from whatever sources, experienced by the subject, and on how the subject interprets or explains this arousal.

Support for this notion comes from a study, by Zanna and Cooper (1974). Subjects wrote a counter-attitudinal essay under instructions that implied either high or low freedom of choice. In accordance with previous findings, it was predicted that subjects should change their opinions to correspond more closely with what they had written under high- than under low-choice instructions. The novel feature of this experiment was that subjects were also given a placebo pill. In one condition they were told that the pill would make them feel tense, in another condition they were told that it would make them feel relaxed, and in a third condition, they were given no information about its likely effects. The dissonance theory prediction of greater attitude change in the high-choice condition was upheld when subjects were given no information about the pill, and even more strongly when they were told it would make them more relaxed (the implication being that, if they felt tense even when given a pill to make them relaxed, they would treat such tension as an even stronger indication that they felt bad about the behaviour).

However, when subjects were told the pill would make them feel tense, no difference between the high- and low-choice conditions was observed, presumably since they could explain their tension as caused by the pill rather than their behaviour.

These results (and those of a related study by Cooper, Zanna and Taves, 1978) are particularly interesting in that they unite themes from a variety of theoretical perspectives. On the one hand, there is the demonstration of the importance of an internal state of arousal, as assumed by Festinger (1957) (see also Nuttin, 1975). On the other hand, there is the evidence of the dependence of attitude change on subjects' own interpretations of their feelings and behaviour, which is broadly compatible with Bem's (1965, 1967) self-perception theory.

If we take a broad view of the literature on cognitive dissonance, therefore, there is good evidence that people will change their attitudes as a consequence of their behaviour. Such attitude change seems particularly likely to occur when the subject is experiencing feelings of tension or unpleasant arousal. Such unpleasant feelings appear to be particularly associated with beliefs in one's own responsibility for a bad behavioural decision leading, actually or potentially, to aversive consequences that one should have been able to foresee.

Consistency and learning

The research we have reviewed in this chapter has all been concerned, in various ways, with how people think of their different attitudes and beliefs in relation to one another and to the way in which they behave. Where such attitudes, beliefs and behaviour are seen as consistent with each other, everything appears much more stable, simple and predictable. Inconsistency, on the other hand, means that it is difficult to make unambiguous judgments about whether something is good or bad, or whether a particular action is right or wrong. But where does this concern with consistency come from? It is here that fundamental divergences occur between different theoretical perspectives.

In the first part of the chapter, we described research which for the most part started from the assumption that consistency is somehow normative, even natural, and that what needs to be explained is why we are sometimes inconsistent. For Heider (1946) consistency is not only *functionally* convenient for purposes of simplification and prediction, it is *intrinsically* desirable, perhaps even beautiful. In short, it is a *Gestalt*. We look for symmetry in our own beliefs and in social relationships, just as we do in physical objects, and if we fail to find it we feel disappointed. Why should we do so? Ultimately the answer must involve some appeal to the ways in which our brains have evolved to deal with information in structural terms. But this is not the only line of speculation that we are forced to follow. Attitudinal issues and social relationships can be looked at from many different points of view, and what appears consistent or balanced according to one set of criteria may appear inconsistent according to another – hence the importance of considering the *salience* of particular attitudes and beliefs.

One thing at least is clear in attitude research. The fact that people can hold a wide variety of opinions shows that we are dealing with repertoires of *learned* reactions, feelings and beliefs. What form does such learning take, and how can it produce consistency? The first part of this question is not especially mysterious. We can acquire many different kinds of evaluative reactions to social objects through general processes of association, reinforcement and imitation. In that many such reactions are acquired through repetitive conditioning they may attain the status of *habits*, the enactment of which requires little direct thought on our part. This can apply not only to the emotional reactions and expectancies but also to overt behaviour. It is for this reason that, in studies such as that by Bentler and Speckart (1979) (see p. 30), past behaviour can directly predict subsequent behaviour, over and above any effect due to present attitude and intention. Verbal behaviour can also be conditioned, and we can acquire habitual ways of talking about particular objects or issues, without having to think deeply about what we are saying.

The question of how we learn to achieve consistency among our separate reactions is more difficult to answer. If we cast the problem, for the moment, in terms of the three-component view of attitudes, there is evidence, even in other animals, that affective, cognitive and behavioural responses can be acquired in ways that produce something very suggestive of what we

41

would recognize as consistency. According to more 'cognitive' views of animal learning (for example, Tarpy, 1982), learning consists essentially of the acquisition of 'if-then' expect-ancies ('cognition'), that may be associated with conditioned emotional responses ('affect') and reflexive or instrumental responses such as approach and avoidance ('behaviour'). Viewed from this perspective, animals are capable of showing a good deal of consistency between their cognitive, affective and behav-ioural reactions. For example, an animal that expects an elec-tric shock to follow a warning stimulus is likely to experience fear and attempt to take avoiding action. The prerequisite for such 'consistency', however, is rather strict: the different modes of response must be acquired within a shared context. To the extent that the different forms of response are based on different histories of learning experience, there is no special reason to expect them to be consistent with one another.

When we try to apply the same analysis to the human case, however, two major difficulties confront us. The first is that our repertoire of responses to any given object may include habits acquired under very different conditions, often without concrete experience of the actual object of our evaluation. It is a common-place to observe that people can sometimes express quite extreme negative reactions towards social groups of whom they have never known a single member. Similarly how we *think* we might react, emotionally and behaviourally, to a new or chal-lenging situation we have not yet encountered may sometimes leave us unprepared for the reality of the experience (as when Breckler's, 1984, subjects were presented with a live snake). In other words, the prerequisite that *verbal* and other modes of response share a history of acquisition is not an issue that arises in the case of animal learning.

It is through language that attitudes can become publicly shared and communicated. But for this to happen, statements of attitude have to be interpreted as *meaningful* expressions of what the speaker feels, believes or intends. However, *we demand at least a modicum of consistency before we accept verbal behaviour as meaningful*. Put another way, we learn that we have to achieve a degree of consistency in what we say if we are to be understood, and a degree of correspondence between what we say and what we do if we are to be believed. A large part of socialization involves internalization of other people's expectations that we should be reasonably predictable (though not inflexible) in our feelings and reactions, and that we may be held *accountable* in what we do for things we say and feel (we should keep promises, be kind to our friends, and such like).

What all this implies, however, is that, in the context of what we feel, think, say and do, *consistency is a social product* (Eiser, 1986, 1987). It is acquired often with difficulty and typically incompletely in response to the demands of *social* communication and interaction. What is more, although we may learn that others expect some consistency from us, there is no general rule that enables us to predict the *specific* form that this expectation may take.

The traditional way of looking at the attitude–behaviour relationship is that attitudes *cause* behaviours, and that if the association between them is not as close empirically as this assumption suggests, it is because other factors intervene that also influence behaviour. The alternative view that we are proposing is that attitude and behaviour are separate response systems. As such, they are *unlikely* to be systematically related to each other unless one of two conditions applies. The first is that they share common learning histories. In other words, we can expect more consistency when a person learns how to interact with another person or object *at the same time* as developing emotional reactions to, and other feelings and beliefs about, that person or object. The second condition is that the person considers what kinds of attitudes and behaviour 'go together' with each other in terms of some higher order category system (e.g. that feelings of 'friendship' and 'friendly behaviour' go together). Such a system of categorization must be learned and will be almost certainly reflected in language. Its function is to group together separate kinds of response to form a recognizable and simplified structure, within which both actual and *socially expected* implications between different reactions and responses are emphasized. Just as people use simpler or more complex categories, so their expectations of consistency imply lesser or greater tolerance for ambivalence. Just as there is always more than one way in which to categorize events, be they subjective or objective, there is always more than one possible form of consistency.

3

Attribution theory

The question of how we perceive and judge our surroundings involves many issues apart from those considered in the previous chapters. Attribution theory deals with the perception of causation and the consequences of such perceptions. It is concerned explicitly with how people try to find appropriate causal explanations for one another's behaviour, and more generally for any event in their social environment. Attributions help us to understand and react to our social surroundings. It matters, for example, whether a person who has been made redundant attributes this to his or her lack of ability, lack of effort, the bias of immediate superiors or the general economic situation. Similarly, it makes a difference whether you see the unexpected, insulting behaviour of a friend as being caused by fatigue or by dislike.

In this chapter we discuss three types of attributional theory: theories that focus on the antecedents of people's perception of the causes of events in their social environment; theories that are based on the assumption that people have preconceptions about causality leading to biases in their attribution; and finally, theories that concentrate on the consequences of attributions. The major theoretical contributions to attribution theory have been provided by Heider (1944, 1958), Jones and his colleagues (Jones and Davis, 1965; Jones and McGillis, 1976) and Kelley (1967, 1972, 1973). We will first describe these three theories and some of the research attempting to test them.

Heider's 'naive' psychology

Attribution theory is usually traced to Fritz Heider and his attempts to describe and explain 'naive' psychology. In *The Psychology of Interpersonal Relations* (1958), Heider noted a similarity between the goals and activities of scientists and those of people in their everyday lives. On the basis of observation, people form beliefs or theories about what is occurring in order to understand, predict and control events that concern them.

Heider assumes that individuals are motivated to see their social environment as predictable and hence controllable, and that they apply the same kind of logic to the prediction of social events as to the prediction of physical events; they look for the necessary and sufficient conditions for such events to occur. Such conditions may either be situational or impersonal, external to the person whose behaviour one is trying to predict and explain, or factors regarded as internal to the person, such as his or her ability or personality. In Heider's words, 'Attributions in terms of impersonal and personal causes, and with the latter, in terms of intent, are everyday occurrences that determine much of our understanding of and reaction to our surroundings' (1958, p. 16).

Heider goes on to stress the importance of the concept of intentionality, arguing that behaviour should only be attributed to personal causes if its outcome is seen to have been intended by the actor (1958, pp. 101–2). There is assumed to be a kind of 'trade-off' relationship between the influence of personal and impersonal factors, so that attributions to a person's character are less likely when the behaviour is seen to be under the control of external constraints. Personal traits (attitudes, needs, beliefs, personality structures) are thus used to explain behaviour that cannot be clearly attributed to external conditions. Even so,

Heider argues, the effect of such environmental conditions may not be fully taken into account: 'It seems that behaviour in particular has such salient properties it tends to engulf the total field rather than be confined to its proper position as a local stimulus whose interpretation requires the additional data of a surrounding field' (1958, p. 54).

This preference becomes more understandable if we try to imagine a social world where people did *not* attribute behaviour to personal traits. People would seem to change at an alarming rate, making them unstable and unpredictable. One of Heider's themes is that people engage in attributional analyses to discern the personal (or dispositional as Heider termed them) and relatively stable properties that underlie the variable behaviour of others.

Heider played a major role in making naive psychology a legitimate field of study in social psychology. Most of his ideas, however, were presented in a relatively discursive fashion. For instance, he suggested that the covariation principle is of crucial importance to the attribution process. This principle entails that an effect is attributed to the cause that is present when the effect is present, and absent when the effect is absent. For instance, if you get a rash every time you wear a particular shirt, that is a high covariation. If you get a rash only sometimes when you wear the shirt and also at other times, that is a low covariation. In trying to understand the cause of a specific effect, we observe its covariation with potential causes and generally attribute the effect to the cause with which it most closely covaries. These and other insights were systematized and expanded upon by Jones and Davis (1965) and Kelley (1967). Their contributions helped develop attribution theory into an explicit, hypothesis-generating set of principles.

Correspondent inference theory

Correspondent inference refers to the tendency to take someone's statement of opinion or other behaviour as a sign of what he or she believes or is really like. Jones and Davis (1965) described how an 'alert perceiver' might infer another's intentions and personal dispositions (personality traits, attitudes, beliefs, etc.) from his or her behaviour. People make correspondent inferences when they infer another's personal disposition directly from behaviour; e.g. perceivers inferring aggressiveness from aggressive behaviour. Jones and Davis described two major stages in the process of inferring personal dispositions: the attribution of intention, and the attribution of disposition.

Firstly, people make dispositional attributions only on the basis of intentional behaviours. In other words, an attribution of intention must precede a dispositional attribution. Perceivers see an act as intentional when they believe that the person who behaved in a certain manner knows that the behaviour would produce the consequences observed, and that this person also possessed the ability to achieve these consequences when he or she desired to. At a conceptual level, there are a number of serious difficulties with the proposed role of intentionality. For instance, we do not assume that stupid people necessarily intend to act stupidly, or that forgetful people necessarily intend to forget things.

The second stage of the inference concerns the attribution of personal dispositions. If an act is seen as intentional, perceivers can begin by comparing the consequences of chosen and nonchosen acts. For instance, you might infer certain attitudes and preferences if someone has chosen to see the latest *Beverly Hills Cop* movie when he or she could just as easily have gone to a Beckett play or a John Huston film. Unfortunately for simplicity, there are various situations in which such a choice is not necessarily informative. For instance, the chosen film might be the only form of entertainment for which tickets are available. In such circumstances you learn little about the person's preferences. As a result, Jones and Davis proposed the principle of 'noncommon' effects. That is, when more than one course of action is available to an individual, one may ask: what did the chosen behaviour produce that some other (nonchosen) behaviour would not have produced? A perceiver makes a correspondent inference (e.g. the inference that the target person prefers easy entertainment) when the chosen action has a few relatively unique or noncommon consequences. Furthermore, if negative consequences are incorporated into the chosen alternative, relative to the nonchosen ones, you may infer that the positive consequences are especially important to the target person. Thus, if the person chooses the latest *Beverly Hills Cop* movie, despite the fact that tickets are available for other forms of entertainment and the particular cinema is expensive, has awful seats and is an hour's drive away from home, you can infer with some confidence why the person chose that particular film.

In summary, then, the analysis of noncommon effects leads to correspondent inferences by identifying the distinctive consequences of a chosen course of action. The fewer the noncommon consequences, the more confident the inference; a perceiver cannot be certain which effect was intended if the chosen and nonchosen acts have many different consequences. The more negative elements associated with the chosen alternative, the more one can infer the importance of the distinctive, noncommon consequences. Generally, alternative courses of action, their consequences and noncommon effects are difficult to ascertain. As a result people have to rely on other cues as well.

Jones and Davis argued that an 'alert perceiver' will also consider whether the behaviour being judged is normative. A person who is aggressive in a situation in which most people would be expected to be aggressive is not seen as an aggressive person. The person will be seen as aggressive, however, if he or she reacts aggressively in a situation in which most people would not react in the same manner. In other words, correspondent inferences are made from non-normative behaviours. The next question concerns the assessment of normativeness. Jones and Davis suggest that it is inferred from the social desirability of the consequences of the behaviour in question. The more desirable or acceptable a consequence is, the more likely it is that people would try to achieve the consequence. Hence, correspondent inferences occur primarily when the consequences of the behaviour are socially unacceptable or undesirable.

Thus, a perceiver will attempt to examine the potential consequences of a target person's chosen and nonchosen behaviours and infer the reasons for the chosen behaviour. Inferred correspondence is supposed to be highest when the consequences of the chosen behaviour are less socially acceptable and/or desirable.

In 1976, Jones and McGillis made a few modifications to their theory. Although these do not alter the basic features of the model, they do result in a more elaborate and conceptually neater version. In this later version correspondence was defined in terms of the degree of information gained regarding the probability or strength of the attribute. The important difference between this and the previous version concerns the factor 'social desirability'. Social desirability is defined in terms of prior probabilities or expectancies. If these are high (e.g. a friend lending you a book) then the particular behaviour tells the perceiver little that is new about the actor. If these are low (i.e. the behaviour disconfirms your expectancies) the behaviour is more likely to result in correspondent inferences. By introducing the concept of expectancy, Jones and McGillis corrected the earlier version where social desirability was simply assumed to be associated with high expectancies and thus to be uninformative with regard to dispositions. Due to the fact that many socially desirable behaviours occur infrequently this assumption was untenable.

The first experiment (Jones and Harris, 1967) devised to test the correspondent inference model created a design model for all that followed. Subjects (in the observer role) read an essay either for or against Castro's Cuba, and on the basis of that single short essay (about two hundred words) were asked to guess the writer's true opinion on Castro's Cuba. The short essay was alleged to have been written under one of three conditions: as an answer to a question on a political science exam asking for (1) a criticism of Castro's Cuba, (2) a defence of Castro's Cuba, or (3) either a defence or a criticism. In short, subjects were led to believe that the essay they read had been either an 'assigned' position or a freely chosen position. In the first experiment all the essays were actually written by the investigators, and so attribution error could not be demonstrated by comparing the true attitudes of authors with attitudes inferred from their essays. It was determined in this experiment that the subjects themselves (the readers of the essays) held clear anti-Castro attitudes. For that reason they would have expected the writers of the essays, who were said to be students like themselves, also to have anti-Castro attitudes. Therefore, the anti-Castro essays can be said to have a high 'prior probability'. They were the expected, the not-surprising thing. The pro-Castro essays, on the other hand, would have been surprising; their prior probability was low. Correspondent inference is shown by the fact that writers of pro-Castro essays were credited with more favourable (pro) attitudes than were writers of anti-Castro essays. The attitudes attributed to essay authors were always in line with the essays themselves; that is, the actions (essays) were attributed to personal dispositions. Subjects assumed not only a greater correspondence between the opinion expressed and the target's true attitude when the opinion was non-normative (low prior probability) rather than normative, but also when the essay was written under high-choice rather than low-choice conditions.

The opinions expressed by the target person, however, affected the attitude attributions of perceivers, even when the opinions were supposedly elicited under low-choice conditions. In other words, a person who was required to write a pro-Castro essay was seen as more favourable towards Castro than a person who was required to write an anti-Castro essay. One could argue that this finding contradicts Jones and Davis's original position since only the consequences of freely chosen behaviours are supposed to be intended and hence lead to correspondent attributions. Some authors interpreted the finding that attributors perceive correspondence even when behaviour is constrained as indicating that perceivers are too ready to attribute causality to internal or personal dispositions. A tendency which was termed 'fundamental attribution error'. Research that followed the first Jones and Harris experiment has definitively shown that the effects are not specific to the issue of Castro's Cuba but are generalizable to a variety of issues.

Correspondent inference is a strong phenomenon, and observers have been shown to make internal, dispositional inferences from an actor's behaviour unless the actor's behaviour is more or less completely controlled. Snyder and Jones (1974) had someone (the actor) simply copy in his own hand an essay supplied by someone else, and observers were asked to guess the real attitude of the copyist on the topic treated in the essay. In that condition correspondent inference finally disappeared. Although the research on correspondent inference made us aware of the strength of this phenomenon, the theory is plagued by a variety of minor and major interpretational problems. Apart from the problems surrounding the role of intentionality the theory has usually been tested with paper-and-pencil tasks (i.e. written descriptions of a target's chosen and nonchosen behaviours). When perceivers are required to extract information from ongoing behavioural sequences it seems much more difficult to decide upon the nonchosen behaviours to be included in the inference process. If we go back to our earlier example concerning the choice of entertainment there seems an infinite number of possibilities. A more serious question is posed by Ross and Fletcher (1985) who rightly point out that related research suggests that perceivers do not pay much attention to nonchosen behaviours and their consequences. The fact that perceivers treat non-occurrences as considerably less important than occurrences when making inferences (e.g. Nisbett and Ross, 1980) contradicts the basic assumption of correspondent inference theory. An important element of Jones and Davis's model concerns the effect of non-normative, unexpected behaviours. This notion is developed more explicitly by Kelley's (1967) theory, which we turn to next.

Kelley's ANOVA model of attribution

Kelley's (1967) analysis of the attribution process concerns the question of how individuals establish the validity of their own or of another person's impression of a stimulus (e.g. behaviour, expressed opinion). The assumption is that the observation of *covariation* of conditions and effects leads to certain attributions. The three aspects that determine the observation of covariation are consistency, consensus and distinctiveness.

In other words, when people judge another person's behaviour they will examine three different kinds of information in their efforts to establish subjective validity: consensus information (do all or only a few people respond to the stimulus in the same way as the person?), distinctiveness information (does the person respond in the same way to other stimuli as well?), and consistency information (does the person always respond in the same way to the stimulus?) Attribution theory assumes that individuals attempt to weigh up different kinds of explanations for behaviour by looking for covariation between presumed causes and effects. For behaviour to be seen as reflecting stable characteristics of the actor, perceivers have to feel able to assume that others would share their impression, that their impression would be confirmed by varied and repeated observations, and that they might have formed a different impression if the actor had behaved differently. For example, suppose you learn that a friend likes the latest Stanley Kubrick film. How do you decide what to think of his or her judgment? For Kelley, this question means that you would like to know whether to attribute the person's appreciation of the film to something about the person or to something about the film. The question is then answered by considering consensus, consistency, and distinctiveness information.

Since we have three information variables, each of which can assume one of two values (low or high), the number of possible combinations is eight, and corresponding to each of these combinations is a distinct type of attribution. Four of these concern more complex attributions (e.g. interactions between the actor and the situation) that are hardly used in everyday thinking about causality. The four remaining, simple types of attributions are listed in Table 3.1 (adapted from Brown, 1986, p. 149).

Table 3.1 Major patterns and related attributions

Type of attribution	consensus	Type of information distinctiveness	consistency
Situation (stable)	H	H	H
Actor (stable)	L	L	H
Situation (unstable)	H	H	L
Actor (unstable)	L	L	L

In the context of our example these four combinations can be worked out as follows. Your friend's judgment of the film (it is a good film) should be perceived as valid if you know that (1) other people like the film (high consensus), (2) your friend seldom likes films (high distinctiveness) and, (3) your friend also enjoyed previous Stanley Kubrick films. In this case you would attribute your friend's liking to something about the film. If consensus is high, distinctiveness is high, but consistency is low (i.e. your friend disliked most of the earlier Stanley Kubrick films) you would probably be more cautious in your attribution. The pattern still suggests a situational attribution (something about the film) but the lack of consistency makes the attribution less stable. For instance, your friend's liking of the film could be due to circumstance.

In contrast, if (1) most people would not like the film (low consensus) (2) your friend has a tendency to like most films (low distinctiveness), and (3) your friend also liked previous Stanley Kubrick films (high consistency), you would be more likely to attribute your friend's appreciation to something about him or her (e.g. he or she simply likes going to the cinema very much) rather than to something unique about the film.

If, however, consensus and distinctiveness were low and consistency was also low, you would again be less certain about the validity of your friend's judgment. The four remaining combinations can all be characterized by a lack of internal consistency (i.e. not all types of information suggest the same type of attribution). For instance, if few other people like the film (low consensus), your friend seldom likes films (high distinctiveness), and he or she disliked most previous Stanley Kubrick films (low consistency), you would also be more likely to make an unstable attribution (e.g. perhaps your friend saw a really bad film the day before and therefore was easy to please).

As can be seen from the above examples the two stable attributions (see Table 3.1) provide relatively clear-cut answers. A lack of consistency will generally yield circumstance attributions, similarly a lack of convergence of the three informational variables (consensus, distinctiveness and consistency) is likely to be more ambiguous in terms of its attributional significance. In his subsequent papers, Kelley (1972, 1973) suggested that people often make attributions on the basis of limited information (i.e. they do not postpone their judgments until they possess information about consensus, distinctiveness, and consistency). These attributions can be made because people have theories or preconceptions about what causes are associated with what effects. These 'causal schemata' include the two stable attributions mentioned above (a) high consensus, high distinctiveness and high consistency for a stimulus or situational attribution (HHH); (b) low consensus, low distinctiveness, and high consistency for a person attribution (LLH); and also, for instance, low consensus, high distinctiveness, and low consistency (LHL) for a circumstance attribution (e.g. few

54

people enjoy the film, John enjoyed the film, John very rarely enjoys this type of film; a pattern suggesting a special circumstance that made John like the film). Causal schemata may lead a perceiver who has only high-consensus information and high-distinctiveness information to presuppose the HHH schema. In other words, Kelley's later work also assumes that people use only a few information patterns in their everyday thinking about social causality. Each of these patterns can be viewed as a causal schema, with which information is compared and integrated.

Empirical tests of Kelley's ANOVA model

The first comprehensive test of the predictions from Kelley's model was conducted by McArthur (1972). In her study subjects were given twelve descriptions of behavioural episodes such as 'John laughs at the comedian' and 'Sue is afraid of the dog' plus some combination of information with respect to consensus, distinctiveness and consistency. The information variable values were also conveyed by sentences such as, for instance, 'Almost everyone who hears the comedian laughs at him' (high consensus) and 'John also laughs at almost any other comedian' (low distinctiveness). Each subject had some value (high or low) for each information variable for each event-depicting sentence, and in the full design all possible combinations were realized. The event-depicting sentence was followed by the question 'Why?' and subjects were asked to choose among types of causal attributions: (a) something about the actor; (b) something about the stimulus (or situation); and so on. The results supported Kelley's model. Other studies, using a format comparable to McArthur's, similarly have found that consensus, distinctiveness, and consistency information play an important role in object, person, and circumstance attribution (e.g. McArthur, 1976; Orvis et al., 1975; Zuckerman, 1978).

However, the above line of research is open to some basic criticisms. The original formulation of Kelley's ANOVA model of attribution always refers to the observation of covariation of conditions and effects. Unfortunately, most studies have not presented subjects with actual series of events which can be seen to covary with certain conditions. Instead subjects have merely been informed about the covariation in terms of consistency, consensus and distinctiveness assuming that they are in fact able to extract consistency, consensus and distinctiveness information when observing the occurrence of natural events (see also Jaspars, Hewstone and Fincham, 1983, p. 19).

Although Kelley based his analysis of the attribution process on the covariation principle there are quite a number of studies suggesting that people are not very skilled at assessing covariation between variables (for reviews see e.g. Crocker, 1981). The studies of Chapman and Chapman (1969) revealed that adults' perceptions of covariation between responses on psychodiagnostic tests and patient symptoms were more dependent on expectations of what ought to go together with what, than on the information subjects were provided with. In general, studies of covariation demonstrate that people will 'see' a correlation between unrelated sets of stimuli when they believe that the sets ought to be causally related (see also Spears, van der Pligt and Eiser, 1986). Conversely, they fail to observe unanticipated relations that do exist. This research makes an important point. Not only are attributions theory-driven, in the sense that covariation information is utilized according to causal schemata, but the observations of the underlying data patterns themselves are also powerfully influenced by the perceiver's *a priori* causal theories.

The difficulty in detecting covariation may explain, in part, why some experiments have produced results less consistent with Kelley's theorizing than those just described. In McArthur-type paper-and-pencil tests the covariation information is provided in an explicit and organized manner. In these relatively sterile contexts, individuals are capable of using the consensus, distinctiveness, and consistency information and so they make attributions more or less as Kelley's theory would predict they should. When subjects have to abstract consensus, distinctiveness and consistency from ongoing behaviour the data provide less clear-cut support for Kelley's theory (Stevens and Jones, 1976; Tillman and Carver, 1980). Nisbett and Ross (1980) have suggested that causal analyses in naturalistic settings are unlikely to follow the normative strategies proposed by attribution theorists. What seemed to be explicit information-gathering processes in Kelley's attributional model seem more appropriately described as cognitive schemata. Attribution, therefore, seems often more influenced by people's own theories and expectations than by a careful consideration of various types of information.

Biases in attribution

Early research on attribution concentrated on information-gathering aspects. Subsequent research suggested that this computational approach did not provide an accurate description of people's judgments. As a consequence, social psychologists have exerted considerable effort investigating the 'shortcomings' of attributional judgment. This research led to the realization that a number of biases exert considerable influence on the type of attribution people make. Four of these biases will be discussed in this part:

(a) self-serving bias (a preference in the actor to attribute desirable actions to internal psychological causes in him- or herself, and undesirable actions to external, situational aspects),

(b) false consensus (a tendency to see one's own attitudes, preferences and behavioural choices as shared with most other people),

(c) actor-observer divergence (a tendency in actors to attribute their actions to external situational causes, whereas observers, by contrast, tend to attribute the same actions to dispositional aspects e.g. personality traits of the actor),

(d) the fundamental attribution error (the observers' tendency to underestimate the impact of situational factors and to overestimate the importance of internal dispositional factors).

Self-serving bias

The self-serving bias concerns the need to view oneself in a favourable way following a success or failure. In other words, if you pass an exam you will tend to attribute it to internal factors (intelligence, talent), if you fail you will prefer to attribute this to the incompetence of the lecturer, the mediocre literature and so forth. A very extensive body of research confirms this tendency (see e.g. Bradley, 1978; Zuckerman, 1979, for reviews of the relevant literature).

Needless to say, a controversy has emerged over the appropriate interpretation of this result. Many authors view the asymmetry as reflecting a motivational bias. It can be argued that people attribute success more than failure to personal factors because they are motivated to enhance or protect their self-esteem. A number of studies confirm this interpretation. For example, McFarland and Ross (1982) provided subjects with false feedback concerning their degree of success at a task and induced them to attribute their performance either to task difficulty (an external cause) or to ability (an internal cause). Failure led to more negative affect and lower self-esteem than success only when the performance was attributed to lack of ability. Miller and Ross (1975) reviewed the literature on the self-serving bias and report substantial support for self-enhancement in case of success but little support for self-protection in case of failure. They offer a cognitive explanation and argue that self-enhancement derives partly from people's (optimistic) expectation that one's behaviour will produce success.

Unfortunately, a lot of research on the self-serving bias requires people to solve puzzles or play games. The fact that people refuse to accept full responsibility for their failure on such tests could partly be due to their refusal to see their failure on these artificial tasks or problems of little consequence as 'my failure', and attribute it instead to external or situational factors. Markus and Zajonc (1985) rightly point out that failing to solve a tremendously difficult puzzle may not be considered a failure at all. An unsuccessful interview for a job you desperately want or failing an exam in one of your favourite subjects is likely to have a different effect.

False consensus

People are frequently found to imagine that their preferences and opinions are shared by most other people. For instance, people who like a specific television programme tend to overestimate the number of people that share this preference. Similarly, people tend to overestimate the number of people that would vote for the candidate they prefer. This phenomenon has been discussed under such labels as 'looking glass perception' (Fields and Schuman, 1976), and the 'false consensus effect' (Ross *et al.*, 1977).

Operationally, false consensus occurs when an individual engaging in a specific behaviour estimates that behaviour to be shared by a larger proportion of some reference group than would be estimated by a person engaging in an alternative behaviour. To give an example, people who are in favour of the building of more nuclear power plants tend to overestimate the number of people sharing this view, as compared to people opposing further expansion of the nuclear industry. As suggested earlier, this overestimation can apply to various reference groups. In the context of the above study on nuclear power stations, the overestimation applied to both the general population and Members of the Dutch Parliament (van der Pligt *et al.*, 1983). The effect has been shown to occur in a wide variety of contexts including not only the perceived popularity of one's own political attitudes, but also estimates of the degree of similarity between one's own and one's partner's views on the causes of conflict in a close relationship (Harvey *et al.*, 1978), judgments of the popularity of one's own behavioural choices concerning energy conservation (van der Pligt, 1984), playing tennis once a week (Ross *et al.*, 1977) and carrying a sandwich board suggesting that people should 'repent' (Zuckerman *et al.*, 1982).

False consensus has been interpreted as a form of wishful thinking, and hence as a motivational phenomenon. This explanation thus sees false consensus as an intended strategy to appear normal, appropriate, and rational. On the other hand, false consensus could represent a non-motivational and unintentional perceptual distortion resulting from a selective exposure to, and, recall of other people who are in agreement with oneself.

A number of authors have tried to test these two explanations (e.g. Mullen, 1983; Ross, 1977; Sherman *et al.*, 1984), but no resolution to this issue has been achieved. The bulk of the evidence, however, suggests that non-motivational explanations are more likely to be correct than motivational interpretations of the phenomenon. For instance, Zuckerman *et al.* (1982) found false consensus effects for both actors and observers. These authors also found that behaviour that is vivid or salient tends to be perceived as more common among group members than less salient, pallid behaviour. In other words, if a person's behaviour is relatively vivid and attention-demanding, other people tend to believe that many others would behave in a similar manner. Other findings suggest that false consensus is augmented for representative targets. Mullen *et al.* (1985) conducted a meta-analysis on a total of 115 tests of the false consensus effect. Their findings revealed a pattern that is inconsistent with motivational explanations for the false consensus effect. Furthermore, the authors suggest that the perceptual distortion explanation is more viable and stress the importance of the availability heuristic, i.e. the tendency to use the ease with which something is brought to mind as a valid index of its probability. This phenomenon can be extended to false consensus in the following way. If subjects in a false consensus study are persuaded to examine the other side of the issue (i.e. the alternative opinion or behaviour they would not choose for themselves), that other side might come to appear more likely. This forced consideration of the opposing point of view would make the opposing view more available and consequently increase people's estimates of the frequency of that point of view. Recent research shows that this effect can occur in the context of false consensus effects (Goethals, 1987). All in all, the false consensus effect is a robust finding obtained in a wide variety of contexts that seems best explained by perceptual biases.

The actor–observer divergence

The actor-observer divergence refers to a tendency in actors to attribute their actions to external situational causes, whereas observers, by contrast, show a relative tendency to emphasize dispositional causes (i.e. characteristics of the actor) in their explanations of the same actions (Jones and Nisbett, 1971). In a number of cases the self-serving bias makes the same predictions as the actor–observer divergence. For instance, when the action is undesirable or evaluated negatively both the self-serving bias and the divergence concept predict a denial of personal responsibility. Harvey *et al.* (1975) provided a demonstration of the actor–observer divergence. Their study used a scenario similar to the famous Milgram (1974) studies on obedience; where people in the role of 'teachers' were required to deliver electric 'shocks' of increasing strength in order to improve the performance of a 'student'. As was the case with Milgram's study, people were prepared to deliver massive electric shocks up to hundreds of volts. Observers in the study conducted by Harvey *et al.* attributed this extreme obedience to authority to internal dispositions of the 'teacher' delivering the shocks. In their study, both actors (those who delivered the shocks) and observers (who witnessed the behaviour of the actors) were asked to rate the responsibility for what was done of the 'teacher' and of the experimenter who gave orders to the 'teacher' to increase the voltage whenever the student failed.

Actors attributed more personal responsibility to the experimenter than to themselves, while observers reversed that pattern and emphasized the responsibility of the actors (the 'teachers') as compared to the experimenter. As argued before, this effect would also be predicted on the basis of the self-serving bias. The most stringent test for the actor–observer divergence will be provided by attributions for successes or desirable outcomes. In this case the self-serving bias makes a prediction for actors (internal, dispositional attribution) contrary to that of the actor–observer divergence. The latter will predict an external attribution for the actor. Attributions for neutral behaviour would also provide an appropriate test of the actor–observer divergence. In this instance, the self-serving bias makes no predictions at all.

A majority of the studies confirm the actor–observer divergence with respect to either successes or neutral behaviours. These (e.g. Nisbett *et al.*, 1973; McArthur, 1972) all found actors preferring external, situational attributions for their behaviour while observers preferred internal, dispositional attributions for the same behaviours. Unfortunately, there are also quite a few studies that did not find an actor–observer divergence (e.g. Miller and Norman, 1975; Miller and Porter, 1980). A number of studies indicate that evaluative factors (i.e. the desirability of the action) can have a strong effect on attributional preferences and diminish actor–observer differences (e.g. Taylor and Koivumaki, 1976; van der Pligt and Eiser, 1983). In these studies no support was obtained for self–other differences in attributional

61

preference, as both actors and observers tended to attribute success and desirable behaviours to dispositional factors while failure and negative behaviours were attributed to situational factors. In other words, some biases (such as the above 'positivity bias') seem to have a stronger influence on attributional preferences than the actor–observer divergence.

The lack of consistency in the results of studies testing the actor–observer divergence has also led to research attempting to specify the determinants that could account for both confirmations and failures to confirm the actor–observer divergence. The above-mentioned positivity effect is an example that applies to behaviours that are clearly desirable or undesirable. Other explanations have a wider scope (i.e. including neutral actions) and tend to emphasize perceptual biases.

For instance, Storms (1973) predicted that actors having a conversation with a stranger will offer different explanations of their own behaviour than observers. In his experiment the conversation lasted five minutes and both the actor and the observer were asked to rate the actor's talkativeness, dominance, friendliness and nervousness in the conversation just completed. Actors and observers were also asked to indicate to what extent the actor's behaviour in the conversation was determined by his or her personal characteristics, personality traits, attitudes, etc., and to what extent by the situation (the behaviour of the stranger, the requirement to get acquainted). Actors attributed less responsibility to themselves and placed greater importance on situational factors than did observers, while observers put more emphasis on personal characteristics than actors did.

Storms's experiment gives some indication of differences between actor and observer that could help explain the actor–observer divergence. Firstly, the actors' visual field was dominated by the external person (the stranger) while the observers were asked to watch the actor; i.e. there was a clear difference in what the actors and observers attended to. Secondly, actors knew about their own past and consequently their friendliness, talkativeness, nervousness and dominance in other situations than the experiment. Thirdly, actors knew how they had behaved but also what they had felt and thought, while observers had to rely upon behavioural evidence only. All three differences –

visual salience, knowledge about the consistency of behaviour in the past and in other situations, and access to private experience – were suggested by Jones and Nisbett (1971) as possible causes for an actor–observer divergence.

The Storms study mentioned above focused on visual salience as a possible explanation and included a cunning experimental manipulation to test this possible cause. Storms exposed all participants to a replay on video of the five-minute get-acquainted conversation. The tapes were being assigned in such a way that some participants saw again what they had seen the first time and others saw the reverse (e.g. the actor now saw a replay from the visual perspective of the observer and watched himself in the conversation). In other words, Storms disentangled two things that in normal life invariably go hand in hand: explanations of one's own behaviour are always accompanied by a visual perspective that is directed outward. Similarly, explanations of another person's behaviour are usually made in a visual perspective dominated by the person displaying the behaviour. Storms's experiment revealed that actors made to look at *themselves* made attributions not normally associated with actors (a preference for situational attributions), but attributions normally made by observers (a preference for dispositional attributions). Similarly, when observers saw a reply of the conversation filmed from the perspective of the actor, they made attributions similar to the actors.

What the Storms's study established was that visual perspective is a determinant of perceived causality. Perceptual salience thus plays an important role in attributional processes. Taylor and Fiske (1978) argued that perceptual salience is not only relevant in the context of the actor–observer divergence. For instance, they showed that one person standing out by reason of, for example, sex or race in a group discussion will attract selective attention, will be salient and hence will be perceived as a particularly important cause of the things that happen in the group.

Regan and Totten (1975) suggested that psychological rather than visual perspective is the crucial antecedent of the actor–observer divergence. They conducted an experiment like that of Storms. All subjects looked at a videotape of a real get-acquainted conversation. Some subjects were simply required

63

to watch one of the two people in the conversation, others were instructed to empathize with a specific actor (e.g. imagine how the person feels in the conversation). After watching the video-tape people were asked to rate the actor's behaviour in terms of friendliness, talkativeness, nervousness, and dominance, and to indicate the relative importance of situational and dispositional factors in explaining the behaviour. Observers given instructions to empathize assigned greater causal efficacy to the situation as compared to those who were only viewers of the conversation.

To summarize, perceptual salience increases the likelihood of situational attributions for the actors and personal dispositions for observers. Perceptual salience is, however, not the only factor that influences the perspective taken by the observer. Empathy could also lead people to share the perspective of the actor and make actor-like attributions. Brown (1986, pp. 190–1) concludes that research findings on the influence of visual orientation and psychological perspective on attribution suggest that there are two ways of looking at someone. If you look simply at behaviour or action in a noninterpretational manner you attribute causality to the actor. This preference is easily reversed by reversing the visual orientation. Most looking is of this kind and, in everyday life, most actors look outward at the situation while observers look at the actor, hence the usually obtained actor–observer divergence. A second type of looking-at is less super-ficial and more interpretative (i.e. focusing on expressive behaviour and attempting to adopt the psychological perspective of the actor). This way of 'looking-at' also seems to reduce the actor–observer divergence in attributional preferences.

The fundamental attribution error

Ross (1977) hypothesized a tendency for attributors (observers) to underestimate the impact of situational factors and to over-estimate the role of dispositional factors in the explanation of behaviour. This he termed the *fundamental attribution error*. Evidence accumulating over the years has supported this hypo-thesis (see Harvey and Weary, 1984, for a review), but some studies have failed to to do so. Examples of confirmations are the earlier-mentioned studies on 'correspondent inference'. The explanations offered by the literature emphasize perceptual salience as a determining factor in the observers' tendency to stress personal causes for behaviour at the expense of possible situational factors. If situational causes of behaviour are somehow made salient, one would expect a bias towards situational attributions. Quattrone (1982) conducted an experiment in which observers did make correspondent inferences to the salient situation and not to the actor. In other words, both the fundamental attribution error and the actor–observer divergence seem to depend on the relative salience of actor and situation. Both have acquired special status because it usually is the case that, when looking at someone's behaviour, the situation is less salient and the person more salient and, consequently, the causal role of situations is underestimated while the causal efficacy of personal characteristics is overestimated.

A number of studies suggest that the fundamental attribution error is (a) not *the* error, (b) not fundamental in the sense of unanalysable, and (c) better described as a *bias* in social judgment. Furthermore, the fundamental attribution error can also be described as a defensible heuristic. Nisbett and Ross (1980) and Markus and Zajonc (1985) argue that personal dispositions are generally more informative and possibly more predictive of people's behaviour than situational elements. When another person's behaviours are observed and interpreted, we tend to take them as instances of some general principle – friendly people smile, careless people have accidents, dishonest people tell lies, etc. Thus, on occasions, the fundamental attribution error is a heuristic helping us to predict and understand people's behaviour. In many cases, however, the emphasis on personal attributions seems to lead to an illusion of predictability.

Two points need to be made with respect to the fundamental attribution error and the actor–observer divergence. Firstly, the internal–external distinction has come to be seen as the most important distinguishing feature of causes. It is not clear, however, that such emphasis is fully warranted. Heider (1958) proposed a hydraulic relation between personal and situational causality: the more the person is seen as causing a specific behaviour, the less causal influence the environment will be perceived to exert. Many researchers have accepted the premise that the two sources of causality operate in a complementary fashion, and some have provided subjects with a single measure in which situational attributions anchor one end of the scale and personal attributions the other end. Studies that looked at the relations between the two attribution dimensions have resulted in less than encouraging results, however, Usually, researchers obtained low and nonsignificant correlations between personal and situational attributions (e.g. Lepper, 1973; Miller, Smith and Uhleman, 1981; van der Pligt and Eiser, 1983). It seems that perceivers will not necessarily consider situational and personal attributions to be inversely related. The failure to observe a hydraulic relationship between personal and situational causality suggests that more complex patterns could also be favoured (e.g. behaviour as an indication of something about the person as well as something about the situation). Interestingly, Kassin and Hochreich (1977) found that people are more likely to employ combinations of person and situation attributions when attributional accuracy is seen as important.

A final point that needs to be raised with respect to attribution concerns the importance of other factors in determining attributional preferences. As we have already seen, attributors may have a variety of goals in mind when making attributions. It could well be that dimensions other than the internality or externality of the cause may be seen as more important in specific circumstances. Dimensions such as stability, predictability and personal control are a few examples. Some of these will be discussed in the next section, in which we discuss consequences of attributions.

Consequences of attribution

In the previous sections we discussed possible determinants of attributions and the possible explanations of a number of attributional biases. People's attributions, however, can also have consequences. These consequences include other cognitions such as expectancies about future events, emotions and affective reactions, and behaviour. In this section we will present a brief review of the consequences of attributions for success and failure.

A research question that is of great practical relevance in the fields of education and of clinical psychology is that of how people explain the achievement, or lack of achievement, shown by themselves and others. If one succeeds, is it because the task was easy, because one was lucky, because of superior skill, or because of extra effort? The answer is likely to affect how much personal credit one should be given for success, and whether one would expect it to be repeated.

The question of whether success or failure should be internally or externally attributed is basic to social learning theory approaches to personality. According to Rotter (1966), individuals differ in the extent to which they expect 'reinforcements' to occur, as a function of their own behaviour ('internal control'), or as a function of luck or forces beyond their personal control ('external control'). The I–E scale devised by Rotter to measure individuals' positions on this dimension of 'locus of control' consists of pairs of statements such as, 'Becoming a success is a matter of hard work, luck has little or nothing to do with it' and 'Getting a good job depends mainly on being in the right place at the right time', subjects having to indicate which statement in each pair is closer to their own opinion. (In this example, endorsement of the second alternative would be taken as indicative of an external orientation.)

How, then, do people's attributions for success or failure influence their expectancies for future success? The attributional distinction to which most attention has been paid in the research so far described is that between internal and external causes. Heider (1958) also discussed achievement-related behaviours in his book. He suggested that a person's level of performance on a task will be attributed either to factors within the person or to factors within the environment. The two major environmental factors are luck (or opportunity) and task difficulty. The two major personal factors are ability and effort. Furthermore, ability is seen as a *stable* element and effort an unstable element. The two environmental factors were also distinguished on the stability dimension. Weiner and his colleagues have conducted the most extensive research programme based on Heider's analysis of achievement attributions.

Weiner (1979) put forward the view that causes may also be classified as controllable or uncontrollable, and as stable or unstable over time. Thus, a person's ability would be an internal but uncontrollable cause, stable over time, the amount of effort expended on a task would be an internal, controllable but unstable cause, the difficulty of the task would be external, controllable and stable, and luck would be external, uncontrollable and unstable. The difference between the two internal causes, ability and effort, seems especially important when evaluating other people's performance. For instance, Weiner and Kukla (1970) found that subjects, instructed to play the role of school-teachers giving rewards and punishments for pupils' examination performance, rewarded pupils more for greater effort than for greater ability. Where pupils of different ability achieved the same level of performance, those with less ability received the greater reward.

In the context of attributions for one's own success or failure, Weiner incorporates these distinctions to revise Atkinson's (1957) concept of achievement motivation. According to Atkinson, the amount of 'pride' obtained from the attainment of some goal is related to the subjective difficulty of the task, so that success at a more difficult task leads to a greater sense of achievement. In terms of the attributional model of achievement motivation (Weiner and Kukla, 1970; Weiner et al., 1971), what is crucial is the degree of perceived personal responsibility for success or failure. Thus individuals high in achievement motivation are assumed to be attracted to achievement-related activities, which allow the attribution of success to ability and effort. Furthermore, they persist in the face of failure, which they tend to attribute to lack of effort rather than ability, and select tasks of intermediate difficulty (since too easy a task will give no sense of achievement, but too difficult a task is likely to lead to failure). Finally, they tend to try hard, in accordance with their assumption that success is at least partly a function of effort. By comparison, people low in achievement motivation are assumed to be less attracted to achievement-related activities, since they would tend to attribute success externally even if they succeeded; give up in the face of failure, which they are more likely to attribute to lack of ability than to lack of effort; select either extremely easy or extremely difficult tasks, since these provide the least information on which to base a self-evaluation; and tend not to try hard, since success, particularly at the kinds of tasks they choose, is assumed to be largely unrelated to effort.

The importance of the stability and locus of causality dimension has been substantiated in other research. Expectancies for success on a task are higher among subjects making attributions to stable causal factors (ability and task ease) rather than unstable factors (luck and effort), but are unaffected by locus of causality (Weiner *et al.*, 1971). Chapter 5 presents illustrations of these phenomena in the context of addictive behaviours. The other important aspects of Weiner's theory concern the affective reactions to successes and failures. These appear to be more strongly connected to the locus of causality dimension. Thus Weiner distinguishes the affective component of achievement motivation (e.g., pride in success or shame at failure) from expectancy for future success or failure. Expectancy is seen to depend primarily on stable *v.* unstable causes. Attribution of success to a stable cause, or of failure to an unstable cause leads to a higher expectancy of success than does attribution of failure to a stable cause, or of success to an unstable cause (Weiner, 1979). For instance, if you did badly on a test and attributed this to unstable factors such as luck and effort, you would expect these unstable factors not to be present again, and simply try again, expecting to succeed. On the other hand, if you attributed your failure to stable factors (task difficulty and lack of ability) your expectations are bound to be lower; neither your ability nor the task's difficulty is going to change the next time you try the task. Attributions to internal *v.* external, or controllable *v.* uncontrollable causes, by comparison, have their main influence on the affective component. Feelings of pride for success and shame for failure are heightened when the performance is seen as caused by internal factors (ability, effort) rather than external factors (luck and task difficulty).

It needs to be noted, however, that the four causes of ability, effort, luck, and task difficulty do not play as dominant a role in common-sense explanations as both Heider and Weiner seem to imply. Open-ended studies of attribution have shown that people often explain performances with reference to ability, task difficulty and effort. On the other hand, luck or chance is rarely mentioned, while people also use explanations such as mood, personality, fatigue, and interest (Darley and Goethals, 1980; Elig and Frieze, 1975, 1979). Research on the affective consequences of achievement-related attributions is still in its infancy but is an important area of future work. More recently Weiner (1985a, 1986) proposed a more comprehensive theory of outcome-dependent emotions, such as happiness and frustration, and dimension-linked (controllability, internal *v.* external) emotions such as pride, anger, pity, gratitude, guilt, and shame. Although his work does not present a complete theory of emotions, the proposed attributional model attempts to deal with some of the most common emotional experiences.

Helplessness, depression and realism

A number of researchers have applied attribution formulations about success and failure to the clinical symptoms of depression. A closely related notion to that of expectancy for failure is 'learned helplessness'. The origin of this notion can be traced to an experiment by Seligman and Maier (1967), who found that dogs which had received a series of shocks from which they were unable to escape, later failed to learn a simple operant response for avoiding shock in a different situation. The interpretation is that the dogs develop an expectancy that responding will be ineffective and so fail to initiate new behaviours that may lead to the termination of shock; or, if they make an occasional response that stops the shock, fail to repeat it. Seligman has since argued (1972, 1975) that this situation may be analogous to depression in humans. An inability to respond effectively may reflect a learned expectancy that any response will be ineffective. Hiroto and Seligman (1975) found that exposing people to inescapable aversive stimuli, or presenting them with insoluble discrimination problems, produced deficits in subsequent performance at tasks involving avoidance behaviour or anagram solving, analogous to the 'learned helplessness' effects found with dogs.

The learned-helplessness model of depression was reformulated by Abramson *et al.* (1978) so as to include attributional concepts. According to Abramson et al., for depression to occur, individuals must not only experience uncontrollable outcomes, they must develop expectations that future outcomes will also be uncontrollable. Depressives are predicted to attribute negative outcomes to internal, global and stable factors, and they may also attribute good outcomes to external, specific and unstable factors (Seligman *et al.*, 1979). The distinctive claim in Seligman's work is the idea that individuals will make causal attributions even when no information about consensus, distinctiveness and consistency is available, and that there will be individual differences in attributional style such that depressives will tend to attribute negative outcomes to internal, global and stable causes.

Just as feelings of lack of control may be implicated in depression, so feelings of positive control may play a part in adjustment to more adverse circumstances. Taylor, Lichtman and Wood (1984) found that, among women being treated for breast cancer, those who showed better adjustment had more positive beliefs about either their own ability, or that of physicians, to control their cancer. Although the great majority of the women made attributions for why they had developed cancer, neither the particular attributions offered, nor whether responsibility was internally or externally attributed, made a difference to level of adjustment.

Anderson *et al.* (1983) found that attributional style is related to depression *and* loneliness. It appears that personal, internal attributions for failure may be associated with depression and loneliness. These authors, however, claim more than a simple association, and posit that a depressive attributional style predisposes individuals to depression. Most of the available evidence, on the other hand, suggests that attributions may not play a causal role in producing depressive symptoms. Studies by Peterson *et al.* (1981) and Lewinsohn *et al.* (1981) suggest that attributional style is a major concomitant of depression, but not a cause.

Similar conclusions are reached by Brewin (1985) in a review that concentrates on clinical as opposed to experimental evidence. He argues that attributions of helplessness may often be a consequence of depressed mood, and that there is little evidence that depression is dependent on the attributions people make for specific life events. On the other hand, Brewin suggests that attributions may reflect positive and negative coping styles that may be quite important predictors of recovery from depressive episodes.

Research and theory in the areas of depression and loneliness continue to shed light on the role of attributions in the development of these phenomena. More research is needed on important issues such as how attributional styles develop and under what conditions attributional style contributes to depression and loneliness. Finally, the study of these phenomena in more realistic everyday settings seems essential for the further development of this area.

Attributions, causality and expectancy

Attribution research has held a dominant position within social psychology over the last fifteen years, and has been applied to many practical fields.

One of the theoretical issues that is of considerable importance to attribution theory concerns the concept of causality. Heider's (1944, 1946) early work derived from an interest in the notion of 'phenomenal causality' – i.e. how objects and people come to be seen as causal origins. The legacy of this concern with phenomenal causality is that there has been a bias towards interpreting attributional responses as causal explanations of events.

One determinant of the extent to which people engage in attributional analysis is their curiosity about the causes of a specific behaviour. Curiosity is most likely to be aroused when a behaviour is unexpected – either because it is discrepant from the actor's past behaviour or from the perceiver's normative expectations. This is confirmed by findings obtained by Weiner and his associates (Weiner, 1985b; Wong and Weiner, 1981). Their studies focus on the kinds of situations in which attributional activity is likely to occur – with the implication that there are many events that we allow to pass by without attributional analysis. Weiner (1985b) reviews seventeen publications showing that people will spontaneously engage in search for explanations without the intervention of a questioner. Most of these studies indicate that such 'causal search' is stimulated primarily by *unexpected* events, particularly those involving loss or failure. Hastie (1984) similarly argues that unexpected events elicit causal reasoning, and that such reasoning can lead to a more elaborate representation of such events in memory.

Another factor influencing willingness to engage in attributional search is the personal relevance of the event or behaviour to the perceiver. This is illustrated by Fletcher (1981, 1983) who studied attributions for marriage separations. Important events such as these can lead to elaborate and complex attributional analysis. Other possible reasons for making attributions are the goal to predict people's behaviour and the need for control. This suggests that attributions do not (just) serve as explanations.

Overall the conclusion seems to be that attributional activity occurs primarily in order to deal with the unwanted or unexpected. This conclusion is not only intuitively compelling, but consistent with Heider's (1958, p. 25) own view that 'Attribution serves the attainment of a stable and consistent environment . . . and determines what we expect will occur and what we should do about it.' Thus, explaining the past is most likely to occur when it helps us to predict and (possibly) control the future.

It needs to be stressed, however, that the importance of phenomenal causality is sometimes secondary to the need for control and prediction. Attribution theory starts from a concern with causal explanations and hypothesizes ways in which information must be weighted and compared in order to make such explanations possible. If, however, people appear prepared to let many events occur without asking *why* they occur, the generality of the theory looks more questionable.

In other words, many aspects of social judgment are not causal in nature. There seems no reason to assume that people are forever pondering or even curious about the possible causes of their own or others' behaviour. Quite often research findings are based on responses to a particular form of question, typically asked by psychologists, but not so typically by anybody else. People have other goals and needs than those related to a causal analysis of behaviour.

In many contexts, however, attributions do matter. Preferences for certain attributions do play a role in many decisions ranging from individual decisions to social policy issues. For instance, the lower educational attainment of some of the ethnic minorities in Western Europe can be related to a variety of causes. Attributing this disparity to the specific ethnic group or to external factors such as lack of facilities and balanced programmes is bound to affect one's preference for solutions to these problems. Similarly, attributing people's inability to find a job to their lack of effort will affect your view on social policy issues.

To a certain extent the above examples suffer from the same drawback as many studies in the field of attribution theory. Too often, it is assumed that the internal-external dimension is important, but frequently we need more than that to explain events and behaviours. People use more causal concepts than the internal-external distinction. Unfortunately, the causal concepts used in the ordinary person's thinking are not well researched. Kelley and Michela (1980) termed this the 'central irony' of attribution research.

The above shortcomings should not be seen as a denigration of attribution theory. Attributional approaches represent a diverse and innovative area of research, and the study of attributions has helped us to understand the different kinds of feelings and behaviours in a wide variety of contexts. It is quite another thing to say that such feelings and behaviours generally *depend* on relatively simple distinctions such as internal versus external causes. For this, the evidence is far less convincing.

Decisions, heuristics and biases

In the previous chapter we discussed a number of judgmental biases as possible explanations for people's attributions. The study of biases and heuristics is one of special importance to the area of decision-making.

A recurrent issue in social psychological research is whether human behaviour can be said to obey 'rational' rules. Discussions of decision-making frequently refer to human rationality versus irrationality, functionality versus maladaptiveness and optimality versus error. Decision-making researchers' concern with rationality is related to the existence of normative models for decision-making. Unlike research on issues such as aggression, helping behaviour, conformity and personal relationships, research on decision-making includes both the development of prescriptive, normative models and of more descriptive accounts. As a result, the discrepancies often found between normative models and actual decision-making have resulted in considerable concern with human rationality. There is a large number of positions on human rationality; these vary from the

human decision-maker as a rationalist whose violations of optimality are simple, correctable slip-ups; to the human decision-
maker as irrational due to uncontrollable emotional or motivational forces. Intermediate positions are those formulated by
Simon (1955) who argued that the decision-maker is rational
but only up to a point, i.e. people choose options that are good
enough. The phrases *satisficing* and *bounded rationality* have been
applied to formulate an alternative to the economist's conception
requiring a complete cost/benefit analysis of each of the decision
options. More recently, research efforts focus on apparent biases
in human judgments arising from the use of *heuristics* (simplifying shortcuts). The majority of this work was inspired by the
work of Kahneman and Tversky (1972, 1984; Tversky and
Kahneman, 1974) and it tends to stress human fallibility. People
are usually seen as trying vaguely to be rational but failing
frequently to appreciate normatively appropriate strategies.

Most decisions are characterized by some level of uncertainty;
in this chapter we will discuss a number of formal models of
the structure of risky decisions. These will be followed by a
short review of factors that in one way or another may exert a
constraining influence on effective decision-making. Finally, we
will discuss ways to improve decision-making.

Models of decision-making

Research on the structure of risky decisions focuses on the
relationship between decisions and expected consequences.
Many of the concepts in this field have been borrowed from
economics and are based on the comparison of expected costs
and benefits.

The simplest theory of decision-making is based on the notion
of expected monetary values. Consider the option of buying a
lottery ticket offering one chance in 1000 of winning a £500
prize. The 'fair' price to pay for such a ticket could be based
on the 'expected value' of the ticket; the probability of winning,
multiplied by the prize to be won. In this case the expected
value would be (1/1000) × £500, or £0.50. The sense in which
£0.50 would constitute a 'fair' price requires a long sequence
of choices. On the average the lottery would pay off once every

thousand offers, and each thousand outlays of the fair £0.50 would balance the £500 prize for the win.

In the above case, as in classical statistics, a probability is simply a long-run frequency. Calculating such probabilities requires taking a large number of samples (rolling a pair of dice 1,000 times, for instance) and noting how often various numbers occur. There is another type of probability, however. This is the *subjective probability* used by the manager when (s)he forecasts a 90 per cent chance of obtaining an order, or by the engineer who estimates that the chance of a nuclear power accident is one in a million. This latter type of probability is not directly based on frequency but represents someone's subjective belief in the likelihood of an event. This subjective belief can, of course, be derived from frequency information, but usually it is a mixture of past experience and educated guesses. The important difference between the two types of probability is not in their method of estimation but in what they stand for – objective frequency counts or subjective belief.

Subjective elements not only play a role in assessing probabilities but also in the assessment of values. For instance, the psychological value of money does not increase proportionally as its objective amount increases. The term 'utility' helps us to differentiate objective monetary value from subjective value. For example, when a rich person and a poor person both bet on the same winning horse at the racetrack, the monetary value of their £100 win is identical, but the subjective utility of this win for the poor person – for whom £100 is a lot of money – is much greater than for the rich person to whom an extra £100 means little. In many decisions, utilities include more than monetary values. They also include intangibles such as pleasure, pain and the quality of life. The subjective element in assessments of probabilities and values is embodied in subjectively expected utility, a concept proposed by Ramsey (1926).

Subjective expected utility

Imagine that you have just finished your first degree at a small campus university in a rural area, and you have a choice of three options for the future: (a) studying for a further degree at your university, (b) studying for a further degree at a university in a major city and (c) a job at a commercial firm in the same city. Confronted with these alternatives you are likely to compare the alternatives in terms of aspects that are important to you (e.g. salary, future career prospects, nightlife, friendships, availability of living accommodation).

A simple and comprehensive rule for making decisions is the following. Firstly, list all the feasible courses of action. For each action, enumerate the possible consequences. For each consequence, assess the attractiveness or aversiveness (utility) of its occurrence, as well as the likelihood that it will be incurred should the action be taken. Next, compute the expected utility of each consequence by multiplying its utility by its likelihood or probability of occurrence. The overall expected utility of a specific action is the sum of the expected utility of all possible consequences. Finally, once all these calculations are completed, choose the action with the greatest expected utility. Subjective expected utility theory (SEU) is a prominent approach to human decision-making and incorporates the above rules. The model can be expressed by:

$$\text{SEU} = \sum_i p_i \cdot u_i \qquad (1)$$

where p_i is the subjective probability of outcome i, u_i is the utility of outcome i. These utilities are multiplied by their probability and summed to obtain the overall subjective expected utility (SEU).

In the decision-making literature, SEU theory is known as a *normative* or prescriptive theory. It provides a set of rules for combining beliefs (probabilities) and preferences (utilities) to make a decision. The terms *normative* and *prescriptive* as used here mean that such theories specify how decisions *should* be made. If you accept the axioms upon which they are based, then the only rational choice is the one specified by the theory.

Subjective expected utility models of human decision-making reduce the universe of decisions to a common set of primitives (outcomes, probabilities, utilities) on the basis of which one can make reasonable decisions. In this context, probabilities are represented on a ratio scale (extending from 0 to 1), and utilities are assumed to exist on an interval scale (extending between two arbitrary points, say 0 to 50 with the property that a score of, say, 30 is twice as far from 10 in extra utility as a score of 20). Finally, people's optimal choice criterion is expected to be maximization of subjective expected utility.

Some writers have argued that simply explaining the rationale behind normative theories should encourage decision-makers to conform to their demands (Estes, 1980). However, conformity to the axioms underlying normative models of decision-making seems more wishful thinking than fact. People do not always behave as normative theories such as SEU claim they should (Edwards, 1955; Lichtenstein and Slovic, 1971). In one study (Lichtenstein, Slovic and Zinc, 1969), subjects ignored expected utility in making their decisions even after the experimenters had carefully explained the concept to them (see also Kahneman, Slovic and Tversky, 1982).

More than two decades of research in cognitive psychology have clear negative consequences for the descriptive validity of SEU models. The major conclusion of this research, going back as far as the early work of Miller (1956) and Simon (1957), is that combining the assumed, quite substantial quantities of information in one's head simply exceeds our computational capacity (cf. Fischhoff, Goitein and Shapira, 1982). Research indicates that, when there are many cues or unusual relation-ships between the cues, people tend to violate decision rules such as those of SEU. Findings obtained by Slovic (1974) suggest that people find it difficult to learn and use a weighted sum decision rule. In other words, people frequently could not use the decision rule assumed by SEU models, even if they tried. Furthermore, evidence presented by Fischhoff et al. (1982) shows that many of the axioms upon which the model is based are contradicted by empirical evidence. For instance, perceptions of values and probabilities are not independent (see also Sundstrom, DeVault and Peele, 1981), probability assess-ments tend to be poorly calibrated (Lichtenstein, Fischhoff and Philips, 1977) and the reliability of utilities of desired outcomes is fairly modest and not consistent across different situations.

Furthermore, there is substantial evidence that many people have difficulty thinking probabilistically. These difficulties are not only experienced by lay people but also by people who deal professionally with probabilistic information. Eddy (1980), for instance, found evidence of misunderstanding of conditional

79

probabilities even by professional physicians (see Chapter 6). Numerous psychological studies have also shown that how decisions are presented, the number of alternatives, and even the presentation of irrelevant information can affect a decision outcome (see Payne, 1982, for a review). Not only do such findings severely limit the applicability of normative theories (which usually assume that decisions are reached the same way across contexts), they also suggest that there are different decision-making strategies for different situations.

All these analyses suggest that the conscious thought preceding a decision may be of a relatively simple nature, given the difficulty of processing complex information. People seem to rely on simple heuristics for making probability judgments and hardly seem to think about more complex combinations of values or utilities involved in a decision. In other words, people's decision processes seem relatively inarticulated and are hardly compatible with the sort of rigorous, systematic thinking required by SEU formulations that involve a considerable number of possible consequences. The model presents an over-intellectualized view of the cognitive processes people go through when making decisions, forming attitudes, or choosing alternative actions. As a consequence, psychologists became more interested in understanding how people actually make decisions in the real world. This research field has come to be known as the 'descriptive' approach to the study of decision-making.

Prospect theory

Kahneman and Tversky (1979) attempted to provide a more general theory of decision-making under uncertainty. Their 'prospect theory' seems the most comprehensive attempt at meeting the various objections to the normative models of decision-making we discussed earlier. Two important assumptions of prospect theory are:

1 Decisions are made not with regard to the desirability of consequences or end-states as such, but with regard to how such end-states relate to some reference point (such as the

present). In other words, outcomes are not evaluated as *absolute* costs or benefits, but as *relative* losses or gains.

2 Expected losses and gains influence decisions in direct *but not exact* proportion to their (subjective) probability. The probability terms in the calculation of SEU are therefore replaced by 'decision weights' reflecting the importance of each possible consequence.

Like subjective expected utility theory, prospect theory assumes that the value V of an option is calculated as a sum of products over its specified outcomes x, each product consisting of a utility $v(x)$ and a weight π attached to the objective probability p of obtaining x, or

$$V = \sum_i \pi(p_i)v(x_i) \tag{2}$$

Prospect theory is unique in the set of assumptions made about the functions v and π and about contextual effects surrounding the choice.

The probability-weighting function. The function $\pi(p)$ is not given in closed mathematical form but, on the basis of inference from Kahneman and Tversky's own empirical work, is assumed to have a shape something like that indicated in Figure 4.1.

One of the noteworthy features of this function is that it changes near the endpoints, where $\pi(0) = 0$ and $\pi(1) = 1$, such that small probabilities are overweighted and large probabilities are underweighted ('objective' weighting would require $\pi(p) = p$).

The sharp increase in π in moving from high probability to certainty contributes to the so-called certainty effect. An example is given by the following task used by Kahneman and Tversky. A group of subjects was asked to choose between options A and B, where A was a win of \$4000 with a probability of .8, otherwise nothing; and B was \$3000 for sure. Only a small minority (20 per cent) chose the gamble (A), with the larger prize, over the sure option (B). Another group of subjects was asked to choose between options C and D, where C was \$4000 with a probability of .2, otherwise nothing; and D was \$3000 with a probability of .25, otherwise nothing. In this case a clear majority (65 per cent) chose to gamble on C, with the larger prize, over D, with a smaller but somewhat more likely prize. This violates the

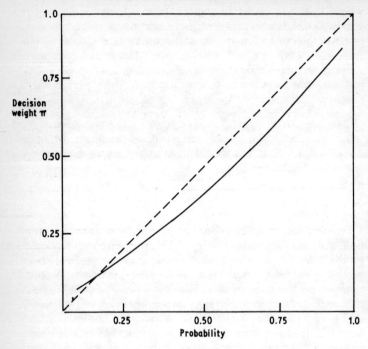

Figure 4.1 Prospect theory: hypothetical probability-weighting function

expected utility principle, which requires consistency in the A versus B and C versus D choices. In the A versus B and C versus D choices the ratio of the probabilities of getting the prizes is the same (.8/1 = .20/.25), yet the preference tends to reverse.

Evidently, the weight given a probability of .8 as a proportion of the weight given a sure thing is psychologically smaller than the weight given a probability of .20 as a proportion of the weight given a probability of .25. In other words, the reduction of probability from certainty to some degree of uncertainty produces a more pronounced loss of attractiveness than does a corresponding reduction from one level of uncertainty to another. Prospect theory attempts to deal with these differences. The previous example can be traced to Figure 4.1: inspection of the probability-weighting function will show that $\pi(.20)/\pi(.25) > \pi(.8)/\pi(1)$.

Another important aspect of the probability-weighting function concerns low probabilities. The overweighting of small probabilities potentially explains the attractiveness of long-shot gambling (as in lotteries), and the tendency to insure against rare potential catastrophes (as in fire insurance). In both cases the rare events – the lottery success or the disastrous property loss – seem to loom larger in the decisions (i.e. gambling or buying an insurance) than the objective probabilities would seem to warrant. The probability-weighting function π of prospect theory is 'regressive with respect to p', as Kahneman and Tversky put it (1979, p. 282). In other words, all uncertainty tends to have a common character, regardless of degree. A probability of .25 is not very different psychologically from a probability of .40 or even .50, at least not as different as it ought to be according to the expectation principles of choice. Even small-probability events partake of what we might call 'possibilityhood' (cf. Abelson and Levi, 1985), enhancing the extent to which they influence decisions. The effects on decisions of possibilityhood can also be enhanced by factors such as dramatic salience. Thus TV images of tragic fire losses, nuclear accidents, chemical disasters, or of delirious national lottery winners could exaggerate the perceived likelihood of these events. Thus *both* overexaggeration and overweighting may characterize some low-probability events.

However, there is also empirical evidence that people tend to ignore extremely low probability events. As a consequence, Kahneman and Tversky (1979) concluded that 'the π-function is not well-behaved near its end-points'. This could be due to people's difficulties in comprehending and evaluating extreme probabilities. Thus, highly unlikely events are either ignored or overweighted, and the difference between high probability and certainty is either neglected or exaggerated.

The probability-weighting function of prospect theory is not only regressive with respect to p (i.e. has a slope generally less than 1 when plotted against p) but is also depressed with respect to p throughout most of the range of p. Mere possibility seems therefore a relatively unpersuasive feature of outcomes. Note for instance, that the weight $\pi(.5)$ associated with the probability of .5 is somewhat less than .5 – somewhere between .35 and .40; a probability of about .65 is necessary to achieve a π of .5. Thus, half a chance is weighted not much better than about a third of a chance, and two-thirds of a chance is necessary to produce a subjective impact halfway between certainty and impossibility. Abelson and Levi (1985) note that the implication of this assertion is that risky ventures with equally balanced potential gains and losses will be seen as rash with objective probabilities of success below two-thirds. A probability above two-thirds will tend to make the venture seem generally sound. A psychological division between perceived rashness and soundness at a probability of around .65 has in fact been found by Myers and Lamm (1977).

The value function. The other major component of prospect theory is the value function, $v(x)$ in Eq. (2). As discussed before, v is defined in terms of gains and losses of wealth or welfare from some reference point or adaptation level. Figure 4.2 presents the shape of the value function.

The region of gains above the reference point is characterized by a concave value function. In other words, each unit increase in gain of wealth has less and less value as gain increases. This type of function disposes towards caution or risk aversion. For instance, one would expect a preference for a sure win of £200 over a 50-50 chance for a win of £400 or nothing. As we have seen before, the subcertainty of the probability-weighting function also leads to a prediction of risk aversion in the above

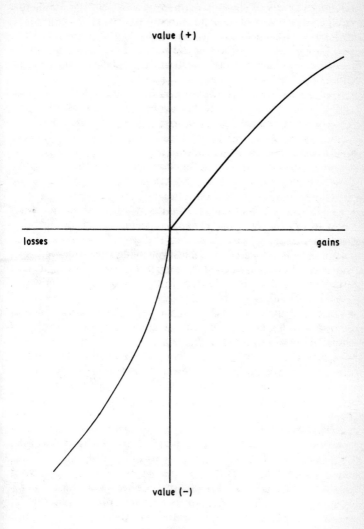

Figure 4.2 Prospect theory: hypothetical value function

example (see Figure 4.1). Thus risk aversion in such choices does not provide evidence for either function without some assumption about the other. In some cases the two functions will lead to opposite predictions. For instance, with prospects in which there is a small chance of a sizeable gain, the probability-weighting function works in favour of the seeking of risk as opposed to the risk aversion due to the concavity of the value function.

In the region of losses (the area below the reference point), each unit increase in potential losses has a decreasing impact on overall (negative) value. For instance, losing £100 is less than twice as unpleasant as losing £50. Thus, the marginal value of both losses and gains generally decreases with their magnitude. The convexity of the value function below the reference point predicts risk-seeking. A 50-50 chance of losing £400 or losing nothing would be preferred to a sure loss of £200. Here, too, the effects of subcertainty are in the same direction as the effects due to the convexity of the value function, i.e. in the direction of risk-seeking. Again these converging tendencies may be in opposite directions when small probabilities are involved. For instance, if an option contains a small-probability loss, subjects may find it less attractive due to their tendency to overweight low probabilities.

Another important aspect of the value function is that it is steeper for losses than for gains. This difference in steepness is related to a salient characteristic of attitudes to changes in welfare, i.e. *losses loom larger than gains*. Generally, the aggravation that one experiences in losing a sum of money appears to be greater than the pleasure associated with gaining the same amount. In other words, losing £200 is more aversive than a gain of £200 is attractive.

The conjunction of risk-aversion for gains and risk-seeking for losses leads to what Kahneman and Tversky (1979) call the *reflection effect*. Reflection of the signs of the possible outcomes of prospects typically reverses the preference order between these prospects. This effect can produce paradoxical effects when the same problem is presented in terms of losses or in terms of gains. These effects will be due to changes in reference point. One of the ways to shift the reference point is by the 'framing' of the choice options. Work by Tversky and Kahneman

(1981) and Fischhoff (1983) provides further insight into the relationships between preference and the 'framing' of a decision problem. Since prospect theory deals with gains and losses relative to a reference point, rather than with absolute outcomes, the same outcomes can be represented alternately as gains or losses, depending on the reference point. One of the hypothetical problems reported by Tversky and Kahneman (1981, p. 453) asks subjects to imagine that the US is threatened with an unusual disease, expected to kill 600 people. A choice has to be made between two alternative interventions, concerning which subjects had to assume the following estimates to be accepted scientific estimates of the consequences of the programmes:

'If Program A is adopted, 200 people will be saved.'
'If Program B is adopted, there is 1/3 probability that 600 people will be saved, and 2/3 probability that no people will be saved.'

When presented with the choice in this form, 72 per cent of subjects opted for 'Program A'. However, a second group were presented with the same problem in the following terms:

'If Program C is adopted, 400 people will die.'
'If Program D is adopted, there is 1/3 probability that nobody will die, and 2/3 probability that 600 people will die.'

In this second group, the majority (78 per cent) chose 'Program D'. Thus when the choice was framed in terms of gains (lives saved), most people opted for the certain outcome, but when the identical choice was framed in terms of losses (lives lost) most people avoided the option of the certain loss. In the first problem the expected 600 deaths have been presupposed, whereas in the second problem they have not. In other words, the reference point is 600 people lower in problem 1 than in problem 2. Thus, the first programme is described as 200 lives saved, rather than 400 lives lost. Similarly, the second programme is described in terms of the chances to save 600 lives, rather than chances to lose 600 lives. This confirms the principle that people tend to be risk-averse for gains and risk-seeking for losses, i.e. sure gains are popular, but sure losses are unpopular. Preference, therefore, seems not deterministically constrained by the prescriptive 'rationality' of SEU theory, but can be strongly influenced (at least in examples of the kind described) by the *frame of reference* in terms of which a problem is defined.

Prospect theory distinguishes two phases in the choice process: an early phase of *editing* and a subsequent phase of *evaluation*. The evaluation phase concerns the assessment of the prospects and the selection of the prospect with the highest value. This phase is described on the previous pages and can be summarized by the value function and the probability-weighting function. The function of the preceding editing phase is to organize and reformulate the options in order to simplify subsequent evaluation and choice. Kahneman and Tversky (1979, p. 274) list six major operations involved in editing. These include *coding* (setting the reference point), *combination* and *segregation* of prospects, *cancellation* of outcomes common to all prospects, *simplification* (rounding possibilities or outcomes) and the detection of *dominance* (i.e. the detection of unattractive alternatives that need no further consideration).

Prospect theory's description of the editing processes under-lying decision-making are relatively sketchy. Editing is, however, a requisite part of any decision, and Kahneman and Tversky acknowledge that many anomalies of preference result from the initial editing of prospects. It is not surprising, therefore, that editing operations figure prominently in lists of factors that may exert a constraining influence on effective decision-making. However, constraints also arise at other stages such as the definition of what is relevant and the integration of the relevant information so as to make the decision.

Most of these constraints are related to the fact that decision-making is a complex performance. It may be costly or impossible to gather all the potentially relevant information, it may be difficult to decide what information is relevant and it may not be easy to combine information from different sources or of different kinds. Furthermore, reasoning about uncertain outcomes or consequences of decisions may prove difficult due to lack of experience or insight. According to Simon (1955, 1957) decision-makers do not necessarily want to find optimum solutions; people quite often choose options that are good enough, i.e. they *satisfice* instead of *optimize*. The phrase '*bounded rationality'* has been applied to the view that people are indeed rational but only up to a point, as an alternative to many normative decision models requiring a complete cost-benefit analysis for any decision. Given this 'bounded' nature of human rationality (Simon, 1955, 1957) it is not surprising that people use various strategies to enable them to handle complex decisions. These include simplified 'problem representations' (subjective models of the real world) which permit us to handle the task with the available cognitive resources (Newell and Simon, 1972).

In addition to simplified problem representations, cognitive load can be reduced by using a number of decision-making strategies. These simplifying cognitive procedures, or rules-of-thumb, are known in the literature as 'heuristics'. Although judgment heuristics can lead to good decisions, this is not always the case. In the past two decades, psychologists have described a number of general judgment heuristics (see Fischhoff, 1975, 1982; Fischhoff and Beyth, 1975; Fischhoff *et al.*, 1977; Kahneman *et al.*, 1982). They have also shown the circumstances under which these heuristics lead to errors in probabilistic reasoning. Because many of these errors result from an attempt to apply the normally useful heuristics to situations in which they are inappropriate, errors are often referred to as cognitive 'biases'. Several of these biases are sufficiently predictable and systematic to have been given names. The next section presents an overview of the major judgmental heuristics and their possible consequences for effective decision-making.

Heuristics and biases

The study of heuristics and biases tends to be dominated by attempts to expose systematic errors and inferential biases in human reasoning. These do expose some of our intellectual limitations. More importantly, errors and biases often reveal the psychological processes that govern judgment and inference and thereby suggest ways of improving the quality of our thinking. The discussion of factors that could affect the quality of decision-making should not be seen as a general indictment of human intelligence. Each of the factors to be discussed relates to potential difficulties in decision and choice processes. Many of them should be taken into account if decisions are to be improved in a wide variety of applied areas ranging from issues such as medical decision-making, decisions about technological innovations and selection interviews.

Probability assessment

Information about the probability of the various outcomes of a decision may be available prior to the decision, be gathered during the decision process or be inferred from similar cases. In all these cases it is important to know how people use information about the probability of outcomes (e.g. relative frequency of the outcomes in the past) or how people estimate the probabilities of specific outcomes.

Availability

The availability heuristic (Tversky and Kahneman, 1973) refers to the tendency for an event to be judged more probable to the extent that it is more easily pictured or recalled. A headline such as '300 people die in air disaster' might increase the 'availability' of information that air travel can be dangerous. An important practical instance of this is when people have to make comparisons between different kinds of risks. Risks from more easily pictured accidents, such as explosions, may contribute more to the judgment that a particular industrial process is dangerous, even though they may happen extremely rarely, than may continuous and cumulative hazards, such as routine emissions into the atmosphere, which have less immediate dramatic effects. Lichtenstein *et al.* (1978) provide evidence that when people judge the frequencies of death from various causes, they overestimate small frequencies whilst relatively underestimating large ones, and exaggerate some specific causes possibly, they suggest, because of disproportionate media exposure or imaginability. For example, when asked to estimate the risk of dying from several different causes, subjects systematically overestimated the death risk posed by 'sensational' events such as homicide and storms and underestimated the risks associated with such mundane killers as asthma and diabetes, which receive much less media attention. Because they are easier to retrieve from memory, sensational causes are judged to have a higher probability than more common, but less available, killers. Slovic, Fischhoff and Lichtenstein (1979) were able to demonstrate a significant relationship between the newspaper column space devoted to a cause of death and subjects' subjective estimates of its likelihood.

Clearly, the availability heuristic can bias judgments by giving easily imagined events more importance than their objective frequency warrants. When the events being estimated are likely to be rare, the availability heuristic can seriously bias judgment. As indicated by the previous examples, the influence of availability has been identified in a wide variety of contexts. Nisbett and Ross (1980) pointed out that increased availability of a mental item could be related to greater attention to the item when presented, more effective coding of the item into memory, more stable storage, or more effective retrieval. Abelson and Levi (1985) put forward the view that the rehearsal of relevant event scenarios may also enhance availability of that specific scenario. For instance, Gregory, Cialdini and Carpenter (1982) found that imagining oneself in plausible scenarios for getting falsely arrested, or for watching a new cable TV service, increased the probability ratings for these events. Moreover, the actual probability of later subscribing to the cable TV was increased by imaginative rehearsal.

Within social psychological research most emphasis has been on attention and encoding effects. Generally, these effects were studied under the heading of the concept of salience. As we have seen in the previous chapter (Chapter 3), perceptually salient events are more easily remembered than nonsalient events. Perceptual salience also influences the type of attributions people make. One would expect salience also to affect estimates of frequency or probability. The effects of salience could be mediated by perceptual vividness or dramatic impact. This would relate the concept more clearly to findings obtained under the rubric of the concept availability. Although the effects of availability on probability estimates are well established, more work is needed to clarify the conceptual framework with which to explain these effects. Concepts such as availability and salience are defined in rather general terms and offer only a limited explanation of the obtained effects.

At any rate, research on the availability heuristic has demonstrated the importance of memory in making judgments. Usually, ease of recall is a relatively valid cue for estimating probabilities, but there are instances when the availability heuristic leads to biased judgments. The same is true of the next heuristic to be discussed, representativeness.

Representativeness

The representativeness heuristic (Kahneman and Tversky, 1972) refers to the tendency to judge the probability that a stimulus belongs to a particular class on the basis of how representative or 'typical' of that class it appears to be, with little regard for the base-rate probability of a stimulus belonging to the class. For example, imagine that one found some wild mushrooms, and wanted to decide if they were edible or poisonous. The representativeness heuristic implies that one will base one's decision on how similar the wild mushrooms appear to be to other mushrooms which one knows to be edible, that is, ordinary cultivated mushrooms, as compared with toadstools which one knows to be poisonous. The weakness of this kind of judgment is that it fails to take account of the probability of any wild fungus, chosen at random, being edible rather than poisonous, with the result that a great number of unfamiliar but edible fungi will be avoided. In this example, of course, the costs of eating a poisonous muchroom are far greater than those of avoiding an edible one, and most people would be unaware of the statistical probability of fungus being edible. The same kind of bias, however, can be demonstrated experimentally when subjects are given incentives for accuracy and are told about the base-rate probabilities. A slightly different example of the representativeness heuristic concerns the perception of randomness. If one knows that a sequence of events is randomly generated, one expects the sequence to *look* random. So, with tosses of a coin, a sequence of heads (H) and tails (T) such as HHTHTTHT is judged to be more probable than TTTTHHHH. Since the first sequence appears more 'representative' it is judged more likely. Tversky and Kahneman (1974) associated the representativeness heuristic with a variety of cognitive errors. These include insensitivity to prior probabilities, misconceptions about randomness, and misconceptions about conjunctive probabilities (the probability of the joint occurrence of two or more events).

A well-known example of how ignoring prior probabilities can lead to biased judgments was reported by Kahneman and Tversky (1973). In their experiment subjects were provided with brief personality sketches supposedly of engineers and lawyers. Next, subjects were asked to rate the probability that each sketch described a member of one profession or the other. Half the subjects were told the population from which the sketches were drawn consisted of 30 engineers and 70 lawyers; the other half were told that there were 70 engineers and 30 lawyers. The findings were an impressive demonstration of the representativeness heuristic in operation. The prior probabilities (the numbers of engineers and lawyers) were essentially ignored. Instead, subjects assigned probabilities by judging how similar each personality sketch was to their stereotype of an engineer ('he likes building things') or a lawyer ('he is a good debater'). This latter effect was confirmed in an elaborate study reported by Fischhoff and Bar-Hillel (1984). They found that prior probabilities were ignored when case descriptions were highly stereotypical. When case descriptions were ambiguous, prior probabilities became more important. It needs to be noted, however, that even in the latter situation, prior probabilities did not exert the influence they should according to normative statistical considerations.

The representativeness heuristic can also be related to misconceptions about randomness and insensitivity to sample size. Kahneman and Tversky described subjects who ignore sample size when making probability judgments as believing in the 'law of small numbers'. For instance, if one asks subjects to indicate how often the daily records of two different hospitals would show more than 60 per cent of babies born to be boys, one would expect different answers depending on the size of the hospital. Given the fact that about 50 per cent of all babies are boys, it is more likely for a small hospital to record days when the percentage of male births exceeds 60 per cent. Most subjects, however, believed that the hospitals were equally likely to record days when the percentage of male births exceeded 60 per cent. In other words, they did not perceive the size of the hospital as relevant, even though larger hospitals, recording many more births, are more likely to produce data reflecting the population mean (50 per cent boys and 50 per cent girls) than are smaller hospitals. The law of small numbers applies to the assumption that any sample, no matter how large, is an equally 'representative' estimate of population parameters. This assumption contradicts the statistically valid law of large numbers which states that the larger the sample, the more accurately it reflects population parameters.

Another consequence of the representativeness heuristic concerns the perception of conjunctive probabilities. It has been suggested that people tend to overestimate the probability of conjunctions of events (Cohen et al., 1971). This conjunction bias refers to the tendency to see the joint occurrence of events A and B as more likely than event B alone. This would violate the rules of probabilistic logic; the joint probability of two events equals the product of the two separate probabilities, this product will always be smaller than each of the separate probabilities. Tversky and Kahneman (1983) termed this phenomenon the *conjunction effect*. An example is the following task (Tversky and Kahneman, 1982, p. 92).

Linda is 31 years old, single, outspoken, and very bright. She majored in philosophy. As a student she was deeply concerned with issues of discrimination and social justice, and also participated in antinuclear demonstrations.

Subjects were asked to rank a number of statements by their probability. These were:

- Linda is active in the feminist movement.
- Linda is a bank teller.
- Linda is a bank teller and is active in the feminist movement.
- Linda is (five other filler items, interspersed with those above).

The obtained estimates of the probability of the conjunction 'bank teller and feminist' significantly exceeded estimates of the probability that Linda is a bank teller. Similar findings have been obtained with different tasks and with different ways to elicit probability judgments. The finding is very robust in situations where a highly representative element (feminist movement) is presented in conjunction with a highly unrepresentative element (bank teller).

The examples presented in this section show that the representativeness heuristic is frequently employed when individuals are required to estimate the probability of events. Although it can take several forms and can produce a variety of different judgmental biases, the representativeness heuristic always involves emphasizing case-specific information while ignoring prior probabilities. Another judgmental strategy that could bias the perception of outcome probabilities concerns 'anchoring and adjustment'.

Anchoring and adjustment
Tversky and Kahneman (1974) demonstrated the effects of anchoring and adjustment by asking subjects to give estimates of various frequencies (the number of African countries in the United Nations, for example). Before making their judgments, subjects were given arbitrary starting points between 0 and 100. The subjects were asked to indicate whether the starting values were too high, too low, or just right and they were also asked to give their own estimates of the true frequency. The results indicated that the randomly derived starting values had an impressive effect on frequency estimates. The higher the initial starting value, the higher the estimate. Although the starting points were totally arbitrary, it seemed that people used them to 'anchor' their estimates; 'adjustments' were made either up or down from the starting point. Typically, these adjustments were crude and imprecise; the crucial point, however, is that the anchor was an important determinant of the final estimate (see also van der Pligt *et al.*, 1987).

Confirmation versus disconfirmation
When people estimate the probability of particular outcomes they may have to rely on past probabilities of success and failure. In this context it is relevant to know whether individuals can keep accurate track of the number of successes and failures of occurrence of a particular outcome over a long sequence of trials. A number of studies indicated a tendency for positive instances to outweigh negative instances in using data to estimate future probabilities. Suppose that a person is scanning evidence

relevant to the proposition 'French cars tend to rust easily'. A positive instance containing a rusty French car may carry more weight towards confirmation than a negative instance (a French car in good condition) may weigh towards disconfirming the proposition. It has been argued that people are not only biased in using positive instances but also tend actively to *look for* potentially positive instances. In other words, people not only tend to emphasize positive instances, they also tend to actively search for confirming instances to the extent that it is less likely for disconfirming evidence to be found. The effect of this strategy is that people may tend to overestimate the validity of their expectations or hypotheses.

In the previous pages we have listed a variety of factors that can affect the accuracy of people's estimation of probability. These factors are all related to the incorrect use of statistical evidence. Prior probabilities, the effect of sample size and conjunctive probabilities seem not clearly understood and are used incorrectly or underutilized in probability estimates. Generally, intuitive judgments of probability seem strongly influenced by relatively concrete, and vivid instances. Both the availability and the representativeness heuristic result in the overweighting of concrete instances. Further factors that can affect probability estimates are the overweighting of positive instances and instances that conform to prior expectations (see also Spears, van der Pligt and Eiser, 1986). All in all, it seems clear that people find it difficult to make probability estimates. This is illustrated by the ease with which concrete instances can affect probability estimates and the substantial effects due to the introduction of anchor values.

Most of these limiting factors seem to operate across a wide range of stimulus materials. Some, however, seem to depend on a combination of judgmental vulnerability and clever stimulus designs highlighting this vulnerability. This raises the more general point that experimental demonstrations of human 'irrationality' may depend to a large extent on the use of hypothetical problems that violate assumptions that people might reasonably make about apparently similar situations in everyday life. While people may seem to use informal decision rules and simplificatory heuristics rather than normative principles of logic or statistics, it is far from obvious that it is always maladaptive to do so. Hogarth (1981) argues that cognitive heuristics may not only be functional, but even a valid basis for decision-making in natural contexts. Although it is important for human beings to be able to predict events in their environment with reasonable accuracy, accuracy *per se* is not the only or even always the most important goal, since different kinds of errors can involve different costs. Is it, for instance, 'irrational' to accept the necessity of safety measures without bothering to test what would happen if no precautions were taken? Furthermore 'judgment is primarily exercised to facilitate action' and 'most actions induce feedback that is often immediately available . . . Receiving and acting on feedback in continuous fashion increases the number of cues and responses available to the organism and thus their intersubstitutability' (Hogarth, 1981, p. 199).

Whereas most studies on heuristics involve discrete judgment tasks at a single point in time, in more natural contexts judgments and actions evolve and influence each other continuously over time. One would expect therefore that the kind of information with which we are best adapted to deal is continuous, redundant and patterned over time. Judgments, then, are typically made on a data base that is redundant rather than randomly generated, and that can constantly be updated. Moreover, because of the possibility of correction through feedback, judgments do not generally have to be made once-and-for-all. It is more typical for people to evaluate decisions with respect to relatively short- or medium-term 'decision horizons' where the link from action to outcome is clearer. It is therefore precisely because many studies fail to simulate the natural context of judgment and action that 'errors' and 'biases' can be experimentally demonstrated with such relative ease. These errors and biases are real enough, and testify to people's tendencies to resolve problems on the basis of rules of thumb rather than recourse to first principles. Such evidence, however, falls short of demonstrating that these rules of thumb, strategies or heuristics are irrational, unreasonable or invalid with respect to the context in which they are more typically used.

In sum, not enough is presently known about the generalizability of the findings obtained in this research area. Questions such as whether the stimuli and designs used in experimental demonstrations are typical or exceptional need further attention.

Another issue that needs to be resolved is whether people can be trained to avoid the various errors and biases in their use of statistical information and their estimates of probability.

Assessing and applying values

As we have seen in the previous sections, probability judgments can often be compared with objectively estimated probabilities. With questions of values, however, standards are typically subjective. There are a number of ways, nevertheless, in which values might be inadequately considered in decision-making. Three will be briefly discussed in this section.

(a) Relevant values may be overlooked.
(b) Uncertainty about relevance of various values may be experienced.
(c) Difficulties in assessing values may occur.

The quality of decisions can be seriously affected if one ignores important positive or negative features of one or more of the choice options. Some researchers (e.g. Janis and Mann, 1977) argue that the quality of decision-making should primarily be judged by the extent to which the processes are complete and unbiased. As discussed in the context of the tendency to look for confirming evidence (see page 96), negative features of favoured options tend to be overlooked. A number of mechanisms lead to the neglect of important values, the most relevant of which will be discussed later.

Apart from the failure to include value considerations, it occasionally happens that people are not sure what values are relevant. Fischhoff et al. (1980) point out that this is especially the case in unfamiliar and complex issues such as those related to the introduction of new technologies. Due to lack of experience and the complexity of the many possible consequences, people might not even know how to begin thinking about certain issues. Many of today's issues such as nuclear energy, the use of chemicals with possible long-term consequences for the environment, and genetic engineering seem to fall in this category.

Even if one knows which values are of relevance to a specific decision, it might be difficult to assess these values. In some decision situations one will have to estimate value outcomes indirectly. Sometimes, however, one may rely upon feature(s) that have little diagnostic significance. Gilovich (1981), for instance, found that football experts are influenced in judging the talent of new players by irrelevant associative similarities with football stars of the past.

Combining information

In the previous two sections we discussed two important aspects of decision-making, i.e. estimation of probabilities and values. Furthermore, we looked at various factors that could potentially distort the estimation or assessment of these 'constituents' of decision-making. Generally, however, the process does not end there; the next step is to combine the relevant values weighted by their probabilities in order to reach an overall evaluation of the possible choices.

The most obvious problem at this stage is related to information overload. There is general consensus about the limits on the number of factors that can be considered simultaneously. Earlier we discussed difficulties of decision-makers with simple operations such as multiplication and adding in the context of subjective expected utility models of decision-making. Abelson and Levi (1985) suggest that since overload provokes a need for simplification, existing heuristics and biases that serve a simplifying function are likely to be most popular under overload conditions. The difficulty of integrating various considerations is usually dealt with by focusing on a limited number of dimensions. Various studies indicate that people are prepared to go quite far in avoiding complicated trade-offs with good and bad features, and frequently limit themselves to one salient dimension while screening out dimensions that suggest a different solution to the problem. This is quite often related to difficulties in considering qualitatively different value considerations. For instance, a delicately balanced choice between a low-salary job that is close to your interests, and a job that pays well but allows less freedom to develop your own interests is more easily resolved when one reduces the relevance of one of these considerations. Since some choice must be made, it seems quite functional to have some mechanism to avoid a permanent stalemate (and possibly no job at all). In the long run, however, it could be less functional. Janis and Mann (1977) point out that in such cases the decision-maker is likely to be more confident of the choice than the various positive and negative considerations warrant, and as a consequence could be less sensitive to changing circumstances that might suggest a reversal of the initial decision.

All in all, the complexity of making trade-offs between different values seems to affect decision quality in two ways. Firstly, individuals tend to use simpler and less optimal choice rules as the information load increases. Usually accuracy declines considerably when the number of features or the number of alternatives increases. Secondly, the reliability with which choice rules are used tends to decrease as the decision-maker's information load increases.

Noncognitive constraints on effective decision-making

The previous sections presented an overview of cognitive factors affecting the assessment of probabilities and values and attempts to combine these two into overall evaluations of choice alternatives. In this section we will look at other influences that could constrain the effectiveness of decision-making. Some of these are of a motivational character, with their own specific consequences for the quality of decision-making, while others are more closely related to the simplifying strategies discussed in the earlier sections.

Commitment

This factor usually refers to some public behaviour on behalf of a decision and can affect the quality of decision-making in the sense that it makes reversal of the initial decision less likely. There are many examples of the constraining effects of commitment at the level of individual decision-making and decisions of groups. Usually commitment goes hand in hand with the denial of negative aspects of the initial decision and, hence, makes it less likely that the initial decision is reversed. Examples of individual commitment are highlighted in the literature on dissonance (Festinger, 1957). At a group level examples such as the doomsday cult studies (Festinger *et al.*, 1956) and the Jonestown commune spring to mind. Finally, decisions such as those concerning the building of the 'Concorde' supersonic passenger aircraft and US involvement in Vietnam, are two familiar examples in the political context.

Defensive avoidance and hypervigilance

Janis and Mann (1977) investigated the role of stress in decision-making. Decision conflicts that involve important goals can lead to stress, and the greater the stress, the more likely it is that one will avoid information about risks associated with the chosen alternative. Another possible consequence is what Janis and Mann call 'hypervigilance'. In this state there is an overactive search for information accompanied by the inability to distinguish between relevant and irrelevant information. This frequently leads to decision paralysis. The state of defensive avoidance is characterized by lack of vigilant search, distortion of the meaning of information, selective inattention and forgetting and the construction of rationalizations. Examples of defensive avoidance are the confirmed alcoholics and smokers who denigrate the various long-term health effects. Janis and Mann argue that these avoiding tendencies are most likely to happen when stress is high. When stress is moderate, interest in information is more likely to be open-minded, accompanied by serious consideration of information emphasizing the potentially serious risks of the present course of action. Overall, research on stress has indicated negative consequences for the quality of decisions, and Janis and Mann's work provides a coherent framework for the analysis of the effects of stress.

Groupthink

Groupthink is a strong psychological drive for consensus within insular, cohesive decision-making groups such that disagreement is suppressed. This can affect the quality of decision-making when social pressures dominate the decision process at the expense of a balanced consideration of the content of the choice alternatives. Janis (1972, 1982) termed this phenomenon *groupthink* and investigated it in the context of elite decision-making groups. Policy blunders such as the Bay of Pigs invasion and the Watergate cover-up were analysed and indicated that otherwise extremely competent members of the decision-making groups tended to overlook or simply dismiss obvious indications of external threats or of flawed reasoning. Groupthink is further accompanied by symptoms such as the illusion of invulnerability, the belief in the inherent morality of the group, the illusion of unanimity, self-censorship when dissenting thoughts arise and the self-appointment of so-called 'mindguards' who try to prevent exposure to dissent. These symptoms may lead to serious shortcomings in decision-making processes. Most of the distorting factors discussed in earlier sections seem to apply to groupthink, i.e. incomplete survey of values and/or possible choice alternatives, poor information search, failure to reappraise rejected alternatives, and failure to work out contingency plans. Rationalizations and excessive confidence in the group's decisions will make a change to more efficient decision-making methods less likely. Janis has documented both antecedents and consequences of groupthink in a number of famous policy disasters, and suggests ways to mitigate the consequences by the introduction of explicit counternorms (e.g. operating procedures that increase the likelihood of alternative views being seriously considered). It needs to be noted, however, that the list of decision defects more or less overlaps with possible short-comings at the individual level. In other words, the phenomena are not unique to cohesive, insular, elite decision groups. The importance of Janis's work is that it makes us aware of the possible enhancement of the effects of distorting factors in a group context.

Improving decisions

In recent years a literature has begun to develop attempting to improve the quality of human decision-making. Approaches include the provision of explicit decision procedures, the use of computerized decision-aids and providing training to overcome flaws in the decision process.

An example of the first category is the use of balance sheets, i.e. listing all the advantages and disadvantages of each decision alternative before trying to make the decision. There is evidence

(Janis, 1982) that this helps to prevent the omission of relevant value considerations and can create an analytical orientation disposing towards caution and scepticism. A further example is cost-benefit analysis. The development of methods for estimating the costs (both economic and personal) and benefits of decisions played an important role in the applicability of this technique. The technique of cost-benefit analysis can be broken down into six steps (Fischhoff, 1977):

1 Enumerate all the adverse consequences of a particular course of action.
2 Estimate the probability that each consequence will occur.
3 Estimate the cost (loss) should each occur.
4 Calculate the expected loss from each consequence by multiplying the amount of loss by its probability of occurring.
5 Compute the expected loss for the course of action by summing the losses associated with the various consequences.
6 Repeat the procedure for benefits.

Cost-benefit analysis is closely related to the SEU approaches to decision-making presented earlier. Probabilities and outcome utilities are estimated, multiplied and summed. Performing a cost-benefit analysis involves several rather strong assumptions. It assumes, for example, that all important consequences of an action can be enumerated in advance, that the probability of their occurrence can be reliably estimated and that different kinds of costs (for instance in the context of rescue operations: financial versus pain, suffering and loss of life) can be compared. All of these assumptions can and have been questioned. But surely the most controversial aspect of cost-benefit analysis is the need to compare disparate costs (e.g. loss of human life versus financial costs in medical decisions). Despite these problems, there is still merit in trying to formalize decision-making. There is no evidence that suggests that intuitive decision-making is superior to the formal approach and quite a lot that suggests that it is not.

Because decision analysis typically requires quantitative judgments from decision-makers, decision-aiding systems can be extended to include routine computations. There are a number of computerized decision-aiding systems available, varying in detail and complexity. Most systems are based on the theoretical principles of decision theory and on the viewpoint that the interaction between decision-makers, decision analysts, and computerized decision-aiding systems should help to improve the quality of decision-making. The underlying procedures involve (a) extracting information from the decision-makers and (possibly) the people who are affected by the consequences of the decision; and (b) helping the individual or the group of individuals in defining and structuring the decision problem so as to decide upon the alternatives and the criteria on which they are to be evaluated and to identify possible courses of action and their consequences. A number of techniques similar to those used in cost-benefit analysis are employed to assist in the assessment of the various constituents of decisions (e.g. values, probabilities, importance of the values and/or utilities). These inputs are then integrated using decision algorithms to derive a preference ordering over the alternatives. Furthermore, quite a few computerized decision-aids include editing facilities and iterative modules that allow the decision-maker to amend existing relationships or judgments, to revise the contributing elements or to insert new information into the problem structure.

The provision of decision procedures and computerized decision-aids assumes a certain degree of deficiency in human decision-making, the impact of which one tries to minimize by structural arrangements. The provision of training designed to overcome flaws in the decision process assumes that relevant experience could improve the quality of human decisions. There is some evidence that experience, in combination with the provision of concepts for appropriately interpreting that experience, can improve learning and, hopefully, the quality of future decisions. Especially training people to avoid specific flaws in specific situations could enhance effective decision-making. Research embodying this strategy has had moderate success.

5

Health attitudes, attributions and addiction

Health as a value

Consider the amount of money expended on medical services in most countries of the developed world, the number of people employed in medical and allied professions, the commercial power of the pharmaceutical industry and the profitability of private practice in both orthodox and less conventional specialisms. The picture that is suggested is surely one of a civilization obsessed with escaping some great evil, be this death, disease, distress or mere discomfort. We idealize good health, even sometimes idolize it, but the other side of this picture is that illness is something we denigrate and disown, even though it is so familiar. Parsons (1951) identified what he called the 'sick role', in terms of the rights and obligations that set the sick person apart from the rest of society. Prototypically, the sick person is excused the obligation to work or to provide for his or her own maintenance. In return for this, however, the sick person must play the part of a 'good patient', who follows doctor's orders.

The status of the patient becomes very much more like that of a child than that of a fully responsible adult.

Our conventional feelings about illness and ill people may be extremely ambivalent. Compassion, pity, dedication and determination to help can most certainly be there, but so can embarrassment, fear, rejection and a wish to ignore. We speak, revealingly, of the sick as 'having something wrong with them'. In short, they are deviants with whom it is difficult to interact normally until they have been 'made whole'. The fact that anyone can become ill is no protection against such rejection. Lerner (1980) has proposed that we are strongly motivated to believe in a 'just world', in which people deserve their fate. He suggests that we find it very threatening to believe in others suffering from undeserved misfortune. Part of the story may be our need to deny any guilt or responsibility we feel for being in a more fortunate position ourselves (Cialdini *et al.*, 1976; Kenrick *et al.*, 1976; Lerner, 1980). Where we can successfully avoid such feelings of guilt, we can accept the fact of injustice more easily. What then happens is that others' misfortunes can be thought of as part of a different world, isolated from anything we do or from anything we are. If we can persuade ourselves that the predictors of death and disability point to our own relative immunity, then, for us at least, the world is very much safer.

We therefore value health highly, but does this relate to the ways in which we behave? There are many things we do that could be – and we know could be – potentially dangerous to our health. Why might this be? One important point is that health may not be the only relevant value that people hold, and for some people in some situations, other values (relating to more immediate consequences) may have far greater importance. This has been frequently overlooked by those health educators who have pinned their main hopes on urging people to 'be healthy'. Kristiansen (1985) has pointed out that, as far as many health-related behaviours are concerned, the value of health may compete with, and even be over-ridden by, other values. Kristiansen adapted Rokeach's (1979) approach to the measurement of people's values by having her subjects rank the importance of a list of values including 'health'. A number of associations were found between how high subjects ranked the importance of health in this list and how much they reported engaging in a number of preventive health behaviours, but such behaviours were often more predictable from values other than health (e.g. 'an exciting life').

One of the most frequently cited reasons why some people continue to behave in ways that put their health at risk, however, is that they no longer have sufficient self-control to change their habits. This is where the concept of 'addiction' comes into play. If someone values health highly but simply appears unable to act in such a way that better health can be achieved, then we must look to more deterministic explanations of behaviour than those embodied in theories of attitudes and decisions. Or so the story goes. Is this story true?

What is addiction?

In simplest terms, an addiction can be defined as any strongly formed habit which someone finds very difficult to break. However, this definition fails to account for some of the more specific connotations that the term carries. The word itself is derived from the Latin for enslavement, or the binding of a slave to a master. In short, the addict is seen as a slave and, like all slaves, longs to be free. The idea of an addict wanting to stay addicted seems as contradictory to common sense as that of a slave or prisoner declining an offer of freedom. In this as in many other fields, however, common sense can fail to do justice to the complexities of reality.

To this connotation of enslavement can be added that of sickness. The implication of this is that addicts should be treated as people with an illness in need of cure. This 'medicalized' way of looking at compulsive or addictive behaviours, however, is of comparatively recent origin. Many of the assumptions in present-day approaches to the treatment of alcoholism derive from Jellinek's (1960) book *The Disease Concept of Alcoholism*. Jellinek described the physical and behavioural symptoms associated with excessive drinking and proposed a taxonomy of different kinds of 'alcoholics'. Alcoholism now became classifiable as a medical condition in its own right, almost irrespective of the physical damage to which it could give rise. As such, it became an appropriate target for medical intervention. It was no longer simply to be regarded as 'bad behaviour' or a moral failing in need of censure.

Another form of 'bad behaviour' that is now widely classified as an addiction is that of cigarette smoking. Compared with the drinking of alcohol, the widespread smoking of manufactured cigarettes dates only from the early part of this century, and the recognition of its serious health consequences is of even more recent origin. Here again, what was first seen as just another form of indulgence, then came to be seen as a behaviour with extremely unhealthy consequences, and later as a sickness in its own right – as a form of 'dependence disorder' (Russell, 1971) or even 'mental disorder' (Jaffé, 1977).

In order to classify something as a disease or disorder, one needs evidence of specific symptoms or reactions. Two such sets of symptoms are widely cited in the case of drug abuse. The first of these is the development of *tolerance* to the effects of the drug. This refers to a process of physiological adaptation to the drug. One can see this clearly in the case of alcohol, where those who drink less frequently can get drunk more easily. The second important sign is the development of *withdrawal* effects. These can vary greatly in severity and persistence, but the term can be used generally to refer to any feelings of discomfort or distress that occur as a kind of 'rebound' as soon as the primary effects of the drug wear off.

Whilst the concept of tolerance is used to explain how consumption can escalate, it is the fear of withdrawal that is commonly assumed to be the main reason why addicts continue to take drugs and find it so difficult to break their habit. Once drug-users regulate their patterns of consumption so that their bodies are not deprived of the drug for any great length of time, there can be a strong presumption that they are, or are becoming, addicted. By this criterion, many powerful and dangerous drugs may not be, strictly speaking, addictive in the contexts in which they are normally used, whereas others, including some that can be legally purchased (such as alcohol and tobacco) or prescribed as medication (such as tranquillizers and antidepressants) can produce symptoms of full-blown dependence.

The opponent-process model

One of the most influential theories of the development of tolerance and withdrawal is Solomon's (1980) opponent-process model. The basic assumption of this model is that addiction results from the way in which emotional reactions can become conditioned to particular stimuli and situations. Starting from the perspective of Pavlovian learning theory, Solomon assumes that particular kinds of stimuli (including drugs) have the capacity to produce an *unlearned* immediate reaction of pleasure or displeasure, to varying degrees. A stimulus that did this would be termed an unconditioned stimulus (UCS), and the response it produced, an unconditioned response (UCR). He further assumes that this immediate response, which he refers to as the 'primary affective process' or 'a process', is automatically followed, after a short while, by a 'b process' that is opposed to the UCR and will eventually suppress it. In other words, Solomon is postulating a homeostatic process, whereby reactions of pleasure are followed by after-reactions of sorrow, and that reactions of pain or fear are followed by after-reactions of relief, and such like. Moreover, these after-reactions can 'overshoot' the baseline representing the normal or neutral emotional state in which the person (or animal) was before presentation of the UCS.

Since the a and b processes overlap in time, the degree of pleasure or discomfort experienced is assumed to be simply the magnitude of the a process minus that of the b process at any moment. During the period immediately following the onset of the UCS, the a process will be stronger and the person or animal is said to be in an A state. With time, the b process will become the stronger and the person or animal is then said to be in a B state. In the case of drug-use, the initial 'high' is the A state and the feeling of withdrawal is the B state. Solomon assumes that the b process (and hence withdrawal) will become stronger and have a shorter latency of onset, the more often the UCS (the drug) has been experienced (see Figure 5.1).

So far this model may be simply regarded as a redefinition of the concepts of tolerance and withdrawal as the net effect of primary and opponent processes. What adds to its predictive power are various assumptions based on principles of

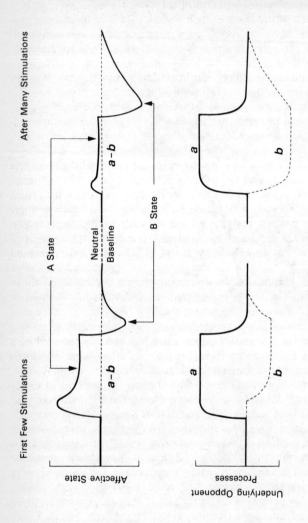

Figure 5.1 The opponent-process model (Adapted from Solomon, 1980)

conditioning. Firstly, a noxious B state (withdrawal effect) is likely to function as a powerful negative reinforcer. Since repeated self-administration of the drug terminates or enables avoidance of the B state, such behaviour will be reinforced and be more likely to recur. However, this repetition will itself increase the potential strength of the B state. Thus an 'addictive cycle' will be set up, in which the addict repeatedly redoses to avoid withdrawal effects, but in so doing increases the strength of such effects that might eventually occur.

Secondly, the A and B states can themselves become conditioned responses (CRs). In other words, they can occur in response to environmental or proprioceptive stimuli with which they have become associated. Thus, actions involved in administration of the drug (e.g. pouring a drink) can produce an anticipatory relief from craving (a conditioned A state). In the same way, environmental cues (including other people, special places or social occasions) that have become associated with feelings of craving in the past may trigger off such feelings again, often long after a drug-user has achieved abstinence. This seems to be one of the major sources of risk of relapse for the reformed addict.

More optimistically, if craving for a drug is partly a conditioned response to environmental stimuli, the strength of such a response may be greatly reduced if important features of the environment are changed. There is evidence that morphine tolerance in rats can decrease when the rats are retested in a changed environment (Siegel, 1977). In the context of human behaviour, one of the most challenging findings is that of Robins, Davis and Goodwin (1974), who studied the patterns of drug-use among American servicemen during the Vietnam war, and followed up a number on their return home. Among a sample of 495 men who had shown signs of opiates in their urine during a medical examination at the time of their discharge from Vietnam, only 7 per cent showed signs of dependence on opiates when recontacted eight to ten months later (although about a third admitted to having had some experience with opiates during this period). This figure rose to only 12 per cent by three years after discharge (Robins, Helzer and Davis, 1975). When set against the fact that three-quarters of this group regarded themselves as having been addicted to opiates while in Vietnam, there are strong grounds for viewing their addiction 'as state-dependent'. When the environmental cues associated with the horrors of war were removed, the men's need for drugs declined or disappeared.

Objections have been raised to the views of Solomon and of other conditioning theorists such as Siegel (1977), principally on the grounds of the importance they attach to the role of withdrawal effects. The assumption is that most addicts persist in taking drugs in order to avoid withdrawal. The clinical evidence, however, is far less simple. As Alexander and Hadaway (1982) point out, many heroin addicts do not experience withdrawal effects when given naloxone, an antagonist to opiates (McAuliffe and Gordon, 1980). Interventions based on the idea of extinguishing conditioned withdrawal effects are far from a complete solution to the problem of prevention of relapse (Teasdale, 1973; Wolpe, Groves and Fischer, 1980). Furthermore, addiction to other forms of drugs such as amphetamines and cocaine, while just as dangerous and compulsive in many ways as opiate dependence, does not seem to depend on the experience of severe physical withdrawal effects (Jaffé, 1980).

Alexander and Hadaway (1982) argue that all approaches that view addiction as a more or less passive response to exposure to drugs fail to take into account the fact that drug-use is a (maladaptive) attempt to cope with problems of various kinds. Whereas they too see addiction as a kind of vicious cycle, unlike Solomon they do not regard this as derived from the escalation of tolerance and withdrawal. Instead, they specify three conditions for the development of an 'addictive cycle':

(a) Opiates are used to adapt to distress, (b) the user perceives no better means of adaptation, and (c) opiate use ultimately leads to an *increase* in the original distress. ... If all three conditions specified by this model did not apply, opiate use, if it occurred at all, would be nonaddictive, even if tolerance and physical dependence occurred ... Therefore, neither tolerance nor physical dependence can be considered essential causal factors in addiction (Alexander and Hadaway, 1982, pp. 376–7).

Alexander and Hadaway argue that addiction, in the behavioural sense of compulsive use, should not be equated with physical dependence, in the sense of vulnerability to withdrawal. The origins of addiction lie, in their view, in the problems or distress experienced by the addict *prior* to first drug-use, and in the tendency of drug-use eventually to make such problems worse rather than better. They are, however, faced with two questions: firstly, why relatively few substances among those available in nature or in manufactured products tend to lead to abuse (suggesting that physiological and metabolic factors cannot be ignored, even though they may be difficult to identify in many cases); and secondly, whether their 'adaptive orientation' can as adequately explain the compulsive use of other drugs such as tobacco which, unlike opiates, are freely and legally available. Whereas the first of these questions is very much within the province of pharmacology, the second relates more closely to psychological issues of motives, attitudes and decisions.

To smoke or not to smoke?

Strong claims have been made not only for the seriously damaging effects of tobacco on health, but also for the addictiveness of nicotine. 'Cigarette-smoking is probably the most addictive and dependence-producing form of object-specific self-administered gratification known to man', according to Russell (1974). The cigarette is also an extraordinarily efficient way of administering nicotine. The speed of delivery from inhalation to the brain – seven seconds or so – is rather faster than that from intravenous injection in the case of heroin. Furthermore, smokers will regulate their patterns of smoking so as to maintain a more or less steady level of nicotine in their bloodstream. Russell (1976) refers to this process as 'nicotine titration'.

Schachter (1978) argues along similar lines, and draws attention to the fact that the rate of excretion of nicotine (and hence the amount that is 'wasted' before it can be metabolized) depends on the pH balance of the urine. The more acid the urine, the higher is the rate of excretion. Thus, factors that increase acidity of the urine should tend to lead to a drop in smokers' blood levels of nicotine, if their consumption of cigarettes remained constant. Two such factors are alcohol and stress, and Schachter's claim is therefore that, when smokers say that they like to smoke when they have a drink, or that

113

smoking helps them cope when they are under stress, they are misinterpreting why they smoke more under such circumstances; they are actually smoking to compensate for the drop in their blood nicotine level.

But is smoking always so much of an automatic reflex? Adult smokers vary considerably in how much they smoke and inhale. There is also the question of why young people start smoking and why experimentation can escalate into dependence. When smokers are asked why they smoke, they come up with a wide variety of reasons. Russell, Peto and Patel (1974) factor-analysed the responses of 175 smokers to a questionnaire containing 34 statements describing different reasons for smoking. On the basis of a second-order factor analysis, they concluded that the smoking habit can develop within the individual in terms of

a progression from non-pharmacological rewards (psychosocial and sensorimotor) to a positive nicotine effect and finally on to nicotine addiction, in which smoking is not so much motivated by a positive effect as by the need for nicotine to avoid unpleasant withdrawal symptoms (Russell *et al.*, 1974, p. 330).

This notion of a progressive change in smokers' motives fits in with epidemiological evidence that the onset of smoking in young people, and the amount that they smoke at a young age, can be best predicted from factors such as the number of friends and family members who smoke (Bynner, 1969; Dobbs and Marsh, 1983). This has been taken to imply that those seeking to deter young people from taking up smoking should concentrate on psychosocial aspects. This at least has meant that health educators have ceased to rely so exclusively on tactics such as showing pictures of cancerous lungs to teenagers or otherwise trying to get them to take seriously the prospect that they might die before they reach 60. However, it has tended to lead to a rather stereotyped representation of the young smoker as not 'really' wanting to smoke, but as pushed into it by 'social pressure'. Based on this view, considerable attention has been given to the development of educational interventions that aim to teach teenagers how to 'resist social pressures' to smoke (Evans *et al.*, 1981).

The social pressures most often considered are those from

commercial advertising, parents and other family members who smoke and, especially, the 'peer group'. The individual adolescent is frequently portrayed as an innocent and passive victim of coercion from the 'bad company' into which he or she has sometimes fallen. There is relatively little attention paid to why adolescents may choose the friends they do, but a great deal of discussion of how they strive to conform to their friends' expectations for fear of rejection from their circle. The evidence for such 'peer group pressure', however, is quite ambiguous. Teenagers who smoke themselves tend to have a higher proportion of friends who are smokers too but, as shown by Eiser and van der Pligt (1984b), smokers are no more likely to be chosen as friends by their age-mates, considered as a whole, than are nonsmokers. It is difficult to argue, therefore, that young smokers are particularly likely to be viewed as 'leaders' or models for imitation by the rest of their peer group. What is more, at all age groups smokers are in the minority, so any general tendency to conform to the conventional forms of behaviour shown by the majority should make young people less, rather than more, inclined to take up smoking.

What this points to is the need to reconceptualize social influence within the context of the relationships that develop within and between different subgroups of friends, rather than treating the 'peer group' as an indivisible monolith, imposing its unhealthy demands on the powerless but innocent individual. Despite attempts to look at the relative importance of different normative influences at different ages (Krosnick and Judd, 1982), it is far from clear that taking up smoking is a simple, direct effect of friendship choice. The evidence could as easily point to a subdivision of the 'peer group' into subgroups or cliques, the members of which share a number of attributes in common, of which smoking status may be only one, and not the most important.

The concept of social influence is of little use as an explanation of behaviour without some assumptions being made about the individual's social identity; that is, his or her subjective identification with a particular social group or category or set of categories at any one time. Research on social identity and intergroup behaviour has stressed the importance attached by individuals to belonging to groups or categories (Tajfel, 1978).

Turner (1982) has used the term 'referent informational influence' to describe the process whereby an individual learns to identify and enact the behaviours that are criterial or defining characteristics of a given kind of group membership. Turner conceives of this process in terms of three stages: (i) individuals define themselves as members of a distinct social category; (ii) they form or learn the stereotypic norms of that category; (iii) they assign these norms to themselves when their membership of that category becomes psychologically salient. According to this view, merely having a fair number of smokers among one's peers should not lead to social pressure to smoke unless one identified oneself as a member of a group of smoking friends, regarded smoking as normative within the group and felt that one should conform to this norm in that membership of the group was an important part of one's self-concept (Hopkins, 1987). The major sources of referent informational influence are people who help one define the criterial norms of membership of the group.

Other members of one's reference group, however, may do more than make smoking appear normative or counternormative. They may provide information about how the experience of smoking itself is to be interpreted. Other people – peers or elders – may not simply provide models for behavioural imitation, but may also communicate expectancies concerning the immediate and long-term effects of cigarettes. Experimental smokers and even still younger children (Eiser, Walsh and Eiser, 1986) are not entirely naive. They already know or believe that smoking can be relaxing, an aid to concentration and coping with tension, more pleasant after a few trials than on the first occasion, difficult to give up, dangerous to long-term health, and such like. Such beliefs are *socially learned* (Eiser, 1985), and furnish adolescents with a repertoire of accounts with which both to justify their own behaviour and interpret their own experience. What this means is that the young smoker may quickly acquire, through a process of social learning, a set of beliefs about their own smoking – even including the belief that they cannot go without cigarettes for any great length of time – in a way that closely resembles the beliefs held by adult smokers. But how may such beliefs be sustainable throughout the long period from the very first cigarette to the stage of full physical dependence (which many regular smokers may indeed never reach)? A possible answer may be found in the literature on self-attributions of mood and emotion.

According to Schachter (e.g. Schachter and Singer, 1962), the subjective experience of an emotional state depends both on the degree of general physiological arousal and environmental cues that allow the arousal to be 'cognitively labelled' as a particular kind of emotion, e.g. anger or amusement. Schachter's own (1978) work on smoking and urinary pH incorporates this same assumption that interpretation of feelings depends on a combination of physiological and cognitive factors. A considerable amount of experimental research has highlighted shortcomings in Schachter's original theory (Leventhal, 1980, 1984; Reisenzein, 1983), but there is still reasonable support for the idea that ambiguous emotional experiences can be influenced by people's expectations.

Whether or not the experimental or irregular smoker is inhaling enough nicotine for a genuine pharmacological effect, the actual experience produced by a cigarette may be very hard to label in the abstract. What is more, the social settings in which experimental smokers try their early (forbidden) cigarettes may well be ones that can give rise to ill-defined and misattributable changes in arousal. Although the concept of 'peer group pressure' may be suspect for the reasons discussed, it is still likely that adolescents may feel a degree of apprehension as a result of the presence of an audience by whom they anticipate being evaluated (Guerin, 1983). Much of this apprehension, as well as the arousal generated by the forbidden or novel nature of the activity, may be dissipated when they take a puff and find that, after all, the sky hasn't fallen down on their heads. In other words, they may feel less tense after their smoke than beforehand. *Ergo*, smoking makes you feel relaxed.

This reinterpretative process may carry on over much longer periods of time. As Marsh (1984) points out, adolescents may be often quite deeply concerned with acquiring control over excessive fluctuations in their mood, 'staying cool' and such like. Part of what counts as greater maturity in adolescence is the achievement of greater emotional self-control and, like other forms of maturity, it comes to most people more or less in the fullness of time. The adolescent smoker, however, is gaining such self-control over the same period as acquiring a habit, one of the supposed benefits of which is a greater ability to remain calm when under pressure. Improvement in coping and self-control thus appears to covary with, and hence be a consequence of, more frequent use of cigarettes. *Ergo*, smoking calms your nerves and helps you cope.

The point of this argument is not that the short-term benefits of cigarette smoking are merely illusory, but only that such benefits are *anticipated* by young people before they are *experienced*. When there is so close a match between what young smokers *expect* to feel (e.g. more relaxed and able to cope) and what, before too long, they *will* feel, it becomes difficult, and perhaps not so very important from a motivational point of view, to determine the point at which their feelings become 'real'.

The self-attribution of addiction

The evidence so far reviewed carries the following general implication. Addiction, as a behavioural syndrome, depends not simply on pharmacological factors but on a whole set of expectancies that drug-users acquire concerning the effects of the drug on their mental state, the pleasure they will obtain from the drug and the pain or discomfort they will experience if deprived of it for any length of time. One aspect of the similarity between the major addictions (smoking, alcoholism and opiate dependence) is the high likelihood of relapse among patients who attend clinics for treatment for their dependence, following a period of initial abstinence (Hunt and Matarazzo, 1973). Schachter (1982), talking about smoking and obesity, makes the important point that such clinic samples are typically self-selected, and that the high rates of relapse that are observed may disguise the fact that many people in the general population may have 'cured' themselves successfully without professional help. Even so, very many smokers report extreme difficulty in staying off cigarettes for long periods, often despite having made many serious attempts to give up the habit, and it is important to ask why.

Much of the earlier work in this area appeared to support the conclusion that attitudes and cognitions had little part to play. In terms of expectancy-value models of attitudes and decisions, it could easily be shown that many smokers already had the right kind of attitudes to make them want to give up smoking. Their subjective expected utility for smoking – that is their calculation of the likely benefits and costs – was consistently found to be negative rather than positive on a variety of self-report measures (e.g. Mausner and Platt, 1971), although less negative, as one might expect, than that held by non-smokers. Attempts have been made to incorporate measures of subjective norms (see p. 26) as well as perceived consequences (Fishbein, 1982), but still the basic paradox remains. Smokers continue to smoke despite the fact that they know it is bad for them, and many (those whom McKennell and Thomas, 1967, once described as 'dissonant' smokers) continue to do so despite professing their wish to stop. The solution to this paradox seemed clear, however, both to investigators and such smokers themselves: they continue to smoke because they are addicted.

Under what conditions, then, do smokers (or other drug-users) make the self-attribution that they are addicted, and what effects does such a self-attribution have on their attitudes and decisions? It seems that quite large numbers of smokers may be prepared to describe themselves as addicted. In a small sample of 115 smokers from a television audience research panel, Eiser, Sutton and Wober (1978) found 61 who thought they were addicted to cigarettes, compared with 54 who thought they were not addicted, or who were undecided. These 61 'addicted' smokers differed from the 'not-addicted' group on a number of variables. In particular, they were much more likely to say that they would like to stop smoking altogether if they could do so easily. This item was the same as that which McKennell and Thomas (1967) had previously used as a criterion for distinguishing 'dissonant' from 'consonant' smokers. Their notion was that continuing to smoke while wanting to stop should give rise to a state of cognitive dissonance (see Chapter 2). Eiser et al. found that those smokers who described themselves as more addicted were more 'dissonant' by this criterion. In other words, they said that they could not stop smoking easily, even though they would like to do so if they could.

Strictly speaking, therefore, the 'addicted' smokers were not in a state of cognitive dissonance. This is not to say that they were entirely happy about their status as smokers. Indeed, they reported a fair amount of concern over the risk to their health. However, as we explained in Chapter 2, the experience of dissonance depends critically on the perception of free choice. If people do not feel in control of their own behaviour, they may experience many other negative thoughts and feelings, but they will not regard themselves as responsible for the aversive consequences of their behaviour and hence will not experience dissonance. Labelling oneself as an addict, therefore, may be functional if one wishes to limit the degree of blame one attaches to oneself for failure at giving up smoking or any other drug.

In that the self-attribution of addiction involves denial of responsibility, it would seem to have a certain amount in common with the concept of the 'sick role' (Robinson, 1972). Eiser and Gossop (1979) studied a group of outpatients at a drug-dependence clinic who were using a variety of drugs, including heroin (which they were able to obtain on prescription). The main findings were from a set of statements to which the addicts had to respond by saying how well each statement described the way they felt about their own drug-use. A principal components analysis revealed two factors. The first, labelled 'Hooked', expressed mainly a felt inability to give up drugs or to resist taking them. The second, labelled 'Sick', involved seeing one's drug-use as a sickness which doctors could cure, concern with health consequences and seeing oneself as needing help with personal problems generally. In other words, it appeared with this group that the acceptance of the definition of their drug-use as a medical condition was independent of the feeling of diminished control over one's own behaviour.

We have found essentially the same distinction in the way smokers describe their smoking (Eiser and van der Pligt, 1986). The sample for this study was drawn from a large number of members of the British public who had contacted a television company in response to an offer of free 'kits' that might help them stop smoking. A subgroup rated 20 self-descriptive items based on those used by Eiser and Gossop (1979). Again, two clear factors emerged, though in the reverse order of magnitude to that found by Eiser and Gossop. The 'Sick' factor was marked by items such as 'I think of my smoking as a sickness which needs to be cured' and 'I'm frightened about what smoking may be doing to me'. Items loading on the 'Hooked' factor included

'I'm not going to be able to give up smoking unless someone helps me', 'If life was easier, I'd have less need to smoke' and 'I don't think I'm really prepared to give up smoking if it proves too difficult or distressing'. This last item is especially interesting, in that it was strongly related to how people responded to the question used by McKennell and Thomas (1967) to identify so-called 'dissonant' smokers. The more the smokers said that they would like to stop if they 'could do so easily', the less they said that they were prepared to try if it proved 'too difficult'. In addition, there was a close relationship between high scores on the 'Hooked' factor and the preparedness to label oneself as more addicted.

Expectancy and change

What implications do such perceptions have for behaviour? A key concept here is that of expectancy: what do people expect to happen if they undertake a given course of action, and how confident are they that they will be able to achieve the ends that they desire? In social psychological research on attribution processes (see Chapter 3), there has been a fairly sharp division between studies that have been concerned with the factors influencing how people explain events in one way rather than another and those concerned with the consequences, for cognitive, emotional and behavioural change, of the particular explanations that people adopt or accept (Kelley and Michela, 1980).

Prominent within the latter category is the work of Weiner (1979, 1985a, 1985b; Weiner and Kukla, 1970) on attributions for success and failure and on the implications of such attributions for achievement motivation. As was described in Chapter 3, Weiner and Kukla (1970) proposed that people's motivation to undertake a difficult task depends on their attributions for their success or failure on similar tasks in the past. These were categorized in terms of two dichotomies: internal v. external and stable v. unstable. When previous success is attributed to stable causes, expectancy of future success will be higher than when it is attributed to unstable causes. Conversely, when previous failure is attributed to unstable rather than stable causes, the person is less likely to feel that such failure is bound to be repeated on future occasions. For example, someone who thought that he or she had failed an examination because of insufficient effort at revision (an unstable factor that could be corrected next time) would be more confident of doing better in future examinations than would someone who put down his or her failure to a lack of intelligence or ability (a stable factor).

The special importance of this research to the problem of addictive behaviours is that few people who manage to break their habit do so at their first attempt. Most smokers, alcoholics and drug addicts – or at any rate most who seek help with giving up – have a history of previous failures at attempted cessation. They are often far from confident that they will ever be able to give up, however hard they try. Before one can ask whether expectancy-value notions are applicable to the decisions made by smokers and other addicts, therefore, one must define exactly what decisions one has in mind. The problem is not one of whether addicts see more or less benefits from continuation rather than cessation of drug-use, but what they expect to be the outcomes of any *attempt* at cessation, granted their failures in previous attempts.

Eiser and Sutton (1977) have argued that, for smokers, the critical decision is not that of whether or not to stop, but whether or not to *try* to stop. For this reason, it is little use convincing smokers that it would be a good idea if they gave up smoking (something that relatively few would deny) if they attach only a minuscule probability to the prospect of their managing to stop if they tried. In expectancy-value terms, the perceived benefits of cessation will need to be multiplied by this minuscule probability in any subjective calculations of the pay-offs from yet another attempt at giving up. Since such attempts are by no means without their costs, it is not 'irrational', from a subjective point of view, for smokers to continue to smoke and not to try to stop, *provided that they are correct in their pessimism about their likelihood of failure if they tried.*

What can produce such pessimism? If Weiner is correct, an important factor will be that of how previous failures are explained. We looked at this in another part of the study (p. 120) of smokers who contacted a television company in response to the offer of help in stopping smoking (Eiser, van der Pligt, Raw and Sutton, 1985). Those responding to our questionnaire were asked to say why 'so many smokers fail when they try to give up smoking'. To answer this question, our respondents had to rank the following possible causes in order of importance:

(a) 'Because it's just too difficult for them.'
(b) 'Because they don't try hard enough.'
(c) 'Because they don't know the best way to set about it.'
(d) 'Because of the kind of people they are.'
(e) 'Because of bad luck.'

Few attached any great importance to luck as a factor, so the analyses were based on the remaining four causes, which were combined to form two separate indices. 'Internality' was represented by the contrast between effort (b) and personality (d) on the one hand and difficulty (a) and knowledge (c) on the other. 'Stability' was derived from the difference between difficulty (a) and personality (d) on the one hand and effort (b) and knowledge (c) on the other. Among the other variables measured were the intention to try to stop smoking 'in the near future', their expectancy of success, or confidence, in their ability to stop ('If you tried to stop smoking altogether, how likely do you think you would be to succeed?') and how addicted they felt that they were to smoking.

A follow-up study was conducted one year later to establish how many of the original sample said that they had tried to stop or cut down, and of those who tried, how many had succeeded. Self-reports of attempts at stopping were strongly related to respondents' declared intentions to stop, as expressed in the questionnaire administered one year earlier. Intention, in turn, was strongly dependent on confidence (expectancy of success). In accordance with Weiner's (1985a) model, confidence was influenced by attributions of (other smokers') previous failures to stable or unstable factors (difficulty/personality v. effort/knowledge), whereas attributions to internal or external factors (effort/personality v. difficulty/knowledge) had no influence on confidence. The measure of self-attributed addiction was related to more stable attributions for failure and lower confidence. It also contributed to the prediction of behavioural outcome: those who saw themselves as more addicted were less likely to manage to stop smoking, even if they tried.

Additional analyses were conducted on the subgroup who responded to the set of self-descriptive statements previously mentioned (p. 120). Those who scored higher on the 'Sick' factor made more 'external' attributions (supporting the notion of a link between external locus of control and the 'sick role'), but had rather greater confidence in their ability to give up. Those with higher scores on the 'Hooked' factor made more 'stable' attributions, had less confidence in their ability to give up, and were less likely to succeed in doing so, even if they tried (Eiser and van der Pligt, 1986).

The importance of confidence (expectancy of success) as a predictor of intention to stop smoking has been confirmed by a number of other studies. Sutton, Marsh and Matheson (1987) have reported analyses derived from a large representative survey (Marsh and Matheson, 1983), in which they show that confidence, perceived costs and benefits of stopping, and prior behaviour (previous attempts at cessations) all contributed to the prediction of smokers' intentions to try to stop. Confidence is also an important variable that can mediate the effects of persuasive communications on intentions. Sutton and Eiser (1984) measured subjects' reactions to a fear-arousing videotape about smoking (originally a television documentary) and used these to predict smokers' intentions to stop smoking. Comparison groups viewed videos on other health topics (alcoholism and seat-belt use). Smokers' intentions to try to stop were influenced both by their confidence and by the levels of fear aroused by the video. Besides providing further evidence of the importance of expectancies, however, this study relates to the more general question of the effectiveness of fear-arousing messages, which is one of the topics to be discussed in the next chapter.

In conclusion, then, the study of health behaviour generally and addictions in particular poses a special challenge for social psychologists. Most theories in social psychology seem better suited to the explanation of unencumbered, one-off behavioural decisions. However, most kinds of health behaviour take the form of strongly learned habits and many are extremely compulsive. If behaviour is beyond 'volitional control' (cf. Fishbein and Ajzen, 1975), the study of attitudes and decisions might be expected to have less relevance to its explanation. Even so, the research reviewed in this chapter clearly shows that social psychological concepts such as attitudes and attributions *are* relevant in this field and that the borderline between voluntary and involuntary action may often be difficult to draw. Even when there are powerful situational and physiological influences at work, it is still essential to understand people's interpretations of their own motives and capabilities.

6

Medical communication and judgment

In this chapter, we shall consider how information can influence behaviour, how it is communicated, and how it is understood by both patients and medical professionals. The theoretical areas to which this research relates include persuasion and attitude change, social power and influence, cognitive development, information-processing and judgment under uncertainty. The applied areas cover a similarly wide range, from health education and preventive medicine to doctor–patient consultations, power structures in the medical hierarchy, and clinical diagnosis.

Fear-arousing messages

A long tradition of experimental research has examined the question of how the amount of fear aroused by a message relates to the amount of attitude and/or behaviour change it produces. The results of this research have penetrated rather incompletely into the thinking of health communicators. It is important to distinguish, in any health warning, between information regarding the *existence* of a risk, information regarding the seriousness or *likelihood* of that risk, and the *manner* in which such information is communicated. It is difficult to conceive of a persuasive health message that does not *in some way* communicate information about possible risks, but the issue is one of *how* such information is conveyed.

Most of the early research on the effects of fear-arousal was based on the framework developed by Hovland, Janis and Kelley (1953). This relied quite strongly on principles of reinforcement. The basic assumption is known as the *fear-drive model*:

> When fear is learned as a response to a new situation, it serves as a drive to motivate trial-and-error behavior. A reduction in strength of the fear reinforces the learning of any new response that accompanies it (Dollard and Miller, 1950, p. 78).

From this, Hovland et al. draw the generalization that 'any intensely disturbing emotion, such as fear, guilt, shame, anger, or disgust, has the functional properties of a drive' (1953, p. 61). What are the responses that may be motivated by fear, and reinforced by fear-reduction? At this point, Hovland et al. part company with the more orthodox behaviourism of Dollard and Miller. Instead, they list three categories of response that are undoubtedly cognitive (cf. Petty and Cacioppo, 1985). These are:

1 attention to the verbal content of the communication;
2 comprehension of the message of the communication;
3 acceptance of the conclusions advocated by the communication.

Fear-arousal is thus assumed to have both an orientating and a reinforcing effect.

Hovland et al. (1953) then proceed to qualify the fear-drive model by introducing the hypothesis that the relationship of fear-arousal to attitude and behaviour change may be curvilinear. The reason that they suggest for this is that intense feelings of anxiety can set off defensive reactions, of which they identify three kinds: (a) a failure to pay attention to what is being said, (b) rejection of the communicator and (c) defensive avoidance of anxiety-arousing thoughts. These themes are developed more fully in later work by Janis (1967) and Janis and Mann (1977; see also Chapter 4). The inference is that greatest attitude change will occur at *moderate* levels of fear, before such defensive reactions come into play.

A frequently cited study by Janis and Feshbach (1953) provides some support for these hypotheses. Janis and Feshbach presented high school students with one of three communications designed to encourage them to take better care of their teeth. In the 'strong appeal' condition, the students received a lecture illustrated by 'highly realistic photographs which vividly portrayed tooth decay and mouth infections' (Hovland et al., 1953, p. 70). They were also given gruesome warnings about the dangers of secondary infection. Compared with this, the 'moderate' and 'minimal' appeal conditions were shown photographs of milder pathology, or X-ray pictures and diagrams of cavities, and were subjected to a greatly 'toned-down' version of the lecture. Manipulation checks revealed that only subjects in the strong appeal condition reported feeling more worried about decayed teeth and decayed gums than did those in a control condition. However, when comparing changes in self-reported behaviour from one week before the communication to one week after, the strong appeal condition showed the least, and the minimal appeal condition the most, change in the direction of more conscientious dental hygiene practice. Only the minimal appeal condition showed a significant difference from the control group, who showed no overall change.

These results do not really confirm the prediction of a strictly curvilinear effect of fear level on change, which would have required the minimal and strong appeal conditions to have been more similar in their effects, with the moderate appeal condition producing most change. The clearer result, however, is the inverse relationship beteen level of fear-arousal and level of change, and this is what has been remembered in the literature. This finding would be clearly inconsistent with a cruder version of the fear-drive model that made no allowance for concepts such as defensive avoidance, but simply assumed that the greater the fear, the greater the drive to change one's beliefs and behaviour.

This pattern of results, however, is by no means typical of

what other researchers have found. Sutton (1982) reviewed the results of 35 studies up to 1980, starting with the Janis and Feshbach (1953) experiment. Considering this group of studies as a whole, Sutton concluded that fear-arousal produced a consistent 'improvement' in intention and behaviour as compared with no-fear control conditions, and furthermore, that higher levels of fear consistently led to *more* change than lower levels. Almost no support was found for the hypothesis of a curvilinear relationship between change and levels of fear. Findings relating to the effects of different kinds of reassurance about the efficacy of protective action were somewhat mixed. Greater reassurance did not always lead to reduction in fear, nor always to stronger intentions to undertake the recommended action (although the overall trend was in that direction). The fear-drive model could be used to generate the prediction that acceptance of a reassuring recommendation should be more rewarding (and hence more likely) at higher levels of fear, but no such interaction was generally observed.

The simplest overall conclusion would therefore seem to be that fear-arousal can and often *does* work in bringing about attitudinal and/or behavioural change. However, one should not underestimate the influence of the Janis and Feshbach (1953) findings on the design of later experiments. Built into the thinking of most researchers has been an awareness of the dangers of setting the fear manipulation at an excessive level, and of leaving subjects without a 'behavioural plan' to enable them to translate their motivation into action. What is very difficult to estimate are the comparative levels of fear produced in studies on different topics with different age-groups at different times.

The effects of fear may also depend on other factors, as has long been recognized, not all of which have been systematically controlled across the different studies. One important distinction, as discussed in Chapter 5, is that between the perceived efficacy of a recommended *action* in reducing the threat and the perceived self-efficacy of the *person*, in other words, the person's confidence is his or her own ability to carry out the recommended action. In the context of smoking, this corresponds to the distinction between believing that giving up smoking will reduce one's chances of getting lung cancer and other diseases, and believing that one will be able to succeed in giving up smoking if one tries (Eiser *et al.*, 1985; Sutton *et al.*, 1987).

Possibly the most disappointing feature of this literature is the lack of any really thorough attempt to relate levels of fear to specific aspects of the content of a communication. The need for an analysis of content cues was recognized by Hovland et al. (1953, p. 59), but their suggestion has not been followed up in any systematic way. Viewed from the perspective of more recent theoretical research (e.g. Petty and Cacioppo, 1985), one would expect any fear-arousing message to give rise to a variety of emotional *and* cognitive responses, of which 'fear' is only one, and perhaps not always the most important. One of the more frequent aspects of fear appeals seems to be the use of more lurid or vivid visual imagery. But is the effect of this merely to be considered in terms of fear, or rather in terms of more cognitive effects such as heightened attention and/or ease of retrieval of information from memory? More vivid presentation has been hypothesized to make information more easily imagined and 'available' for retrieval, and hence to increase the subjective probability of the events or outcomes described (Nisbett and Ross, 1980; Tversky and Kahneman, 1973). The suggestion is that people tend to overestimate the number of deaths from causes that receive considerable media coverage and to under-estimate the toll of less newsworthy accidents and diseases (Lichtenstein *et al.*, 1978; see also Harding and Eiser, 1984; Harding, Eiser and Kristiansen, 1982). The possibility that more vivid presentations increase the subjective probability of a threat could produce a direct relationship between levels of 'fear-arousal' and change, but without needing to attribute this effect to the drive properties of increased emotional 'tension'.

There is also the variable of perceived self-relevance to consider. It could well have been that the pictures of grotesque oral decay and infection shown by Janis and Feshbach (1953) in their strong appeal condition were so extreme that perceived self-relevance was undermined. If this were so, such a reaction could be interpreted as a form of defensive avoidance in terms of their theory, but it could also be the case that, irrespective of such motivational factors, the extremity of the appeal simply led to subjects making different self-attributions about their behaviour:

> a subject exposed to the high-fear appeal . . . would tend to believe that improper dental care leads to having teeth pulled, to cancer, paralysis, blindness, and sore, swollen, and inflamed gums . . . Since it is unlikely that his own oral hygiene practices have resulted in any of these consequences, he would probably infer that he has been taking proper care of his teeth and thus he has no need to change his tooth-brushing behavior (Fishbein and Ajzen, 1975, p. 502).

Self-relevance can also lead to an increase in subjective estimates of probability. As mentioned in Chapter 4, Gregory *et al.* (1982) found that subjects who were led to imagine themselves experiencing one of a number of positive or negative events subsequently gave higher estimates of the likelihood of such events occurring. Sherman *et al.* (1985) found the same effect for subjective estimates of the likelihood of contracting a disease.

What all this amounts to is the fact that it is very difficult to produce a 'pure' measure of fear-arousal. Other things being equal, if effective reassurance and a behavioural plan for the avoidance of threat are offered too, the evidence suggests that more fear-arousing information *can* produce more change. However, other things usually are *not* equal even in the experimental laboratory and still less in the world of mass media campaigns. Probably the greatest danger is that of a 'fear-arousing' message being construed as a personal attack by the target groups whose behaviour the communicators are trying to change (consider, for example, the possible reactions of homosexual men to campaigns on AIDS). This relates directly to our general argument throughout this book, that people with different attitudes may interpret information in different ways, and see different aspects of an issue as salient.

Communicating with patients

A considerable body of research has looked at the factors determining the quality of communication between medical personnel and their patients. These include ensuring that messages are given to patients in a form that they can understand, something that is by no means universally achieved, even with printed messages (Ley, 1982). Although awareness of this problem seems to be improving, there are still mistakes made. A recent example is provided by an evaluation by Sherr (1987) of the first stage of the British Government's campaign against AIDS, which involved a whole-page advertisement in every national newspaper. Sherr concluded that, according to the formula devised by Flesch (1948), only 24 per cent of the population would have been able to understand the whole text of the advertisement. In addition to problems of complex vocabulary, there were instances of plain ambiguity. For example, 'intimate kissing' was identified as a practice to avoid. Even a group of gynaecologists questioned by Sherr could not provide an agreed definition of what this phrase meant!

Many of the most important factors influencing medical communication, however, are interpersonal. Much conventional medical training involves coaching future doctors in a style that combines sensitivity to the patient's needs with a professional detachment from personal considerations. The success of such training can be uneven, and the fact that it is needed at all suggests that it may not always come naturally. A recent textbook for medical students (Mendel, 1984) contains a long list of guidelines for proper professional conduct. These include not keeping patients waiting, not discussing 'cases' disrespectfully on ward rounds, making sure one's hands are warm and dry, accepting everything they say as potentially useful information and monitoring one's own performance even in terms of details such as tone of voice.

Unfortunately, many medical consultations fall short of these ideals. There are far too many reports from patients of long waits for brief and brusque encounters, often involving little verbal exchange or even eye-contact. It is clear that poor communication is often cited as a reason for patient dissatisfaction and poor compliance by the patients with their doctors' advice (Pendleton and Hasler, 1983). Discourtesy aside, however, one of the most significant features of doctor–patient interactions is the inequality of the power relationship. This carries with it implications for the obtaining or withholding of information. Whereas Mendel is clear that doctors should try to gain as much information as possible from their patients, he takes a far from egalitarian view on what the patients themselves need to be told:

> you can have no preconceived notions about 'what you always tell your patients'. Rather, you tell them the minimum amount which will satisfy them and you do not overload them with information that they would rather not have heard ... You must have your answers pat, and it is more important that your story should be consistent, logical and directed towards getting the patient well, than that it should be the whole truth or scientifically accurate (p. 120).

This frankly patriarchal attitude is based on certain premises about the doctor's role and the patient's needs that may not always apply. This passage implies that the adequacy of any communication should be judged purely pragmatically, in terms of how it makes the patient feel and how it assists the process of treatment. However, the patient's requirements from a consultation may not always be cure, alleviation of pain, or even reassurance, but simply information. Patients whose primary need is to discover as much as possible about their condition could well come away dissatisfied from a consultation of the kind recommended above.

In fact, studies of patient satisfaction tell a rather different story. Many patients are remarkably tolerant of a lack of technical excellence and expect neither omnipotence nor omniscience in their physician. On the other hand, poor communication of information is the single most frequently cited cause of dissatisfaction both in the UK and USA (Locker and Dunt, 1978). An early review by Ley (1972) reported rates of dissatisfaction with communication varying between 11 and 65 per cent across a number of studies of inpatients in British hospitals. Why should this be? One possibility is that doctors find it more difficult to communicate with certain kinds of patients, or to communicate certain kinds of information. Another is that the patients are in fact given adequate information, but fail to retain it for reasons of heightened anxiety or whatever. Another is that the information is given in too complex a form to be readily understood.

There are well-documented inequalities in health care

provision that covary with the economic prosperity of different regions. More disturbing is the possibility that such inequalities may be reinforced by different forms of doctor–patient communication within a single practice. Pendleton and Bochner (1980) conducted a study which involved videotaping consultations conducted by six GPs with practices in the south of England. There were 79 adult patients, all white, 34 of whom were male. The patients were divided into three categories on the basis of socio-economic status. Various aspects of the communications were coded quantitatively and the three groups were compared. Overall, it was found that higher-status patients received longer consultations, more information and explanations spontaneously volunteered by the doctor, and more information and explanations in response to questions they themselves asked. No differences were found between the status groups in the complexity of the medical problems presented. These findings are not interpreted as evidence of deliberate discrimination by the doctors, but rather as reflecting the fact that they felt more comfortable and informal with members of their own subculture. Thus, the quality of doctor–patient communication can be influenced by how easy doctors feel about talking to particular kinds of patients, which may doubtless reflect more or less well-founded presumptions about the patients' abilities to understand more elaborate explanations or instructions.

It has also been remarked that medical staff find it especially difficult or upsetting to give 'bad news' to patients and their families, in particular diagnoses of fatal illnesses and cancer generally. The diagnosis of cancer is not always directly communicated, or if it is, it may not be described in so many words; phrases like 'lump' or 'growth' may often be used instead. Even so, conventions have changed considerably over recent years. For instance, Oken (1961) found that 90 per cent of a sample of physicians would usually not or never tell their patients that they had cancer, whereas in a study by Novack et al. (1979), the figure was as low as 2 per cent (both studies were in the USA).

The policy of generally withholding information in the patient's own interest is essentially unsupported by empirical research. Gilbertsen and Wangensteen (1962) followed up a group of cancer patients who had been informed of their diagnosis. Of those who had been successfully treated, 93 per cent reported that the information had been advantageous to them. The figure was only slightly lower (87 per cent) among those whose condition was terminal. When attention is shifted to broader categories of patients, the same conclusion holds that the provision of fuller information is widely welcomed, and leads to no real difficulty, even when patients are given full access to their case records (Stevens, Staff and Mackay, 1977). Ley (1982) lists fourteen such studies that found little or no adverse effect of more open communication. It therefore appears that much of the reluctance of physicians to give more complete information, however convinced they may be that this may be justified by their 'clinical experience', serves their own preferences more than those of their patients.

Explaining illness to children

Different groups of patients may need to be talked to in different ways, but nowhere would this seem to be more obvious and important than in the case of children. It has been estimated that something over one in ten of school-aged children have some form of chronic illness (Pless and Douglas, 1971). With many of these conditions, diabetes being a prime example, children must learn at quite a young age to take responsibility for various aspects of their own treatment. However, Johnson et al. (1982) concluded that the level of theoretical and practical knowledge of a sample of diabetic children was inadequate to enable them to cope independently with the everyday demands of the disease. Martin, Landau and Phelan (1982) similarly concluded that a group of young adults who had suffered from asthma since childhood were generally unaware of a number of risk factors (such as smoking) that could exacerbate their respiratory difficulties. So why do many paediatric patients remain underinformed about their illness? One possibility is that they are in fact given the necessary information, but do not have the necessary cognitive maturity to understand and remember it. Another possibility is that insufficient information is specifically given to the children themselves. Pantell et al. (1982) videorecorded 115 consultations involving a physician, a child and a parent. Although some of the physicians' questions were directed at the child, most of the feedback about diagnosis and treatment was directed to the parent. More information was given directly to older children and more to boys than to girls!

Paediatricians tend to have rather little appreciation of how much young children can and cannot understand, tending to overestimate understanding in young children and underestimate it in older children (Perrin and Perrin, 1983). Communication that takes account of the child's level of understanding should be more effective, but how is such a matching of message content to cognitive level to be achieved? Most attention has been paid to finding better ways of explaining more abstract concepts to children at the 'concrete-operational' stage. For instance, Whitt, Dykstra and Taylor (1979) recommended the use of metaphor to link illness with events in the child's everyday experience. Thus, the need for regular food and injections in diabetes may be likened to needing to put petrol in a car. All cars need petrol, but a diabetic is like a car that needs to make more frequent stops for refuelling. Epileptics can be told that the brain is like a telephone exchange, and a fit is like getting a wrong number. The empirical support for these suggestions, however, is rather mixed.

Two studies on healthy children by C. Eiser, Eiser and Hunt (1986a,b) investigated this question. The first (1986b) found age differences in the kinds of similes children spontaneously used to describe parts of their body, with 14-year-olds being inclined to describe bodily functions in rather concrete, mechanistic terms. However, the younger children (in the 7 to 11 age-range) did not produce analogies of the kind suggested by Whitt et al. (1979), but instead emphasized attributes such as colour, shape, sound and movement. The Eiser et al. (1986a) study compared metaphorical explanations of illness (either diabetes or cancer) as suggested by Whitt et al. with explanations in more straightforward medical terms. Although understanding of either of these illnesses was higher for older children, the type of explanation (medical or metaphorical) had no overall effect.

At the simplest level, the problem with conveying information to children is not that they are stupid but that they are naive. Like adults, they will attempt to understand new experience by comparing it with previous experience, and will look for the best fit available. Unlike adults, however, they will generally have rather little previous experience to use in this way. The Whitt et al. (1979) idea of using metaphors based on supposedly everyday experience seems to concede part of this argument, but goes astray on a crucial point. There is no direct reason to suppose that children find the idea of filling cars with petrol (let alone the workings of an internal combustion engine) any more familiar or comprehensible than that of eating to give oneself energy. The neural pathways in one's brain *may* be more difficult to visualize than the wires in a telephone exchange, but how clear an idea do children have of how telephones work anyway? The appropriateness of particular metaphors as an aid to understanding is thus dependent on how well the metaphors themselves are understood, and indeed on the child's ability to understand that they *are* only metaphors. The challenge is not to find different concepts that can act as imperfect *substitutes* for those that one wants the child eventually to acquire, but to find a way of communicating a set of broad categories out of which more differentiated concepts will develop with more learning and experience. The literature on cognitive development gives us every reason to suppose that, where children choose to work up a degree of expertise on a particular topic, they can acquire a degree of sophistication far beyond their years (e.g. Chi and Koeske, 1983). This runs counter to the idea proposed by Bibace and Walsh (1981), but open to a number of empirical and theoretical objections (C. Eiser, 1985), that children's understanding of health and illness is constrained by the stage of cognitive development, defined in terms of Piaget's (e.g. 1930) theory.

The clear implication of this is that, if suitably handled, young children can become quite expert with respect to aspects of their disease and its management that relate closely to what they themselves have experienced. On the other side, it is clear that sickness often imposes not only a physical but also an emotional strain on young children and their families. If families adopt a strategy of denial or of defensive avoidance of talk or thought about the illness in order to cope with such anxiety, far less learning will take place. It must also be remembered that children with chronic illness can miss a good deal of schooling, which may likewise impede their rate of acquisition of cognitive skills and knowledge generally, quite apart from possible side-effects of the treatment some of them receive (C. Eiser, 1980).

There is in fact some confusion in the literature with regard to whether children with chronic illness, who consequently have greater experience of hospitals and procedures, are better informed about such issues than are healthy children. Some early work supported the suggestion that the emotional stress of chronic illness impeded children's capacity to learn and that sick children were therefore less well informed (Lynn, Glaser and Harrison, 1962). Against this, more recent work has tended to show that sick children have a better practical and conceptual understanding *of their own specific illness* than healthy children, but that this advantage does not generalize to improved under-standing of other aspects of health and illness (C. Eiser, Patterson and Tripp, 1984). Furthermore, there may be an interaction with age. With the younger child, the opportunity to learn may be impeded by restricted mobility, increased anxiety and parental protectiveness, whereas the older child may actually gain intellectually from the experience of hospitalization.

This leads on to another general problem of communication in paediatric medicine, which is not restricted just to the needs of the chronically sick. This is the question of how best to prepare children for hospital admission. Children can ordinarily have quite distorted views of what goes on in hospitals. There are reports of the difficulty young children, even if they have been frequently hospitalized, have with understanding why it is necessary for doctors to do things to them that cause them pain (Brewster, 1982). As a result, those under 5 years old may think that the doctors actually *want* to hurt them, whereas slightly older children may feel that the doctors simply do not care about the pain they inflict. There is also the trauma of unfamiliar surroundings, and separation from friends and family.

Educational preparation for hospital admission is obviously impossible for emergencies such as road accidents unless a more general programme of health education has been introduced into schools. Most evaluations of preparation programmes have therefore concentrated on cases of acutely sick children and others admitted for planned but routine surgery. Although generally any preparation seems to be better than none, there have been some surprising results where researchers have tried to evaluate specific methods. Peterson and Ridley-Johnson (1984), for example, compared a traditional lecture with a film about hospitalization in terms of their effects on children's attitudes and knowledge about hospitals. While both methods succeeded in reducing children's fears, an increase in knowledge was demonstrated only for the lecture. At the same time, it cannot necessarily be assumed that all patients will benefit from being more fully informed. A point may come when too many gory details can be disturbing and make the patient more anxious. Melamed and Siegel (1975) found that preparation for surgery (by means of a film showing another child coping well with the experience) was successful for children who had never been previously hospitalized, but was counterproductive for children with a history of previous admissions.

This is therefore clearly an area that would benefit from more theoretically directed research. Although desensitizing children to potentially stressful stimuli is a very important goal, the young patient's needs are informational as well as emotional. As with communication with chronically sick children, the need would seem to be for the provision of broad categories, schemata or 'script headers' (cf. Abelson, 1981), that allow patients to recognize their own experiences as examples of some more general rule.

Professional compliance

So far our emphasis has been on how communication can influence the knowledge, attitudes and behaviour of actual and potential patients, but of course the behaviour of professionals can often be far from blameless. We may conclude that paediatric patients need to be educated out of the view that doctors deliberately hurt people and that you go to hospital to be ill, but in fact there is good evidence that often hospitals can seriously damage your health.

The term 'nosocomial' is used to refer to infections contracted in hospitals. Most of these should be eliminated by the observance of proper hygiene procedures. However, according to Raven and Haley (1982), about 15,000 hospital patients in the USA die each year from infections contracted in hospital. Raven and Haley describe one response to this problem – the appointment of an 'Infection Control Nurse' (ICN), supported by a 'Hospital Epidemiologist' (HE) who would usually be a physician. The responsibility of the ICN would include not only the monitoring of infection within the hospital, but also advising other staff on proper hygiene procedures and ensuring compliance with such advice. Raven and Haley evaluated the success of this system in a sample of 433 hospitals. The data included comparisons of how the ICNs saw themselves and how they were seen by their colleagues (specifically staff nurses) and also responses to hypothetical examples of nonadherence to infection control policies.

One of the main variables considered was that of status. Staff nurses and HEs were asked to estimate the likelihood of different target persons – head nurses, staff nurses, laboratory technicians and attending physicians – adhering to each of two accepted infection control policies. Both groups of raters estimated that nurses and, to an only slightly less extent, technicians would almost certainly comply with both policies. The compliance of attending physicians with either policy, however, was rated as more 'probable' rather than 'definite' by both groups. Another question asked ICNs whether they would speak up to someone who violated different control policies. Whereas the ICNs said that they would speak up to nurses or technicians in almost every instance, they were much less likely to confront a physician who violated these policies.

Raven and Haley (1982) then addressed the question of what strategies the ICNs used to enforce compliance. Different possible strategies were identified in accordance with theories of *social power* (French and Raven, 1959; Raven, 1974). These were defined as follows:

(1) *Coercive power*, depending on the ICN's ability to initiate disciplinary action.
(2) *Reward power*, depending on the ICN's ability to use her influence in another's favour.
(3) *Legitimate power*, depending on acceptance of the ICN's position of authority.
(4) *Referent power*, involving the use by the target person of others as a frame of reference – essentially, an emphasis on the normativeness of adherence.

(5) *Expert power*, depending on acceptance of the ICN's specific expertise.

(6) *Informational power*, depending on provision of specific persuasive information, such as hospital data.

ICNs rated the likelihood of their using each of these power bases when dealing with physicians or nurses, and how effective each would be. Although there was a strong preference for informational power for either target, ICNs were much less likely to use coercive or reward power, and more likely to use expert power, with a physician than with a nurse. Although 74 per cent chose informational power as the most effective strategy for dealing with other nurses, coercive power came second, with 18 per cent of the first preferences. However, when staff nurses were asked which strategies they themselves would find most persuasive, coercive power was distinctly unpopular. The most votes went to expert (56 per cent) and informational power (37 per cent).

Although these data all refer to hypothetical interactions, the message seems clear. One of the major barriers to effective monitoring of standards of professional competence by other professionals is, or is seen to be, the differences in status between different grades of medical and paramedical staff. Those whose lapses can be potentially most damaging – the physicians – are the same people who are least likely to be taken to task for apparent incompetence.

Diagnosis and accuracy

Possibly the most important area of medical decision-making is that of diagnosis. Thanks to modern technology, there is a vast range of tests that can be applied to assess a patient's condition. However, there remains the question of whether the information from all these separate tests can be incorporated into a single diagnostic decision. Any clinical judgment involves the implicit or explicit weighting of probabilities. As we saw in Chapter 4, however, people are rather bad at handling probabilistic information in statistically normative ways. Doctors are no exception. The errors they make are similar to those demonstrated in other contexts and include those arising from neglect of base-rates, from confusion about conditional probabilities and from the use of cognitive heuristics (see pp. 89–98).

The importance of base-rate probabilities can be illustrated by the following example (from Applegate, 1981). Suppose there was a test for colon cancer that was initially validated on a sample of patients, half of whom were known to have cancer and half of whom were known to be healthy. The probability of a positive test result if a patient had cancer and the probability of a negative test result if the patient did not could both be calculated. Suppose each of these probabilities was 0.90. Would this mean that the test was '90 per cent accurate'? Not exactly. The reason for this is that the above probabilities were based on a sample in which the incidence of colon cancer was pre-set at 50 per cent, compared with, say, about 1 per cent in the population at large. Thus, out of a general population sample of 1000, one would expect 10 cases of colon cancer, 9 of which could be identified by the test (a good 'true-positive' rate), but 99 of the remaining 990 individuals *without* colon cancer would also have a positive test result (a quite high rate of 'false-positives'). Thus the percentage of true-positives out of all positive results – that is the probability of an individual who had a positive test result also having cancer – would be only 8.3 per cent (9/108).

These kinds of measures of test accuracy can therefore be quite misleading. Better measures can be derived from *signal detection theory* (e.g. Swets, 1973), widely used in the study of perception. This deals with the accuracy with which a perceiver can discriminate the presence *or absence* of an uncertain stimulus under noisy conditions (much of the original work being conducted on radar operators). In terms of this theory, a decision-maker's performance (or that of a diagnostic instrument) can be represented by plotting against each other the probabilities of false-positive and of true-positive responses observed under different conditions of noise and signal strength. The first performance parameter is referred to as *discriminating ability* or *sensitivity*, and reflects the overall probability that any 'signal' will receive a more positive response than any instance of 'noise'; for example, that someone with cancer would be more likely to be positively diagnosed than someone without. Such sensitivity is distinguished from the spurious accuracy that could be produced by simply increasing the probability of a positive response (or diagnosis) where the signal/noise ratio (or incidence of a disease) is low, thereby increasing the number of true positives at the price of an inflated number of false-positives. The second parameter of decision-making reflects the cut-off point, on a continuum of increasing certainty that a signal (or disease) is present, above which the decision-maker is prepared to make a positive response (or diagnosis). This is referred to as the *criterion* or *response bias*.

There have been numerous applications of signal detection theory to the evaluation of diagnostic procedures and expertise. One example is a study by Berwick and Thibodeau (1983), who asked physicians working in an emergency clinic to predict the outcome of chest X-ray and throat culture tests that they ordered for their patients. The focus of these tests was on the diagnosis of pneumonia and streptococcal infection, respectively. The main finding was that more experienced physicians showed more discriminating ability in their predictions than those who were less experienced, particularly in relation to X-rays.

Another influential theoretical framework has been *Bayes' theorem*, which deals with the impact of new information on the revision of probability estimates. Unlike signal detection theory, it is a *normative* rather than a descriptive model. This means that it describes the ideal or mathematically correct way of drawing inferences from probabilistic information. In practice, however, people may make inefficient or inappropriate use of such information and even draw inferences without obtaining the right kinds of information at all. The theorem thus provides a benchmark against which decision-making performance can be evaluated. In the context of diagnosis, the theorem may be defined as follows (Schwartz and Griffin, 1986, p. 57):

$$P(\text{H/Proc.+}) = \frac{P(\text{H}) + P(\text{Proc.+/H})}{P(\text{H}) \times P(\text{Proc.+/H}) + P(\text{Alt.H}) \times P(\text{Proc.+/Alt.H})}$$

The basic logic of the theorem rests on the distinctions between different conditional and base-rate probabilities. Thus, H is the hypothesis being evaluated, and Alt.H is an alternative hypothesis (e.g. disease and no disease respectively). $P(\text{H})$ is the base-rate (or in Bayesian terms, the *prior*) probability of H being correct (e.g. the incidence of the disease). $P(\text{H/Proc.+})$ is termed the *posterior* probability. This is the conditional probability that one's hypothesis is correct (the patient has the disease), if a given test is positive. It is defined as a function of the base-rate probability (without such a test result) of the hypothesis being correct $[P(\text{H})]$ or incorrect $[P(\text{Alt.H})]$ and the conditional probabilities of obtaining a positive test result, if the hypothesis was correct $[P(\text{Proc.+/H})]$ or incorrect $[P(\text{Proc.+/Alt.H})]$. These last two probabilities are equivalent to the true-positive and false-positive rates, respectively.

One implication of this theorem is that it is important to have tests that not only increase true-positive rates, but enable one to eliminate alternative hypotheses. Prediction will be improved if the false-positive rate is low. However, the importance of 'negative' procedures that rule out alternative hypotheses seems often poorly understood by clinicians (Christensen-Szalanski and Bushyhead, 1983). Beyth-Marom and Fischhoff (1983) tried to identify factors that influenced (nonmedical) subjects to have a greater appreciation of the relevance of false-positive rates. Overall, subjects tended to disregard information relevant to false-positive rates. This bias was stronger when they were simply asked to say whether the main hypothesis was true than when they were asked to choose between the main and alternative hypotheses. Even so, Beyth-Marom and Fischhoff concluded that their subjects could revise their estimates in reasonably appropriate ways if they were actually *provided* with different kinds of probabilistic information. The problem seems to be that people will not necessarily seek out such information spontaneously for themselves.

Eddy (1982) provides strong evidence that doctors are often confused about the nature of conditional probabilities. With respect to the use of mammography for the diagnosis of breast cancer, for example, he cites many published articles in which posterior probabilities are treated as equivalent to the likelihood of a positive test result. In other words, the true-positive rate, $P(\text{Proc.+/H})$, is used as though it was the same as $P(\text{H/Proc.+})$, the posterior probability of the patient having cancer, granted a positive test result. This is a serious error. What physicians want to know is the probability that the patient has cancer if the test is positive, which is quite different from the proportion of patients with cancer who show positive test results.

Heuristics and clinical judgment

Since doctors fail to act like normative statisticians, it should come as little surprise that their judgments can be shown to be vulnerable to the influence of heuristics of the kind described in Chapter 4. Detmer, Fryback and Gassner (1978) found evidence of an *availability* bias in surgeons' estimates of mortality rates. Those in low-mortality specialities (plastic surgery, orthopaedics and urology) gave lower estimates of overall hospital death rates than those in high-mortality specialities (cardiovascular, neurosurgery and general surgery). Comparable results were found by Christensen-Szalanski, Beck, Christensen-Szalanski and Koepsell (1983), who asked doctors to estimate the mortality rates of forty-two different diseases. The doctors appeared to overestimate the numbers of people who died from those diseases that featured more prominently in medical publications.

The *representativeness* heuristic seems to be reflected in diagnostic judgments based on the degree of similarity between an individual case and previous or prototypical examples of patients with a particular condition. The resulting confidence in 'knowing a case of X when I see one' could be misplaced if some of this similarity depends on the coincidence of irrelevant attributes, or if the symptoms were also compatible with another disease Y. The comparative frequency of cases of X and of Y is obviously a crucial factor.

Neglect of base-rate frequencies was demonstrated by Bennett (1980) in a modified replication of the Kahneman and Tversky (1973) study described in Chapter 4. Bennett's subjects were nurses who were told that a panel of doctors and nurses had examined cases of post-operative haemorrhage and peritonitis following abdominal surgery. Five case histories were described, supposedly drawn from a random sample of 100. The nurses had to estimate the probability that each patient had a haemorrhage. As in the Kahneman and Tversky experiment, the prior probabilities were systematically manipulated, so that some subjects were told that there were 30 haemorrhage and 70 peritonitis cases in the sample, and others were told that there were 70 haemorrhage and 30 peritonitis cases. Other groups were presented with more extreme prior probabilities (10 v. 90 per cent). Bennett also manipulated the extent to which the case histories resembled each of the conditions. Some case histories were ambiguous, whereas others were strongly indicative of one of the conditions. The findings suggested that the nurses relied on a representativeness heuristic, ignoring prior probabilities in favour of case-specific information. In other words, they attended more to whether the case histories resembled 'typical' cases of either condition than to whether either condition was more frequent than the other. However, this tendency was weaker if the case histories were more ambiguous or the prior probabilities were more extreme.

Nonetheless, doctors and nurses might not make the same mistakes in real life as they do when presented with artificially constructed problems. More frequent experience of previous instances of a particular condition or disease category should also influence the availability, or accessibility from memory, of thoughts related to that category. Since the availability heuristic (i.e. using imaginability or ease of recall as an index of likelihood) would lead clinicians to place a higher probability on diseases which they had observed more frequently, more familiar conditions should be more easily recognized and ambiguous symptoms should tend to be interpreted as signs of a common rather than rare disease. This could serve to counteract any bias arising from exclusive reliance on the representativeness heuristic.

Amount of information can lead to inflated confidence in the accuracy of one's judgments, even if the extra information does not help one to distinguish between different possibilities. Oskamp (1965) found that clinical psychologists were more confident in their assessments when they were given extra case material, but were no better at predicting outcomes. There is considerable evidence of the practice of ordering redundant and even repetitive diagnostic procedures in clinical medicine, something that can be costly, painful and even hazardous to the patient (Schwartz and Griffin, 1986). Clinicians may also mistakenly recall the presence of symptoms that would have been consistent with their eventual diagnosis, and forget discrepant details in the original case material (Arkes and Harkness, 1980).

Despite this, we should hesitate before assuming that clinicians are always behaving 'irrationally' if they require more data to feel confident in their decisions. In a general critique of experimental research on cognitive heuristics, Hogarth (1981) argues that heuristics may provide both a functional and a valid basis for decision-making in natural contexts. A major difference between experiments and real life is the dimension of time. Experiments typically require discrete judgments on the basis of information presented all at once at a single point of time. In real life, judgments lead to actions which frequently provide feedback on the basis of which previous judgments can be modified and new actions planned. Thus, information is accumulated *over time* through continuous interaction with the environment. Although once-and-for-all decisions do need to be made from time to time, this is by no means true of all medical judgments. Whatever may apply in, say, neurosurgery, in general practice telling patients 'Try this and come back next week if you don't feel any better' may often be a sensible strategy. What is often more important in real life than the absolute level of uncertainty is whether time and cost allow such uncertainty to be *reduced* through further information search.

Costs, benefits and feedback

On the one hand, then, there are many contexts in which decision-making might be improved if we were able to process probabilistic information in closer accordance with normative principles, and clinical diagnosis seems to be one of these. On the other hand, our adaptation to the environment depends primarily on our ability to learn and to anticipate events, rather than on our (demonstrably limited) capacity for handling abstract statistical data. Accuracy, moreover, is not the decision-maker's only concern. Different errors may carry very different costs, and this can be especially true in medicine. This point is taken into account in signal detection theory and a number of other models. Within the original context of radar detection, there are costs in a false-negative response of failing to challenge an attack by enemy bombers, but there are also costs in a false-positive response of scrambling a fighter squadron to scare off a flock of geese. It is assumed that the balance of benefits and costs of different correct and incorrect decisions mainly influences 'response bias', that is to say, whether a decision-maker takes greater or lesser risks under conditions of uncertainty. For instance, a treatment with fewer side-effects may be more readily recommended, even if its effectiveness as a cure for a particular patient may be somewhat uncertain.

In the context of medical diagnosis, the costs of failing to respond to early indications of a malignancy could be fatal for the patient. However, there are also costs in distressing the patient by premature announcements of the form 'I don't know, but you just *might* have cancer'. This illustrates one of Hogarth's (1981) main points. The clinician's response to uncertain but possibly sinister symptoms will be to try and obtain more information to resolve the uncertainty – something that is eminently reasonable when the costs of a false-positive decision could be devastating. The issue that then arises is whether clinicians generally look for the right kind of information to resolve such uncertainty and whether they interpret additional information appropriately. Here, as Schwartz and Griffin (1986) point out with many examples, there is real cause for concern.

The goal of clinical diagnosis is not the interpretation of symptoms *per se*, but the choice of an appropriate form of treatment to reduce danger or alleviate distress. It is a form of decision-making that is tied to action, and the action chosen will have both costs and benefits. Cost-benefit analysis (see Chapter 4) can provide a useful formal device for ensuring that enough options are taken into account and that due consideration is given to the risk of various complications. Many people, however, find it difficult to apply such statistical notions of risk and uncertainty to the individual case. The preference of many doctors for more heuristically driven, rather than statistically based, styles of decision-making may have its compensations. Technically derived probabilities may not always provide convincing representations of risks that are aggravated by human error and other unconsidered factors, as we shall see in the next chapter. However, confidence in doctors' 'clinical experience' is well placed only if doctors can indeed learn from their experience and receive adequate feedback on the quality of their decisions. This is where the quality of communication, not only between doctors and patients, but also between fellow professionals, can be so important. As Mendel (1984, pp. 106–7) warns his students,

> Learning from experience is made more difficult because patients and their diseases are so varied that the outcome in an individual patient is uncertain. Frequently, the patient will or will not get better regardless of what you do. In those cases where a doctor's judgement plays an important role in the outcome, it is difficult for even the most sensible doctor to know whether the outcome in a particular patient would have been different if he had acted differently ... There is no external assessor. The opinion of patients is misleading because they confuse kindness, the amount of time the doctor spends with them and a successful outcome, with excellence. For all these reasons the feedback, which is so important for learning, is usually not available. Furthermore, if nobody is in a position to monitor your performance, it is easy to imagine that you are actually doing rather well.

7

Nuclear energy, risk perception and attitudes

For decades energy policy was an area for experts only. Initially, the introduction of nuclear power as a source for generating electric power did not seem likely to change this. A number of nuclear accidents and many uncertainties associated with this technology resulted in demands by the public to be more involved in energy policy matters. For the first time, a traditionally closed industry was confronted with the necessity to be more open and accept the entrance of 'the public' into the once-exclusive domain of policy-making. The recognition of the fact that the future of nuclear energy will not only depend on technical and economic factors, but also on public acceptability of this technology, led to an increasing demand for psychological studies on the issue of public reactions to nuclear energy.

This chapter is intended to give an overview of psychological studies on nuclear energy. A brief summary of public opinion research will be followed by cognitive and social psychological approaches to this issue. Special attention will be given to two important aspects of the nuclear energy debate: the building of more nuclear power stations and the problem of nuclear waste.

Public opinion

Since the mid-1970s there has been a dramatic increase in public concern about nuclear energy. Until then the debate had largely centred on technical issues. Changes in public awareness and involvement led to the recognition that public acceptance of nuclear energy could play an important role in the future of this technology.

Over the past decade public support for nuclear energy has gradually been eroded. This increase in public concern is reflected in various developments. For instance, several national referenda on the issue have been decided by narrow margins (Austria, Italy, Sweden and Switzerland). The results of a series of state initiative votes in the USA provide a further illustration of increased public concern. Several countries reacted to the increased public involvement by organizing national debates and/or national information campaigns (e.g. Austria, 1976–7; the Netherlands, 1982–3). The increasing length of public inquiries into the issue of nuclear energy (e.g. the recent inquiries in the UK into the building of nuclear facilities in Sellafield and Sizewell) is another example of the public's concern about nuclear issues. These developments were accompanied by a substantial number of public opinion polls on a variety of nuclear issues. A brief summary of these findings will be presented below.

The USA has a long tradition of public opinion research and the more comprehensive accounts of changes in public acceptance of nuclear energy are all based on US surveys. There have been many surveys in Europe as well, but most of these efforts were uncoordinated, resulting in data that are very difficult to compare due to differences in the wording of questions and/or response categories.

Prior to the mid-1970s survey data showed consistently high levels of support for nuclear energy. This majority eroded in the late 1970s. Although the decline was apparent prior to the Three Mile Island accident in 1979 (the most serious accident in the history of nuclear energy before the Chernobyl disaster), it was accelerated by that event. Immediately following the Three Mile Island accident public support for nuclear energy in the USA decreased, uncertainty about taking a stand on the nuclear issue decreased, and opposition towards nuclear energy increased. Although there has been some rebound towards pre-Three Mile Island levels of support and opposition, the return has not been complete. Not surprisingly, this rebound was more complete in countries further removed from the location of the accident. For instance, in a number of Western European countries, it took some six months before public acceptance returned to the levels of before the accident. Recent figures show that the percentage of the USA public that supports the continued building of nuclear power plants is, on average, 5–10 per cent higher than the percentage of the public that opposes such construction. These levels of support and opposition were obtained before the Chernobyl accident (see Nealy, Melber and Rankin, 1983, for an overview). Furthermore, a majority of the public believed that more accidents like that at Three Mile Island were likely to happen.

Recent European Community (EC) surveys confirm this trend. In most EC member states there has been a decline in public support between 1978 and 1982. The 1982 findings show a number of countries with marginal differences between the numbers of opponents and supporters. In most EC countries, however, opponents outnumber supporters, with the exception of France which shows a sizable majority in favour of expanding the nuclear industry. It should be noted that these studies were all carried out before the series of incidents at Sellafield in NW England and, more importantly, the major accident at Chernobyl in 1986. The latter is bound to have a major impact on public opinion and this effect will probably be more prolonged than that of the Three Mile Island accident, especially in the European countries that were exposed to significantly higher radiation levels and their immediate consequences (disposal of cattle, dairy products and certain vegetables). For instance, recent surveys carried out in the Netherlands show a considerable shift in public opinion immediately after the Chernobyl accident; more than 80 per cent of the public opposed further expansion of the number of nuclear power plants in the Netherlands (as compared to approximately 50 per cent just before the Chernobyl accident; Verplanken, 1987).

Results of public opinion surveys in both the USA and Europe show that people are less willing to approve the construction of nuclear facilities close to their community than to approve the construction of these facilities in general. Local support for the building of nuclear power plants has been in decline since the mid-1970s. In the USA support decreased from 47 per cent in 1977 to 28 per cent in 1980 (Nealy *et al.*, 1983). Findings obtained in the SW of England are in accordance with these results (van der Pligt *et al.*, 1986).

Unfortunately, most opinion-poll data are based on a limited number of questions and do not allow clear and firm conclusions about the various beliefs underlying public attitudes. The opinion polls do show, however, that the public is divided, both in Europe and the USA. Research on public perception of the various potential benefits and costs of nuclear energy could provide further information on public concern about nuclear energy. Issues of risk perception and the attitudinal structure underlying public beliefs about nuclear energy have been extensively studied in recent years, partly with the aim of helping to formulate policy decisions on risk regulation and risk-bearing technologies.

Antecedents of public acceptance of nuclear energy

Risk perception

Although the experts' assessments of the risks of nuclear energy indicate that these are not greater than, and perhaps substantially less than, those of other generally accepted technologies, the public distrust of nuclear energy is considerable. Research consistently reports qualms about the release of radioactivity, potential catastrophic accidents and the disposal of nuclear waste. Both operational hazards and possible adverse environmental impact due to routine emissions seem major public worries.

Early research on risk perception focused on the contrast between expert judgment and lay people's intuitive assessments of risks. The experts' risk assessments were regarded as objective and quantifiable and public fears were interpreted as biased and irrational. Initially, attempts focused on the errors and biases of lay people's perception of risks. It was assumed that normative models of decision-making and a definition of risk in terms of expected losses constituted the only tenable approach. Furthermore, taking the mean losses (usually of human lives) was assumed to provide a correct way to infer risks from past experience, even when this experience was limited. In this context, the study of lay people's biases and errors was expected to help educate the public about risks and convince them that the experts were right.

Public disagreement among scientists over methodological aspects of risk-assessment techniques led to the realization that experts' assessments were less 'hard and fast' than previously assumed. Furthermore, experts also disagreed over what constitutes acceptable risk. As a consequence, more research paid attention to the study of possible factors influencing the acceptability of risks and attempted to develop a framework with which to explain public reactions to technological risks such as those associated with nuclear energy.

Several studies attempted to establish whether the public's intuitive assessments are related to the criterion of expected losses used in technical risk assessments. As we have seen in Chapter 4, people find it difficult to deal with very low probabilities. It needs to be noted, however, that apart from an overestimation of risks with low expected losses and an underestimation of risks with high expected losses, the intuitive assessments of lay people are not that far out. This led to the necessity to focus on other possible explanations for the limited public acceptance of the risks associated with nuclear energy.

A number of studies have revealed that the lay public defines risks in much broader terms than the expert. One of the conclusions of this line of research was that nuclear energy elicits extraordinary levels of concern, particularly because of the characteristics of the hazards that it poses (Fischhoff *et al.*, 1978; Vlek and Stallen, 1981). Most prominent among these are the potentially catastrophic and involuntary nature of possible accidents, and the fact that the hazard poses an unknown threat which is difficult to combat (i.e. unlike other hazards such as a fire it is difficult to imagine what one can do to reduce the possible consequences in case of an accident). The public's concept of risk, therefore, seems to be heavily influenced by the catastrophic nature of conceivable consequences and a number of qualitative risk characteristics such as voluntariness, possibilities of personal control and the fact that the hazard is relatively unknown.

Summarizing, it seems fair to conclude that both the catastrophic characteristics of the risks of nuclear energy and a number of qualitative aspects of the risks associated with this technology play a more important role in the level of acceptability of these risks than the assumed low probability of the possible negative consequences of nuclear energy. The concept of risk, however, does not embrace all the relevant terms of acceptance. The public's perceptions of risks are built on values, attitudes and sets of attributes which need not be similar to the representations of the experts and those involved with energy policy. In the next section we will discuss a number of social psychological studies that attempted to analyse people's perception of costs and benefits of nuclear energy.

Attitudinal structure: costs and benefits

Attempts to analyse the structure of people's attitudes towards nuclear energy are usually based on expectancy-value models of attitude formation which broadly assume that the more a person believes the attitude object has good rather than bad attributes or consequences, the more favourable his or her attitude tends to be. Most of the work in this area is based on the model of attitude formation proposed by Fishbein and his colleagues (Fishbein and Ajzen, 1975), which analyses attitudes in relation to the anticipated consequences accompanying the attitude object. Results of these studies show that individual attitudes are based upon perceptions of a limited number of potential negative and positive aspects of nuclear energy.

A further conclusion of this research is that separate dimensions of the issue of nuclear energy appear differentially salient for different attitude groups. Otway, Maurer and Thomas (1978) report the results of a factor analysis on thirty-nine beliefs about nuclear energy. Their results pointed at a number of dimensions underlying the way people think about nuclear energy. These can be summarized as follows:

(a) beliefs about economic benefits;
(b) beliefs about environmental and physical hazards due to routine low-level radiation and possible accidents;
(c) beliefs about the socio-political implications of nuclear power (e.g. restrictions on civil liberties, increased security measures); and,
(d) beliefs about psychological risks (fear, stress, etc.).

In the Otway *et al.* study, subgroups of the fifty most pro- and fifty most anti-nuclear respondents were compared in order to determine the contribution of each of the four factors to respondents' overall attitudes. For the pro-nuclear group, the economic and technical benefits factor made the most important contribution, whereas for the anti-nuclear group, the various risks were more important.

Woo and Castore (1980) also found that nuclear proponents attached greater value to potential economic benefits, while the nuclear opponents were more concerned with potential health and safety issues. Results obtained by Eiser and van der Pligt (1979) and van der Pligt et al. (1982) provide further support for the view that individuals with opposing attitudes tend to see different aspects of nuclear energy as salient, and hence, will disagree not only over the likelihood of the various consequences but also over their importance. In other words, each group has its own reasons for holding a particular attitude; the proponents stressing the importance of economic benefits and paying less attention to the various risks, while the opponents attach greater value to environmental and health risks and pay less attention to possible economic benefits. An important finding of these studies was that the overall attitude of respondents was more closely related to ratings of – in their view – important aspects than to their ratings of subjectively less important aspects. Thus, a consideration of both the perception of the various consequences and the subjective importance or salience provides a more complete picture than could be obtained from a consideration of either factor alone. The finding that separate dimensions of the issue appear differentially salient (both subjectively and in their contribution to the prediction of overall attitude) for the different attitude groups has important practical implications for theories of attitude and our understanding of why people hold different attitudes towards nuclear energy. In the next section we will present a more detailed discussion of the possible role of salience and also relate it to issues described in earlier chapters.

Salience, attitudes and decisions

As discussed in Chapter 4, the manner in which people form judgments and evaluations has been the subject of much research interest in recent years. This research has identified several judgmental heuristics that function as adaptive strategies of selective effort. This tendency of the perceiver to attend selectively has been studied in a wide variety of research areas under the heading of *salience*. Salient stimuli are assumed to have a disproportionate influence on people's judgments. The idea of differences in the salience of information has a long history and has been applied to attitudinal judgment (Chapter 1), decision-making and attribution processes. Attribution research focuses on salience in context, and shows that people attribute causality to distinctive and hence salient stimuli (Taylor and Fiske, 1978; see also Chapter 3).

The concept of salience is thus implicit in many theories in social psychology. Most of the research just cited defines salience in terms of stimulus properties (e.g. negative or distinctive stimuli are more salient). In the current analysis we will focus on salience in relation to a person's attitude towards particular issues. In Chapter 1 we focused on dimensional salience and its role in attitudinal judgment. In this section we investigate salience effects in the context of expectancy-value formulations of decision-making. Expectancy-value approaches usually attempt to trace the causes of behaviour through a series of intervening processes to the person's salient beliefs. The considerable appeal of the expectancy-value approach has made it the cornerstone of applied research on decision-making. Unfortunately most research in applied settings is mainly concerned with *prediction*. For researchers working in applied settings, such as consumer behaviour, the predictive power of a model provides a highly useful tool. As a consequence, the descriptive validity of the model receives less attention and seems to be taken for granted. As long as one can predict, it seems irrelevant to understand how decisions are made. The major argument to be put forward in the present section is that increasing the predictive validity of a model does not necessarily lead to improved understanding of the decision-making process. It will be argued that a more explicit incorporation of belief salience could improve our understanding of how people come to their decisions.

As we have seen in Chapter 4, a substantial body of research suggests that the conscious thought preceding a decision may be of a relatively simple nature, given the difficulty of processing complex information. People seem to rely on simple heuristics for making probability judgments and hardly seem to think about more complex combinations of values or utilities involved in a decision. In other words, people's decision processes seem relatively inarticulated and are hardly compatible with the sort of rigorous, systematic thinking required by expectancy-value formulations that involve a considerable number of beliefs.

Expectancy-value models of human decision-making usually employ considerable numbers of belief statements. For instance, Fishbein and Ajzen's (1975) theory of reasoned action traces the causes of behaviour through a series of intervening processes to the person's salient beliefs. Fishbein and Ajzen suggest one should obtain the *modal salient beliefs* in a given population, by simply asking a representative sample to elicit their beliefs about a specific attitude object. The most frequently elicited beliefs are then considered *modal* salient beliefs. However, most research in this area places little weight on the distinction between salient and nonsalient beliefs; responses to nonsalient belief statements are regarded as inferences consistent with the salient beliefs held by the person, and are seen as predictive of his or her attitude.

A rather unfortunate consequence of this type of reasoning is the tendency to use considerable numbers of belief statements. Most applications of expectancy-value models use twenty or more belief statements concerning possible consequences or attributes. These statements then have to be rated in terms of likelihood and valence (see also Chapter 4). Usually this type of research shows a reasonable predictive power of the model. Unfortunately, it is difficult to know what this proves. Does it prove that the individual used the model? Or have we finally stumbled upon a set of items that correlates well with the actual decision, without reflecting the decision process? As we have seen, research in cognitive psychology suggests that the latter interpretation is more likely to be correct than the former.

The crucial question that remains, however, is *why* a person holds a particular attitude. The inclusion of a measure of perceived salience could provide more information concerning why a person holds a specific attitude. Furthermore, inclusion of this variable enables the researcher to reduce the analysis of the decision-making process to manageable and more realistic proportions. Finally, incorporating perceived salience does not necessarily reduce the predictive power of the model. In the next section we will present some empirical evidence suggesting that a simplified version of the model, allowing for individual differences in perceived salience, leads to a more concise and informative representation of individual judgment and decision-making without reducing the predictive power of the model.

Salience and nuclear energy

A number of studies on the issue of nuclear energy have shown that separate dimensions of the issue appear differentially salient for different attitude groups. Some of these were briefly mentioned in a previous section. In this section we will discuss some of our own studies in more detail.

Eiser and van der Pligt (1979) conducted a study on the development of a nuclear waste reprocessing plant at Windscale (now Sellafield) in NW England. Subjects rated a list of eleven possible consequences (selected from pro- and anti-nuclear literature) of the proposed development, and were also asked to rank the five possible consequences they personally thought to be most important. The percentages of pro- and anti- subjects choosing each of the consequences among the most important five showed marked differences. The pro- subjects most frequently chose the strength of the UK economy (75 v. 17 per cent for the anti- group) and the UK's ability to meet future energy demands (92 v. 22 per cent). The anti- subjects focused on the possible restriction on civil liberties (83 v. 17 per cent) and the risk of nuclear terrorism (72 v. 4 per cent). The rank correlation between the two sets of percentages was −.50, indicating that the two attitude groups saw the issue in very different terms. The relationship between an overall measure of subjects' attitude and an index score based on their ratings of the eleven possible consequences was strongly affected by their perceived importance of the belief statements. The index score based on the five items perceived as most important correlated .86 with subjects' attitudes. A similar calculation on the six remaining (less important) items for each subject resulted in a correlation of only .44. Results of this study show that a simple measure of salience or importance does provide interesting information on the structure of people's attitudes toward an issue. Inclusion of this variable shows that different attitude groups will tend to disagree not only over the likelihood and evaluation of certain attributes or consequences but also over their importance. Similar findings were obtained by van der Pligt *et al.* (1982) and van der Pligt *et al.* (1986). In these studies samples of the general population were asked to select the possible consequences of nuclear energy which they found most important. Again, findings showed a close relationship between salient aspects and attitudes. No significant gains in predictive power were found when less salient beliefs were included.

Summarizing, results of these studies indicate that individuals with opposing attitudes see different aspects of the issue as salient, and hence, disagree not only over the likelihood of the various potential consequences but also over their importance. Attitude scores based on this subset of subjectively important aspects were generally more strongly related to subjects' standpoint on the issue than attitude scores based on less salient beliefs. Generally, the pro- group saw the potential economic benefits of nuclear energy as most important, while the anti- group attached greater value to environmental and public health aspects. This finding has important practical implications for communication and mutual understanding between the protagonists in the nuclear debate. Nuclear opponents not only question the economic benefits of nuclear energy, but also regard these as less important. Similarly, the nuclear proponents not only regard the risks as less probable but also regard environmental and political risks as less important. In other words, information campaigns stressing the economic benefits of nuclear power and simply stating that it is safe, without providing more information, are bound to have a limited impact on nuclear opponents.

Beliefs and values

The different perspectives of nuclear opponents and supporters seem related to more general values. Public acceptance of nuclear energy is not only a matter of perceptions of risks and benefits but is also related to more generic issues. Eiser and van der Pligt (1979) addressed this point and asked 47 participants attending a one-day workshop on nuclear energy to select the five factors from a list of nine which they felt 'would contribute most to an improvement in the overall "quality of life" '. Table 7.1 summarizes these findings and shows marked differences between nuclear opponents and supporters. The pro-nuclear group stressed the importance of 'advances in science and technology', 'industrial modernization', 'security of employment' and 'conservation of the natural environment'. The anti-nuclear respondents put even more emphasis on the last factor and stressed the importance of 'decreased emphasis on materialistic values', 'reduction in scale of industrial, commercial and governmental units' and 'improved social welfare'.

Table 7.1 The importance of general values as a function of attitude

	Percentage of respondents selecting each factor	
	Pro-nuclear subjects	Anti-nuclear subjects
Decreased emphasis on materialistic values	36	100
Reduction in scale of industrial, commercial, and governmental units	22	86
Industrial modernization	68	6
Security of employment	77	40
Improved social welfare	31	80
Conservation of the natural environment	77	100
Advances in science and technology	82	13

Adapted from Eiser and van der Pligt (1979).

Similar findings were obtained in the Netherlands (van der Pligt et al., 1982). Pro-nuclear respondents generally stressed the importance of economic factors and law and order issues, whereas anti-nuclear respondents put more emphasis on conservation of the environment and the reduction of energy use. The latter also attached more importance to increased public participation in policy decisions. Not surprisingly, this research also showed a relation between these value differences and people's position on a political left–right dimension. Political preference was significantly related to both the above values, and to people's attitudes towards the building of more nuclear power stations in the Netherlands. Large-scale opinion research confirmed this relationship between political preference and attitudes towards nuclear energy.

The above findings serve as a reminder of the fact that the issue of nuclear energy is firmly embedded in a much wider moral and political domain. Not surprisingly, the nuclear debate is a polarized one. Compared to other issues there is only a small percentage of the public that has no opinion about issues such as the expansion of the nuclear industry and the building of nuclear waste facilities. Generally, attitudes towards nuclear issues seem quite stable. In our longitudinal study in SW England we did not find major shifts in attitudes towards the building of nuclear power stations in the SW. In the next section we will discuss some of the consequences of these relatively polarized attitudes. Under the heading of 'perseverance' we will give some examples of mechanisms that are likely to make attitude change difficult.

Perseverance of attitudes

In the course of this book various biases in the sampling, processing, and interpretation of stimuli in one's environment have been described. These biased strategies and procedures produce initial impressions about oneself, other people or issues that can be premature and are often erroneous.

One mechanism is especially relevant to account for perseverance phenomena, i.e. *distortion* in the judgment of potentially pertinent data. That is, the weight people assign to evidence is determined, in large measure, by its consistency with initial impressions and/or existing attitudes. More specifically, the possibility that evidence seemingly consistent with existing impressions may nevertheless be irrelevant or tainted is often neglected; similarly, one too readily conceives and accepts challenges to contradictory evidence. As a result data considered subsequent to the formation of a clear impression typically will seem to offer a large measure of support for that impression. Indeed, even a random sample of potentially relevant data 'processed' in this manner may serve to strengthen rather than challenge an erroneous judgment or decision. The capacity of existing impressions and expectations to bias interpretations of social data is, of course, a well-replicated phenomenon in social psychology (see also Chapters 1 and 4). The effects of distortion may be further enhanced by what Ross (1977, p. 206) calls the autonomy achieved by distorted evidence. Once formed, an initial impression or decision may not only be enhanced by the distortion of evidence, it may even be sustained by such distortion. The autonomy enjoyed by distorted inferences may further contribute to the perseverance of nonoptimal theories and decision-making strategies. In the next section we will give a few examples of the distortions of evidence and of biased impression.

Attitudes, consensus, and person perception

One way to bolster one's attitudes is to think that they are shared by many others. People seem to have a tendency to perceive a 'false consensus' (cf. Ross et al., 1977; see also Chapter 3) with respect to the relative commonness of their own responses, i.e. people overestimate the commonness of their own behaviour/ attitude, relative to other behaviours or attitudes. Such biased estimates play an important role in people's interpretation of social reality. Not only can they bolster one's own opinions and preferences but they seem also related to processes of stereotyping and attribution. Ross et al. (1977) argued that individuals judge those responses that differ from their own to be more revealing of the other's personality traits than those responses which are similar to their own. In other words, people tend to ascribe relatively simplified personality traits to people holding different attitudes towards an issue. This is one way of discounting one's opponent, and can be regarded as the basis of stereotyping.

In a study conducted in the Netherlands (van der Pligt *et al.*, 1982) subjects with different attitudes towards nuclear energy were asked to estimate:

(a) the percentage of the Dutch population in favour of increasing the number of nuclear power plants;
(b) the percentage of Members of Parliament in favour of increasing the number of nuclear power plants;
(c) the percentage of the Dutch population that would not object to living near a nuclear power plant; and
(d) the percentage of residents from their local community that would not object to living near a nuclear plant.

Next, subjects were asked to select from a list of twelve trait-descriptive terms any that they thought best described firstly a typical pro-nuclear person, and then a typical anti-nuclear person. This list contained, in a random order, six adjectives relatively positive in evaluation (responsible, realistic, environment-conscious, level-headed, humanitarian and rational) and six relatively negative adjectives (ill-informed, short-sighted, weak-willed, complacent, selfish and alarmist). The selection was based on words used in the various publications for and against nuclear power and on the Eiser and van der Pligt (1979) study.

Results confirmed this prediction. The more pro one's attitude towards nuclear energy, the higher one's estimate of the percentage of the Dutch population in favour of expanding the nuclear programme. Extremely pro-nuclear subjects thought 58 per cent of the population would be in favour, while extremely anti-nuclear subjects estimated only 29 per cent to be in favour. Similarly, the first group estimated 56 per cent of Members of Parliament to be in favour, while the anti-nuclear group estimated this percentage to be 43 per cent. In other words, both groups saw their own choices and judgments as relatively common. The fact that there was no clear-cut majority for or against nuclear energy in Parliament (an issue that received widespread attention in the media) did not preclude people from biased estimates, although the effect was less pronounced for estimates of MPs than for estimates of the general population.

The same effect was observed with various other measures (e.g. estimates of the number of people in subjects' community who would object to living near a nuclear power plant). The effect has been reported in over 45 published papers (see Marks and Miller, 1987) all confirming this tendency to see one's own choice as relatively common. It has been proposed that this bias also implies that people see their own choice as appropriate to existing circumstances while viewing alternative responses as uncommon, deviant or inappropriate. According to attribution theory (see Chapter 3) high estimated consensus should lead to reduced willingness to infer personality traits. Was this indeed the case, i.e. did people attribute more traits to others with differing views than to those with opinions similar to one's own viewpoint?

Subjects' selections of trait-descriptive terms to describe the typical 'pro'- and 'anti'-nuclear person revealed, as predicted, a strong tendency to describe their 'own side' positively and the opposition negatively. A composite score was calculated by counting the number of positive adjectives minus the number of negative adjectives attributed to the two target persons. Results of this evaluative score are shown in Figure 7.1, with subjects' attitudes towards building more nuclear power stations indicated on the five-point scale ranging from 'strongly in favour' to 'strongly opposed' on the horizontal axis. These results show clear differences in evaluation as a function of own attitude, and contradict the prediction derived from attribution theory that high consensus should be accompanied by a relative absence of trait attributions. The findings illustrate the importance of evaluative factors and are in accordance with studies mentioned in Chapter 3. These studies indicated that evaluative factors can have a strong effect on attributional preferences and diminish various attributional biases (e.g. the actor–observer divergence).

It is interesting to take a closer look at the ratings of the more extreme attitude groups, i.e. the role of affective intensity in perceptions of consensus and person perception. The results (as summarized in Figure 7.1) suggest that people with extremely committed attitudes on an issue engage in little or no information processing, as assumed by attribution theory. Their consensus estimates are not related to their willingness to infer personality characteristics. Results show a clear valence effect in trait attri-

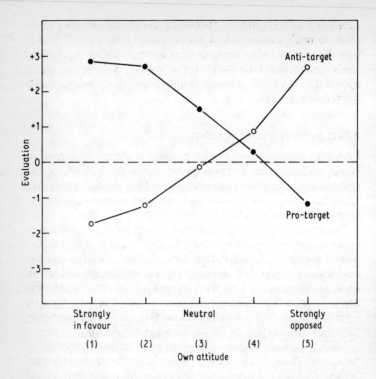

Figure 7.1 Evaluation of a typical pro-nuclear and an anti-nuclear target-person as a function of own attitude
(From 'Attitudes to nuclear energy: beliefs, values and false consensus' by J. van der Pligt, J. van der Linden and P. Ester, 1982, *Journal of Environmental Psychology*, 2, p. 228. Copyright 1985 by Academic Press. Reprinted with permission)

butions, and suggest that this effect is mediated by attitude extremity. In other words, people's preference for trait attributions is primarily determined by evaluative factors, and this effect is especially strong for those with relatively extreme and involved attitudes.

These data reveal other striking differences between the two attitude groups. Firstly, there are the very different 'images' each group has of one another. Encountering others who disagree with one's own committed opinions presents a continuing challenge to one's conception of social reality. One way of dealing with this is to use what amounts to *ad hominem* arguments against one's opponents. One looks for a way of discounting one's opponents' opinions through imputations of stupidity, short-sightedness or bias.

Siting nuclear power stations

Localities confronted with the possible building of a nuclear power station in the neighbourhood generally show a majority of the local population opposing such plans. As a consequence siting nuclear power stations has met with considerable delays in most Western countries (with the exception of France).

In a recent study we attempted to investigate the relationships between people's attitudes towards the building of a nuclear power station in their locality, their specific beliefs about the *local* consequences and their perception of the importance of these consequences. This study (van der Pligt *et al.*, 1986) was carried out in three localities that were shortlisted by the UK Central Electricity Generating Board (CEGB) as possible sites for a new nuclear power station in SW England.

We will summarize the findings concerning the perception of the various potential costs and benefits of a nuclear power station in one's locality. Participants were generally opposed to the construction of a nuclear power station in their neighbourhood. It needs to be added, however, that most respondents were also opposed to other industrial activities such as the building of a chemicals plant.

In order to investigate people's perception of the various potential costs and benefits of a nuclear power station we presented subjects with two sets of 15 potential consequences. The first contained 15 immediate effects of the construction and operation of a nuclear power station in the locality, while the second set focused on long-term consequences. Subjects were split into three attitude groups on the basis of their answer to the question whether they were opposed to or in favour of the building of a new nuclear power station in their locality. A discriminant analysis revealed that the three attitude groups (pro, neutral and anti) differed significantly in their assessment of a number of immediate consequences. The aspects that were most differentially perceived concerned the area of land fenced off, the conversion of land from agricultural use and the prospect of workers coming into the area. Opponents generally thought these developments to have a negative impact on the quality of life in the locality, while proponents thought the impact of these factors would be relatively minimal.

We also asked people to select the five (out of 15 immediate consequences) aspects they thought to be the most important. Results showed three aspects that were rated very differently as a function of own attitude. Of the pro subjects, 67 per cent regarded road building an important aspect, while only 20 per cent of the anti subjects selected this item among the five most important. A similar difference was obtained concerning the prospect of workers coming into the area (53 per cent of the pros and 18 per cent of the antis). The antis, on the other hand, attached more importance to the possible conversion of land from agricultural use than the pros (58 v. 27 per cent).

The mean ratings by the three attitude groups of the 15 (mainly long-term) effects of the building and operation of a nuclear power station in their neighbourhood also showed highly significant differences. Again, we conducted a discriminant analysis to find out which aspects most distinguished the three attitude groups. The results revealed three aspects which had considerable predictive power in separating the three attitude groups. These were the perceived effects on one's 'peace of mind' and the effects on the environment and wildlife. The first aspect corresponds to what we called 'psychological risk', while the other two aspects are related to what we termed 'environmental and physical risk'.

Again we asked the respondents to choose the five consequences they regarded as most important. The results showed very marked differences between the three attitude groups. The most striking difference concerned the possible effects on employment opportunities, 73 per cent of the pros selected this item among the most important, while only 15 per cent of the antis considered this aspect as important. Overall, the pro respondents stressed the importance of economic benefits to the locality, while the antis stressed the risk factors (both environmental and psychological risks). Table 7.2 presents a summary

Table 7.2 Perceived consequences of the building and operation of a nuclear power station as a function of attitude

n =	Impact[a]			Importance[b]		
	Pro (n=30)	Neutral (n=40)	Anti (n=209)	Pro (n=30)	Neutral (n=40)	Anti (n=217)
Economic factors						
Employment opportunities	8.3	7.6	6.0[c]	73	57	15[c]
Business investment	6.7	6.0	4.2	27	28	11
Environmental factors						
Wild life	4.7	2.6	1.5	40	57	67
Marine environment	5.1	3.6	2.3	13	17	38
Farming industry	4.6	3.0	1.9	17	45	56
Landscape	4.3	2.6	1.3	23	50	66
Public health and psychological risks						
Health of local inhabitants	5.0	4.4	2.6	20	29	48
Your personal peace of mind	5.4	4.3	1.7	27	17	47
Social factors						
Social life in the neighbourhood	6.9	5.7	3.9	30	7	11
Standard of local transport and social services	6.8	6.3	4.9	40	17	5
Standard of shopping facilities	6.6	5.8	4.9	20	14	4

(a) Possible range of scores from 1 (consequence will affect life in the neighbourhood very much for the worse) to 9 (very much for the better).
(b) The scores represent the percentage of subjects selecting each factor among the five most important.
(c) The differences between the 3 attitude groups were significant in all cases ($p < .05$) as indicated by the linear F-term.
From 'Public Attitudes to Nuclear Energy: Salience and Anxiety' by J. van der Pligt, 1985, *Journal of Environmental Psychology*, 5, p. 93. Copyright 1985 by Academic Press. Reprinted with permission.

of the differences in the perception of the various long-term consequences. A closer inspection of these differences underlines the importance of including both beliefs and salience in one's conception of attitude. Even though the attitude groups, for example, showed relatively minor differences in their evaluation of the effects of potential employment opportunities in the locality, a majority of the pros but only a small minority of the antis regarded this aspect as being of importance.

Results of this study showed that the major differences

between the attitude groups concerns the less tangible, more long-term nature of the potential negative outcomes. Our findings further suggested that the perception of the psychological risks are the prime determinant of attitudes, as indicated by a very high correlation (.80) between this factor and attitude towards the building of a new nuclear power station. Other studies (e.g. Woo and Castore, 1980) did not find such a strong relation between psychological risks and attitude. One reason for this could be that our research concentrated on people living very close to the proposed nuclear power station (all within a 5-mile radius). Most other studies used much wider areas around proposed nuclear power stations.

In summary, opponents and proponents of nuclear energy have *very different* views on the possible consequences of nuclear energy. The most significant difference, however, concerns the perception of psychological risks (anxiety, stress). This factor becomes more important when people are (or will be) more directly exposed to the risks, for instance when their locality is shortlisted as a possible site for a nuclear power station. The importance of stress-related variables has been shown in a wide variety of studies of local reactions to technological and environmental hazards. Studies conducted around Three Mile Island (e.g. Baum, Fleming and Singer, 1982) and research in residential areas confronted with contaminated soil (de Boer, 1986) are just two examples of a growing field of research that tries to apply findings obtained in research on stress and coping patterns in public reactions to a variety of hazards.

Decisions, coping patterns and stress

Janis and Mann (1977) mention various coping patterns of which defensive avoidance, hypervigilance and vigilance are particularly relevant in the present context. Awareness of possible serious losses together with loss of hope of finding a satisfactory solution are important conditions for defensive avoidance. Janis and Mann relate defensive avoidance to closed-mindedness and biases in information preference. Examples are the avoidance of information, shifting of responsibility (e.g. leave it to the expert) and selective exposure (preference for information supporting one's viewpoint). Hypervigilance is the most likely strategy when people believe that there exists a satisfactory solution, but insufficient time to search and deliberate. If this is the case, people tend to display an indiscriminate openness to all information and usually fail to differentiate between information that is relevant or irrelevant, reliable or unreliable, supportive or nonsupportive. As a consequence, the person becomes overwhelmed by information, is unable to find a solution and is bound to experience anxiety and stress due to the decisional stalemate. When the conditions for vigilance are present (i.e. awareness of serious risks, along with a belief that a satisfactory solution can be found and that there is sufficient time for search and evaluation), the individual will tend to have a discriminating and open-minded interest in both supportive and opposing information. Janis and Mann argue that the above coping patterns and their relations with characteristic modes of information processing should improve our understanding of decisional stress. Research on environmental stressors confirms the importance of some of the coping strategies included in Janis and Mann's conflict model for information preferences. The literature contains many examples of avoidance techniques and hypervigilance. An important contribution of this type of research is that it could enable us to locate people who are most at risk. People differ widely in the ways they cope with risks and uncertainty, and some coping patterns are more likely to lead to anxiety and stress-related complaints.

In a series of studies in the aftermath of the Three Mile Island accident, Baum and his colleagues investigated people's reactions to this stressful event. Findings suggested that emotionally-focused coping and self-blame were associated with less stress than were problem-focused coping and denial. In other words people who chose to attend to their emotional response (i.e. focus inward and attempt to control fears and emotional responses associated with exposure to stress) experienced less stress than people who tended to address the source of stress (danger) in order to reduce or remove the threat that was posed. One should take into account that, in extreme circumstances such as the immediate aftermath of the TMI accident, the situation is highly resistant to attempts at change by individuals, and those changes that are made usually take a long time. Furthermore, the complexity of the issue and the uncertainties associated with possible consequences lead to the recognition that the situation is relatively impervious to manipulation or control. In other words, in these specific situations even problem-oriented coping strategies that are 'well balanced' (such as the vigilant coping pattern described above) are less effective. Baum *et al*. (1982) emphasize the importance of personal control in public reactions to technological mishaps such as that at Three Mile Island. They argue that the use of emotionally-focused coping and the assumption of blame may reflect control-relevant concerns. Concern with emotion management may provide sufficient success to bolster one's general feelings of control. In contrast, the use of problem-oriented coping in situations impervious to manipulation or control may result in frustration and in further failures at establishing a sense of control. Furthermore, problem-centred coping is generally related to the denial of responsibilities for one's own difficulties in dealing with the situation. Results indicated that people who denied responsibility for their predicament also reported more feelings of helplessness and less confidence in their ability to control things that happened to them. The latter group also showed higher levels of stress as indicated by self-reports, biochemical measures and task performance (i.e. ability to concentrate).

Results obtained in later studies (Baum, Gatchel and Schaeffer, 1983) revealed that, more than a year after the nuclear accident at Three Mile Island, residents of the area still exhibited more symptoms of stress than did people living under different circumstances. The intensity of the problems seemed 'subclinical', but the possible persistence of stress leading to a chronic aftermath inhibiting recovery may be cause for concern.

It is clear that in order to understand local reactions to nuclear power stations and possible accidents, both cognitive aspects such as risk perception and perceived importance of costs and benefits, as well as emotional aspects such as stress-related reactions and coping styles, should be taken into account. The study of emotional reactions is especially important in the context of accidents such as those in Harrisburg (Three Mile Island), Sellafield, and Chernobyl. Increased understanding of how people cope with these technological calamities should increase our ability to help future victims of such accidents.

The nuclear waste issue

The siting of radioactive wastes poses a significant planning challenge to most Western countries. The public is generally extremely apprehensive about radioactive wastes, and this has led to substantial delays in siting much-needed waste facilities. As a consequence, the 'back end' of an industry that started some three decades ago still poses serious problems to its further development. Scientists still disagree about the best technical means for permanently isolating radioactive wastes from the biosphere. Moreover, most governments have not yet resolved many of the relevant political and institutional issues surrounding the waste management problem. The siting problems do not only affect the nuclear power industry; the controversies surrounding the siting of low-level radioactive wastes affect a wide variety of other industries, biomedical research facilities and hospitals.

One of the conclusions of survey studies on public acceptability of nuclear energy is that opinions concerning nuclear waste management must be seen in the wider context of more general attitudes toward nuclear energy. The two matters have become linked in public discussions. Nealy *et al.* (1983) report that since 1976 over twice as many people have indicated that they oppose nuclear power because of waste-management problems than was previously the case. Furthermore, when nuclear power problems were directly compared, waste management was still believed to be a bigger problem than reactor safety. The relationship between the two issues is also apparent in the context of *local* opinions about nuclear developments such as nuclear power plants and waste facilities.

As discussed earlier in this chapter, public opinion surveys in both the USA and Europe show that people are less willing to approve construction of new nuclear facilities in their neighbourhood than to approve the construction of these facilities in general. This is also the case when localities are confronted with hazardous waste facilities. Most studies indicate that a substantial majority of the local public opposes such facilities. For instance, Cook (1983) found that 74 per cent of the local population in Steele Creek (Charlotte, NC) opposed a proposed waste facility. Similar findings were obtained by Bachrach and

Zautra (1985). Other findings indicate that the public hardly differentiates between toxic chemical disposal facilities and nuclear waste facilities; both are accompanied by extremely unfavourable local reactions (Lindell and Earle, 1983).

The reasons for the public opposition to nuclear waste facilities are bound to be similar to those discussed earlier in this chapter. These will not be discussed in detail again, but instead we will focus on another element that plays a major role in siting policy: the issue of equity. This issue is of crucial importance. As compared to nuclear power stations, the economic benefits (e.g. employment opportunities) of waste facilities are marginal. This leads to situations where some members of society are exposed to risks without receiving sufficient compensation for these potential costs.

Kasperson (1985) addressed the widely held opinion that inequity is the crucial problem for hazardous waste facility siting. Once a locality is shortlisted, the community objects to being the dumping ground for waste from elsewhere. Furthermore, the affected locality is likely to oppose the facility because the benefits will flow to others (waste-generating industries, the general public and the owners of the facility) while the risks will be concentrated locally.

This geographical dissociation of costs (risks) and benefits cannot easily be balanced. As discussed earlier in this chapter, the perceived risks, and the qualitative nature of these risks associated with considerable fear, dominate local acceptance of nuclear facilities. These aspects simply overwhelm any prospect of restoring the original conditions of equity through the enlargements of benefits.

This view is supported by recent experiences where the relevant authorities attempted to increase local acceptance of a nuclear waste facility by providing compensation to the locality. The purposes of (financial, economic) compensation are to change local motivation to oppose the facility, increase the efficiency of facility planning because costs and benefits are better accounted for, and finally, to promote negotiation as opposed to confrontation (see e.g. O'Hare, Bacow and Sanderson, 1983). Because the environmental and health risks so dominate public reactions, the prospect of compensation does not effectively increase the degree of local acceptance or engender a propensity among local residents to 'trade off' concerns. Moreover, compensation tends to be viewed as a 'bribe', exacerbating the equity issue and increasing suspicion and distrust of the relevant authorities (see e.g. Kasperson, 1985; Kunreuther, Linnerooth and Vaupel, 1984).

In the USA, a number of states have used compensation strategies in cases of siting hazardous nonradioactive wastes. Massachusetts adopted an approach based upon the work of O'Hare *et al.* (1983) with the following key ingredients. The two primary parties in the bargaining process are the host community and the developer; these are required to reach a settlement (via negotiation or arbitration) including mitigation and compensation to the host community. The community has only a limited basis on which to refuse the construction of the facility, and impasses between developer and the affected community are submitted to an arbitrator.

Three assumptions are of particular interest in the context of the approach discussed by O'Hare et al. (1983). First, voluntary consent is assumed to be achievable through sufficient provision of incentives and through direct bilateral negotiations between the community and the developer. Second, the long-term consequences of the facility can be defined with sufficient precision to formulate an acceptable and appropriate compensation package (e.g. economic benefits, financial help, provision of other facilities that benefit the community). Finally, it is assumed that both the developer and/or the relevant regulatory authorities can rely upon sufficient social trust to reassure local fears and to prevent a conflict-laden decision-making process.

The last assumption seems rather optimistic, given the erosion of public confidence in a wide variety of major social institutions. Portney (1983) conducted a survey in Massachusetts indicating that lack of trust in both the management of companies that operate the facilities, and the government regulators who monitor whether proper procedures are followed, is a significant source of concern for the community. Similar remarks can be made about the second assumption. The literature on social and environmental impact assessment acknowledges the limited ability of planners to identify and/or measure the possible consequences of the building and operation of a siting facility. A further problem concerns the difficulties in translating health and environmental risks into compensating economic measures or financial benefits. It is not surprising, therefore, that siting efforts based on compensation measures have had mixed success. This lack of success provides further support for the view presented earlier that local opinion near proposed nuclear facilities tends to be dominated by perceived environmental and health risks. Economic benefits and compensation are of secondary importance to residents of communities confronted with the possible location of a nuclear waste facility in their neighbourhood.

The above discussion suggests that public acceptance may well depend more on the characteristics of the *process* that allocates risks than on the relationship between risk and benefits. Compensation does not seem a sufficient condition to increase public acceptance of nuclear facilities. Lack of public acceptance could well be related to the limited *public participation* in decision-making processes concerning siting nuclear wastes and to the *communication* between the experts (and relevant authorities) and the public.

Conclusions

The fact that public attitudes towards nuclear energy issues are relatively stable and embedded in a wider context of values suggests that large-scale attitude conversion may be more difficult than often assumed. People may, however, change their attitudes as a function of serious accidents that attract widespread attention, such as those of Three Mile Island (1979) and Chernobyl (1986), especially if they have not committed themselves strongly to one of the two sides. With regard to safety-related aspects of public acceptance of nuclear power, it seems much easier for nuclear attitudes to become suddenly more anti-nuclear because of a major accident or a series of smaller accidents (e.g. the recent events at the Sellafield reprocessing plant) than it would be for nuclear attitudes to become more pro-nuclear as a longer-term result of an extensive period of safe operations. Changes in a pro-nuclear direction are more likely to result from events related to energy supply, e.g. developments that would make nonnuclear energy much more expensive.

Since safety-related issues play a crucial role in public acceptance of nuclear facilities, it seems necessary to improve the
relationship between the expert and the lay public. For the
experts this poses an important challenge: to recognize the limitations and fallibility of risk-assessments, and to be aware of the
fact that important qualitative aspects of risks influence the
responses of lay people. For lay people it seems necessary to
accept the necessity to be better informed and to be aware of
the influence of these qualitative aspects.

The high level of concern and involvement of residents of
communities confronted with the possible construction of a
nuclear facility poses a further challenge to risk communication.
Earle and Cvetkovich (1985) pointed out the importance of
developing a common framework appropriate to the particular
hazard and acceptable to all involved parties. Development of
this framework is a necessary condition for risk communication
(e.g. information about the specific health and environmental
risks, information about possible ways to reduce the effects
of the hazard) to be successful. Experience has shown that
communication about risks is extremely difficult and often frus-
trating to those involved. Government officials and experts
frequently complain about the lack of understanding of lay
people and the distorted and biased media coverage. Individual
citizens, on the other hand, often perceive a lack of interest in
their concerns, and a reluctance to allow them to participate in
decisions that intimately affect their lives. Recent experiences in
a number of Western countries are in accordance with the above
view. In the Netherlands, attempts to inform the public in a
number of communities shortlisted as possible sites for radioactive wastes were largely unsuccessful and were frequently
accompanied by demonstrations by the local residents. Recent
events in three villages in different counties in England where
contractors were prevented from starting test drilling for the
dumping of nuclear wastes provide a further illustration of the
gulf between citizens and the nuclear industry.

Communication will play an important role in increased public
participation in decisions about siting nuclear facilities.
Increased participation could improve the fairness of the risk-
allocation process and increase the degree of trust in the authorities responsible for the siting problem. Experience with

approaches that incorporate public participation is limited. This approach entails more than a public relations task. It demands more openness of a traditionally closed industry, a different distribution of knowledge and expertise, and substantially improved communication between experts and the public. A necessary condition for the latter is more mutual understanding and respect for the concerns and representations of the parties involved in the siting problem. Psychology could help clarify the many differences of opinion about facts and values that play a role in siting disputes. In the face of growing evidence that the current approaches are failing, increased public participation could well be the only way to reach acceptable solutions and increase the dramatically eroded trust and credibility of the nuclear industry.

8

Conclusions

During the course of this book we have referred directly and indirectly to a variety of attitudinal and judgmental issues and their applications. In this final chapter we will briefly discuss the central themes of this book.

Attitudes, attributions and salience

Attitudes involve an evaluation of something or somebody. People can agree and disagree in their attitudes and this is usually reflected in language. In the first chapter we developed the notion that attitudinal and judgmental processes are closely interrelated. When people express their attitudes they prefer to use labels that are compatible with their preferred mode of talking or thinking about the issue. Another way of putting this is that our view of social issues is selective, so that some aspects of the issue are *salient* to us whereas other aspects are not. Differences in salience may then be reflected in the kind of language we prefer to use to describe our opinions and those of other people. People who prefer to talk about the same issues in terms of different kinds of language will generally be regarding different aspects of the issue as salient – in other words, as they selectively experience it, it will be a different issue for those on either side.

In this book we have discussed many examples of perceived salience in the context of the nuclear debate and health behaviours. For instance, people with opposing attitudes towards nuclear energy tend to see different aspects of nuclear energy as salient, and hence, will disagree not only over the likelihood of the various consequences but also over their importance. In other words, each group has its own reasons for holding a particular attitude; the proponents stressing the importance of economic benefits and paying less attention to the various risks, while the opponents attach greater value to environmental and health risks and pay less attention to possible economic benefits. Moreover, attitudes are often more closely related to ratings of subjectively important aspects than to ratings of subjectively less important aspects. Thus, a consideration of both the perception of the various consequences and the subjective importance or salience provides a more complete picture than could be obtained from a consideration of either factor alone.

Salience and selectivity also play an important role in people's perception of the causes of their own and other behaviour. Both visual perspective and psychological perspective increase the likelihood of situational attributions for actors and dispositional attributions for observers. Although people are prepared to let many events occur without asking *why* they occur, attributions can help to understand the different kinds of feelings and behaviours in some specific contexts. Overall, attributions are most relevant when people try to deal with the unwanted or unexpected. In such circumstances attributions may influence expectations *and* future behaviours, as we have seen in our studies on people trying to give up smoking.

Salience and selectivity are not only studied in the context of attitudes, judgment and attribution. Research on human decision-making tends to be dominated by attempts to describe and explain a variety of biases and heuristics in decision-making processes.

Decisions: salience and selectivity

The evidence presented in this book suggests that the conscious thought preceding a decision may be of a relatively simple nature, given the difficulty of processing complex information. People seem to rely on simple heuristics for making probability judgments and hardly seem to think about more complex combinations of probabilities and values or utilities involved in a decision. Most decisions requiring complex combinations of values and probabilities do not seem to follow normative models of decision-making. Furthermore, if people are asked explicitly to use the various (normative) decision rules, they experience great difficulty following these rules. In other words, people's decision processes seem relatively inarticulated and are hardly compatible with the sort of rigorous, systematic thinking required by normative decision models. Most models present an overintellectualized view of the cognitive processes people go through when making decisions, forming attitudes, or choosing alternative actions.

Given the complexity of decision-making, it may be costly or impossible to gather all the potentially relevant information, it may be difficult to decide what information is relevant and it may not be easy to combine information from different sources or of different kinds. Furthermore, reasoning about uncertain outcomes or consequences of decisions may prove difficult due to lack of experience or insight. Given the 'bounded' nature of human rationality, it is not surprising that people use various strategies to enable them to handle complex decisions. These include simplified 'problem representations' (subjective models of the real world) which permit us to handle the task with the available cognitive resources.

In addition to simplified problem representations, cognitive load can be reduced by using a number of decision-making strategies. These simplifying cognitive procedures, or rules-of-thumb, are known in the literature as heuristics. Although judgment heuristics can lead to good decisions, this is not always the case. Psychologists have shown the circumstances under which these heuristics lead to errors in probabilistic reasoning. Because many of these errors result from an attempt to apply the normally useful heuristics to situations in which they are inappropriate, errors are often referred to as cognitive 'biases'. An illustration of these biases is provided by the study of people's perception of probability. This research area deals with factors that can affect the accuracy of people's estimation of probability. These factors are all related to the incorrect use of statistical evidence. Prior probabilities, the effect of sample size and conjunctive probabilities seem not clearly understood and are used incorrectly or underutilized in probability estimates. Generally, intuitive judgments of probability seem strongly influenced by relatively concrete, vivid, and hence salient instances. This reliance upon salient information can be useful in many everyday situations but is less appropriate when estimating probabilities. Salience thus not only influences the type of attribution people make but also affects estimates of frequency or probability. This effect of salience seems mediated by perceptual vividness or dramatic impact.

The study of heuristics and biases tends to be dominated by attempts to expose systematic errors and inferential biases in human reasoning. These do expose some of our intellectual limitations. On the other hand, errors and biases often reveal the psychological processes that govern judgment and inference and thereby suggest ways of improving the quality of our thinking. The discussion of factors that could affect the quality of decision-making should not be seen as a general indictment of human intelligence. The factors indicate potential difficulties in decision and choice processes, many of them should be taken into account if decisions are to be improved in a wide variety of applied areas. In Chapter 6 we discussed the possible contributions of this field of study to medical decision-making.

A cautionary note seems in order, however. Whereas most studies on heuristics involve discrete judgment tasks at a single point in time, in more natural contexts judgments and actions evolve and influence each other continuously over time. One would expect, therefore, that the kind of information with which we are best adapted to deal is continuous, redundant and patterned over time. Because of the possibility of correction through feedback, judgments do not generally have to be made once-and-for-all. It is more typical for people to evaluate decisions with respect to relatively short- or medium-term 'decision horizons' where the link from action to outcome is clearer. It is therefore precisely because many studies fail to simulate the natural context of judgment and action that 'errors' and 'biases' can be experimentally demonstrated with such relative ease. These errors and biases are real enough, and testify to people's tendencies to resolve problems on the basis of rules of thumb rather than recourse to first principles. Such evidence, however, falls short of demonstrating that these rules of thumb, strategies or heuristics are irrational, unreasonable or invalid with respect to the context in which they are most typically used.

Research on the quality of human decision-making is not only relevant to the field of medical decision-making. The relation between stress and decision-making helps us to understand public reactions to technological risks such as those of nuclear energy. We have argued that, in order to understand local reactions to nuclear power stations and possible accidents, both cognitive aspects such as risk perception and perceived importance of costs and benefits, as well as emotional aspects such as stress-related reactions and coping styles, should be taken into account. The study of emotional reactions is especially important in the context of accidents such as those in Harrisburg (Three Mile Island), Sellafield, and Chernobyl. Increased understanding of how people cope with these technological calamities should increase our ability to help future victims of such accidents.

Frames of reference and communication

An important conclusion of this book concerns the tension between theoretical development and applied value. Too often, it seems, popular theoretical approaches are accompanied by a tendency of researchers to try and explain too many phenomena in terms of one specific theory.

In this respect, our remarks about differences in salience as an important factor in the creation and maintenance of misunderstanding between groups and/or individuals also seem to apply to the relationship between researchers and the people and groups being studied.

Salience and implicit expectations in their own minds may have led attribution theorists to overestimate the role of attributions in everyday life, decision-analysts to expect people to employ the researcher's normative statistical models of decision-making, and researchers on decisional biases to develop tasks that were bound to find shortcomings in human decision-making. Fortunately, this initial optimism and the occasional tendency to relate all possible social phenomena to a single model are usually followed by more realistic assessments of the scope and generalizability of specific theories.

In this book, we have attempted to show that theories of judgment, attitudes, attribution and decision-making can make important contributions to social issues such as the employment of nuclear energy, the storage of nuclear waste, health behaviour and medical decision-making. These contributions are most clear-cut when the frame of reference or psychological perspective of the people being studied is taken seriously and explicitly incorporated in research efforts. Usually, this will be accompanied by a tendency to use a variety of theoretical approaches, as we have attempted to show in the applied chapters of this book.

For instance, for social psychology to make a contribution to the nuclear debate, it should incorporate elements of theories of judgment, equity, attitudes and decision-making in order to improve communication between the various groups involved in this debate *and* the quality of (policy) decision-making processes. Similarly, communication and decision-making in the context of health and illness can best be served by applications of a variety of theoretical approaches. In this way social psychology is relevant to a wide variety of social issues. This relevance does not depend on a single theory or some vague expression of concern. It derives from the theoretical and distinctive methods that social psychology has developed.

References and name index

The page numbers in italics at the end of each entry indicate the position of the publication's citations in this book.

Abelson, R.P. (1959). Modes of resolution of belief dilemmas. *Journal of Conflict Resolution*, 3, 343–52. *33*.

Abelson, R.P. (1981). Psychological status of the script concept. *American Psychologist*, 36, 715–29. *139*.

Abelson, R.P. and Levi, A. (1985). Decision making and decision theory. In G. Lindzey and E. Aronson (eds), *Handbook of Social Psychology*. vol. 1, New York: Random House. *83, 91, 99*.

Abramson, L.Y., Seligman, M.E.P. and Teasdale, J.D. (1978). Learned helplessness in humans: a critique and reformulation. *Journal of Abnormal Psychology*, 87, 49–74. *70*.

Ajzen, I. and Fishbein, M. (1977). Attitude-behavior relations: a theoretical analysis and a review of empirical research. *Psychological Bulletin*, 84, 888–918. *26*.

Ajzen, I. and Fishbein, M. (1980). *Understanding Attitudes and Predicting Social Behavior*. Englewood Cliffs, N.J.: Prentice-Hall. *27*.

Alexander, B.K. and Hadaway, P.F. (1982). Opiate addiction: the case for an adaptive orientation. *Psychological Bulletin*, 92, 367–81. *112*.

Anderson, C.A., Horowitz, L.M. and French, R.D. (1983). Attributional style of lonely and depressed people. *Journal of Personality and Social Psychology*, 45, 127–36. *71*.

Applegate, W.B. (1981). Decision theory for clinicians: Uses and misuses of clinical tests. *Southern Medical Journal*, 74, 468–73. *142*.

Arkes, H.R. and Harkness, A.R. (1980). The effect of making a diagnosis on subsequent recognition of symptoms. *Journal of Experimental Psychology: Human Learning and Memory*, 6, 568–75. *147*.

Atkinson, J.W. (1957). Motivational determinants of risk-taking behavior. *Psychological Review*, 64, 359–72. *68*.

Bachrach, K.M. and Zautra, A.J. (1985). Coping with a community stressor: the threat of a hazardous waste facility. *Journal of Health and Social Behavior*, 26, 127–41. *176*.

Baum, A., Fleming, R. and Singer, J.E. (1982). Stress at Three Mile Island: applying social impact analysis. *Applied Social Psychology Annual*. Beverley Hills Ca.: Sage. *171–2*.

Baum, A., Gatchel, R.J. and Shaeffer, M.A. (1983). Emotional, behavioral and physiological effects of chronic stress at Three Mile Island. *Journal of Consulting and Clinical Psychology*, 51, 565–72. *172*.

Baumeister, R.F. (1982). A self-presentational view of social phenomena. *Psychological Bulletin*, 91, 3–26. *38*.

Bem, D.J. (1965). An experimental analysis of self-persuasion. *Journal of Experimental Social Psychology*, 1, 199–218. *36–7, 40*.

Bem, D.J. (1967). Self-perception: an alternative interpretation of cognitive dissonance phenomena. *Psychological Review*, 74, 183–200. *36–7, 40*.

Bennett, M.J. (1980). Heuristics and the weighting of base rate information in diagnostic tasks by nurses. Unpublished doctoral dissertation. Monash University, Australia. *145–6*.

Bentler, P.M. and Speckart, G. (1979). Models of attitude-behavior relations. *Psychological Review*, 86, 452–64. *30–2, 41*.

Berwick, D.M. and Thibodeau, L.A. (1983). Receiver operating characteristic analysis of diagnostic skill. *Medical Care*, 21, 876–85. *143*.

Beyth-Marom, R. and Fischhoff, B. (1983). Diagnosticity and pseudo-diagnosticity. *Journal of Personality and Social Psychology*, 45, 1185–95. *144*.

Bibace, R. and Walsh, M.E. (eds) (1981). *Children's Conceptions of Health, Illness and Bodily Functions*. San Francisco: Jossey-Bass. *137*.

Bradley, G.W. (1978). Self-serving bias in the attribution process: a re-examination of the factor fiction question. *Journal of Personality and Social Psychology*, 36, 56–71. *57*.

Breckler, S.J. (1984). Empirical validation of affect, behavior and cognition as distinct components of attitude. *Journal of Personality and Social Psychology*, 47, 1191–205. *23, 25, 42*.

Brewin, C.R. (1985). Depression and causal attributions: what is their relation? *Psychological Bulletin*, 98, 297–309. *71–2*.

Brewster, A.B. (1982). Chronically ill hospitalized children's concepts of their illness. *Pediatrics*, 69, 355–62, *138*.

Brown, K. (1986). *Social Psychology*, 2nd edn. New York: The Free Press. *53, 64*.

Budd, R.J. and Spencer, C. (1984). Latitude of rejection, centrality and certainty: variables affecting the relationship between attitudes, norms and behavioural intentions. *British Journal of Social Psychology*, 23, 1–8. *26*.

Budd, R.J. and Spencer, C. (1985). Exploring the role of personal normative beliefs in the theory of reasoned action: the problem of discriminating between alternative path models. *European Journal of Social Psychology*, 15, 299–313. *26*.

Bynner, J.M. (1969). *The Young Smoker* (Government Social Survey). London: HMSO. *114*.

Chaiken, S. (1980). Heuristic versus systematic information processing and the use of source versus message cues in persuasion. *Journal of Personality and Social Psychology*, 39, 752–66. *18*.

Chapman, L.J. and Chapman, J.P. (1969). Illusory correlation as an obstacle to the use of valid psychodiagnostic signs. *Journal of Abnormal Psychology*, 74, 271–80. *56*.

Chi, M.T.H. and Koeske, R.D. (1983). Network representation of a child's dinosaur knowledge. *Developmental Psychology*, 19, 29–39. *137*.

Christensen-Szalanski, J.J.J. and Bushyhead, J.B. (1983). Physicians' misunderstanding of normal findings. *Medical Decision Making*, 3, 169–75. *144*.

Christensen-Szalanski, J.J.J., Beck, D.E., Christensen-Szalanski, C.M. and Koepsell, T.D. (1983). The effect of journal coverage on physicians' perception of risk. *Journal of Applied Psychology*, 68, 278–84. *145*.

Cialdini, R.B., Kenrick, D.T. and Hoerig, J.H. (1976). Victim derogation in the Lerner paradigm: just world or just justification? *Journal of Personality and Social Psychology*, 33, 719–24. *106*.

Cohen, J., Chesnick, E.I. and Haran, D. (1971). Evaluation of compound probabilities in sequential choice. *Nature*, 32, 414–16. *94*.

Cook, J.R. (1983). Citizen response in a neighborhood under threat. *American Journal of Community Psychology*, 11, 459–71. *173*.

Cooper, J. and Fazio, R.H. (1984). A new look at dissonance theory. In L. Berkowitz (ed.). *Advances in Experimental Social Psychology*, vol. 17. New York: Academic Press. *36, 39*.

Cooper, J. and Goethals, G.R. (1974). Unforeseen events and the elimination of cognitive dissonance. *Journal of Personality and Social Psychology*, 29, 441–5. *35*.

Cooper, J. and Worchel, S. (1970). The role of undesired consequences in arousing cognitive dissonance. *Journal of Personality and Social Psychology*, 16, 199–206. *35.*

Cooper, J., Zanna, M.P. and Taves, P.A. (1978). Arousal as a necessary condition for attitude change following compliance. *Journal of Personality and Social Psychology*, 36, 1101–6. *40.*

Crocker, J. (1981). Judgment of covariation by social perceivers. *Psychological Bulletin*, 90, 272–92. *56.*

Croyle, R.T. and Cooper, J. (1983). Dissonance arousal: Physiological evidence. *Journal of Personality and Social Psychology*, 45, 782–91. *39.*

Darley, J.M. and Goethals, G.R. (1980). People's analyses of the causes of ability linked performances. In L. Berkowitz (ed.). *Advances in Experimental Social Psychology*, vol. 13. New York: Academic Press. *70.*

Davidson, A.R. and Jaccard, J.J. (1975). Population psychology: a new look at an old problem. *Journal of Personality and Social Psychology*, 31, 1073–82. *26.*

Davidson, A.R. and Jaccard, J.J. (1979). Variables that moderate the attitude-behaviour relation: results of a longitudinal survey. *Journal of Personality and Social Psychology*, 37, 1364–76. *26.*

de Boer, J. (1986). Community response to soil contamination: risk and uncertainty. In J.W. Assink and W.J. van der Brink (eds). *Contaminated Soil*. Dordrecht, Netherlands: Martinus Nijhoff. *170.*

Detmer, D.E., Fryback, D.G. and Gassner, K. (1978). Heuristics and biases in medical decision-making. *Journal of Medical Education*, 53, 682–3. *145.*

Dobbs, J. and Marsh, A. (1983). *Smoking among Secondary School Children* (Government Social Survey). London: HMSO. *114.*

Dollard, J. and Miller, N.E. (1950). *Personality and Psychotherapy*. New York: McGraw-Hill. *127.*

Earle, T.C. and Cvetkovich, G. (1985). Failure and success in public risk communication. Paper presented at the Air Pollution Control Association Conference on Avoiding and Managing Environmental Damage from Major Industrial Accidents. Vancouver BC, Canada, November. *177.*

Eddy, D.M. (1980). *Screening for Cancer: Theory, Analysis and Design*. Englewood Cliffs, N.J.: Prentice Hall. *79.*

Eddy, D.M. (1982). Probabilistic reasoning in clinical medicine: Problems and opportunities. In D. Kahneman, P. Slovic and A. Tversky (eds). *Judgment under Uncertainty: Heuristics and Biases*. Cambridge: Cambridge University Press. *144.*

Edwards, W. (1955). The prediction of decisions among bets. *Journal of Experimental Psychology*, 50, 201–14. *79.*

188

Eiser, C. (1980). How leukaemia affects a child's schooling. *British Journal of Social and Clinical Psychology*, 19, 365–8. *138*.

Eiser, C. (1985). *The Psychology of Childhood Illness*. New York: Springer-Verlag. *137*.

Eiser, C., Eiser, J.R. and Hunt, J. (1986a). Comprehension of metaphorical explanations of illness. *Early Child Development and Care*, 26, 79–84. *136*.

Eiser, C., Eiser, J.R. and Hunt, J. (1986b). Developmental changes in analogies used to describe parts of the body: implications for communicating with sick children. *Child: Care, Health and Development*, 12, 277–85. *136*.

Eiser, C., Patterson, D. and Tripp, J.H. (1984). Illness experience and children's conceptualisation of health and illness. *Child: Care, Health and Development*, 10, 157–62. *138*.

Eiser, C., Walsh, S. and Eiser, J.R. (1986). Young children's understanding of smoking. *Addictive Behaviors*, 11, 119–23. *116*.

Eiser, J.R. (1971). Enhancement of contrast in the absolute judgment of attitude statements. *Journal of Personality and Social Psychology*, 17, 1–10. *10–13*.

Eiser, J.R. (1976). Evaluation of choice dilemma alternatives: utility morality and social judgement. *British Journal of Social and Clinical Psychology*, 15, 51–60. *14*.

Eiser, J.R. (ed.) (1984). *Attitudinal Judgment*. New York: Springer-Verlag. *9*.

Eiser, J.R. (1985). Smoking: the social learning of an addiction. *Journal of Social and Clinical Psychology*, 3, 446–57. *116*.

Eiser, J.R. (1986). *Social Psychology: Attitudes, Cognition and Social Behaviour*. Cambridge: Cambridge University Press. *11, 15, 43*.

Eiser, J.R. (1987). *The Expression of Attitude*. New York: Springer-Verlag. *43*.

Eiser, J.R. and Gossop, M.R. (1979). 'Hooked' or 'sick': addicts' perceptions of their addiction. *Addictive Behaviors*, 4, 185–91. *120*.

Eiser, J.R. and Mower White, C.J. (1974). Evaluative consistency and social judgment. *Journal of Personality and Social Psychology*, 30, 349–59. *14, 17*.

Eiser, J.R. and Mower White, C.J. (1975). Categorization and congruity in attitudinal judgment. *Journal of Personality and Social Psychology*, 31, 769–75. *14–17*.

Eiser, J.R. and Pancer, S.M. (1979). Attitudinal effects of the use of evaluatively biased language. *European Journal of Social Psychology*, 9, 39–47. *16–17*.

Eiser, J.R. and Ross, M. (1977). Partisan language, immediacy, and attitude change. *European Journal of Social Psychology*, 7, 477–89. *16*.

Eiser, J.R. and Stroebe, W. (1972). *Categorization and Social Judgement.* London: Academic Press. *9–13.*

Eiser, J.R. and Sutton, S.R. (1977). Smoking as a subjectively rational choice. *Addictive Behaviors,* 2, 129–34. *122.*

Eiser, J.R., Sutton, S.R. and Wober, M. (1978). 'Consonant' and 'dissonant' smokers and the self-attribution of addiction. *Addictive Behaviors,* 3, 99–106. *119.*

Eiser, J.R. and van der Pligt, J. (1979). Beliefs and values in the nuclear debate. *Journal of Applied Social Psychology,* 9, 524–36. *156, 159, 161, 164.*

Eiser, J.R. and van der Pligt, J. (1982). Accentuation and perspective in attitudinal judgment. *Journal of Personality and Social Psychology,* 42, 224–38. *14.*

Eiser, J.R. and van der Pligt, J. (1984a). Accentuation theory, polarization, and the judgment of attitude statements. In J.R. Eiser (ed.). *Attitudinal Judgment.* New York: Springer-Verlag. *10, 14.*

Eiser, J.R. and van der Pligt, J. (1984b). Attitudinal and social factors in adolescent smoking. In search of peer group influence. *Journal of Applied Social Psychology,* 14, 348–63. *115.*

Eiser, J.R. and van der Pligt, J. (1986). Smoking cessation and smokers' perceptions of their addiction. *Journal of Social and Clinical Psychology,* 4, 60–70. *120, 124.*

Eiser, J.R., van der Pligt, J., Raw, M. and Sutton, S.R. (1985). Trying to stop smoking: effects of perceived addiction, attributions for failure and expectancy of success. *Journal of Behavioral Medicine,* 8, 321–41. *122, 130.*

Elig, T.W. and Frieze, I.H. (1975). A multidimensional scheme for coding and interpreting perceived causality for success and failure events: the CSPS. *Catalog Sel. doc. Psychol.,* 5, 313. (MS 1069). *70.*

Elig, T.W. and Frieze, I.H. (1979). Measuring causal attributions for success and failure. *Journal of Personality and Social Psychology,* 37, 621–34. *70.*

Estes, W.K. (1980). Comments on directions and limitations of current effort toward theories of decision-making. In P.S. Wallsten (ed.) *Cognitive Processes in Choice and Decision Behavior.* Hillsdale, N.J.: Erlbaum. *79.*

Evans, R.I., Rozelle, R.M., Maxwell, S.E., Raines, B.E., Dill, C.A., Guthrie, T.J., Henderson, S.H. and Hill, P.C. (1981). Social modeling films to deter smoking in adolescents; Results of a three-year field investigation. *Journal of Applied Psychology,* 66, 399–414. *114.*

Fazio, R.H. (1986). How do attitudes guide behavior? In R.M. Sorrentino and E.T. Higgins (eds). *Handbook of Motivation and Cognition: Foundations of Social Behavior.* New York: Guilford Press. *29.*

Fazio, R.H., Powell, M.C. and Herr, P.M. (1983). Toward a process model of the attitude-behavior relation: Accessing one's attitude upon mere observation of the attitude object. *Journal of Personality and Social Psychology*, 44, 723–35. *29.*

Fazio, R.H. and Zanna, M.P. (1981). Direct experience and attitude behavior consistency. In L. Berkowitz (ed.). *Advances in Experimental Social Psychology*. New York: Academic Press, 14, 161–202. *25.*

Fazio, R.H., Zanna, M.P. and Cooper, J. (1977). Dissonance and self-perception: An integrative view of each theory's proper domain of application. *Journal of Experimental Social Psychology*, 13, 464–79. *37.*

Festinger, L. (1957). *A Theory of Cognitive Dissonance*. Evanston, Ill.: Row, Peterson. *33, 36, 39, 40, 100.*

Festinger, L. and Carlsmith, J.M. (1959). Cognitive consequences of forced compliance. *Journal of Abnormal and Social Psychology*, 58, 203–10. *33, 34, 36, 38.*

Festinger, L., Riecken, H. and Schachter, S. (1956). *When Prophecy Fails*. Minneapolis: University of Minneapolis Press. *101.*

Fields, J.M. and Schumann, H. (1976). Public beliefs about the public. *Public Opinion Quarterly*, 40, 427–48. *58–9.*

Fischhoff, B. (1975). Hindsight and foresight: the effect of outcome knowledge on judgment under uncertainty. *Journal of Experimental Psychology: Human Perception and Performance*, 1, 288–99. *89.*

Fischhoff, B. (1977). Cost benefit analysis and the art of motorcycle maintenance. *Policy Sciences*, 8, 177–202. *103.*

Fischhoff, B. (1982). For those condemned to study the post: heuristics and biases in hindsight. In D. Kahneman, P. Slovic and A. Tversky (eds). *Judgment under Uncertainty: Heuristics and Biases*. Cambridge: Cambridge University Press. *89.*

Fischhoff, B. (1983). Predicting frames. *Journal of Experimental Psychology: Learning, Memory and Cognition*, 9, 103–16. *87.*

Fischhoff, B. and Bar-Hillel, M. (1984). Diagnosticity and the base rate effect. *Memory and Cognition*, 12, 402–10. *93.*

Fischhoff, B. and Beyth, R. (1975). I knew it would happen: remembered probabilities of once-future things. *Organizational Behavior and Human Performance*, 13, 1–16. *89.*

Fischhoff, B., Goitein, B. and Shapira, Z. (1982). The experienced utility of expected utility approaches. In N.T. Feather (ed.). *Expectancy, Incentive and Action*. Hillsdale, N.J.: Erlbaum. *79.*

Fischhoff, B., Slovic, P. and Lichtenstein, S. (1977). Knowing with certainty: the appropriateness of extreme confidence. *Journal of Experimental Psychology: Human Perception and Performance*, 3, 522–64. *89.*

Fischhoff, B., Slovic, P. and Lichtenstein, S. (1980). Knowing what you want: measuring labile values. In T.S. Wallsten (ed.). *Cognitive Processes in Choice and Decision Behavior*. Hillsdale, N.J.: Erlbaum. *98.*

Fischhoff, B., Slovic, P., Lichtenstein, S., Read, S. and Combs, B.

(1978). How safe is safe enough? A psychometric study of attitudes toward technological risk and benefits. *Policy Sciences*, 8, 127–52. *154*.

Fishbein, M. (1967). Attitude and the prediction of behavior. In M. Fishbein (ed.). *Readings in Attitude Theory and Measurement*. New York: Wiley, 477–92. *26, 28*.

Fishbein, M. (1982). Social psychological analysis of smoking behavior. In J.R. Eiser (ed.). *Social Psychology and Behavioral Medicine*. Chichester: Wiley, 179–97. *26, 32, 119*.

Fishbein, M. and Ajzen, I. (1975). *Belief, Attitude, Intention and Behavior: An Introduction to Theory and Research*. Reading, Mass.: Addison-Wesley. *26–9, 32, 124, 131, 155, 158*.

Fishbein, M. and Ajzen, I. (1984). Predicting and understanding consumer behavior: Attitude-behavior correspondence. In I. Ajzen and M. Fishbein (eds). *Understanding Attitudes and Predicting Social Behavior*. Englewood Cliffs, N.J.: Prentice-Hall. *26*.

Flesch, R. (1948). A new readability yardstick. *Journal of Applied Psychology*, 32, 221–33. *132*.

Fredricks, A.J. and Dossett, D.L. (1983). Attitude-behavior relations: a comparison of the Fishbein-Ajzen and the Bentler-Speckart models. *Journal of Personality and Social Psychology*, 45, 501–12. *32*.

French, J. and Raven, B.H. (1959). The bases of social power. In D. Cartwright (ed.). *Studies in Social Power*. Ann Arbor, MI: Institute for Social Research. *140*.

Frey, D. and Wicklund, R.A. (1978). A clarification of selective exposure: The impact of choice. *Journal of Experimental Social Psychology*, 14, 132–9. *35*.

Gilbertsen, V.A. and Wangensteen, O.H. (1962). Should the doctor tell the patient that the disease is cancer? *Ca: A Cancer Journal for Clinicians*, 12, 82–6. *134*.

Gilovich, T. (1981). Seeing the past in the present: the effect of associations to familiar events on judgments and decisions. *Journal of Personality and Social Psychology*, 40, 797–808. *99*.

Goethals, G.R. (1987). Fabricating and ignoring social reality: self-serving estimates of consensus. In J. Olson, C.P. Herman and M.P. Zanna (eds). *Relative Deprivation and Social Comparison: The Ontario Symposium on Social Cognition: IV*. Hillsdale, N.J.: Erlbaum. *60*.

Goethals, G.R., Cooper, J. and Naficy, A. (1979). Role of foreseen, foreseeable, and unforeseeable behavioral consequences in the arousal of cognitive dissonance. *Journal of Personality and Social Psychology*, 37, 1179–85. *35*.

Greenwald, A.G. (1975). On the inconclusiveness of 'crucial' cognitive tests of dissonance versus self-perception theories. *Journal of Experimental Social Psychology*, 11, 490–9. *37*.

Gregory, W.L., Cialdini, R.B. and Carpenter, K.M. (1982). Self-relevant scenarios as mediators of likelihood estimates and compliance: does imagining make it so? *Journal of Personality and Social Psychology*, 43, 89–99. *91, 131.*

Guerin, B. (1983). Social facilitation and social monitoring: a test of three models. *British Journal of Social Psychology*, 22, 203–14. *117.*

Harding, C.M. and Eiser, J.R. (1984). Characterising the perceived risks and benefits of some health issues. *Risk Analysis*, 4, 131–41. *130.*

Harding, C.M., Eiser, J.R. and Kristiansen, C.M. (1982). The representation of mortality statistics and the perceived importance of causes of death. *Journal of Applied Social Psychology*, 12, 169–81. *130.*

Harvey, J.H. and Weary, G. (1984). Current issues in attribution theory and research. *Annual Review of Psychology*, 35, 427–59. *64.*

Harvey, J.H., Harris, B. and Barns, R.D. (1975). Actor–observer differences in the perception of responsibility and freedom. *Journal of Personality and Social Psychology*, 32, 22–38. *60–1.*

Harvey, J.H., Wells, G.H. and Alvarez, M.D. (1978). Attribution in the context of conflict and separation in close relationships. In J.H. Harvey, W. Ickes and R.F. Kidd (eds). *New Directions in Attribution Research*, vol. 2. Hillsdale, N.J.: Erlbaum. *59.*

Hastie, R. (1984). Causes and effects of causal attribution. *Journal of Personality and Social Psychology*, 46, 54–6, 73.

Heider, F. (1944). Social perception and phenomenal causality. *Psychological Review*, 51, 358–74. *46, 72.*

Heider, F. (1946). Attitudes and cognitive organization. *Journal of Psychology*, 21, 107–12. *20–2, 33, 41, 72.*

Heider, F. (1958). *The Psychology of Interpersonal Relations*. New York: Wiley. *46–7, 65, 67, 69, 73.*

Hinckley, E.D. (1932). The influence of individual opinion on construction of an attitude scale. *Journal of Social Psychology*, 3, 283–96. *7, 8.*

Hiroto, D.S. and Seligman, M.E.P. (1975). Generality of learned helplessness in man. *Journal of Personality and Social Psychology*, 81, 311–27. *70.*

Hogarth, R.M. (1981). Beyond discrete biases: functional and dysfunctional aspects of judgmental heuristics. *Psychological Bulletin*, 90, 197–217. *97, 147–8.*

Hopkins, N.J. (1987). Group prototypicality and 'threatened identities': Non-conformity and the intra- and inter-group determinants of social influence. Paper presented to the 7th General Meeting of the European Association of Experimental Social Psychology. Varna, Bulgaria (May). *116.*

Hovland, C.I., Janis, I.L. and Kelley, H.H. (1953). *Communication and*

Persuasion: Psychological Studies of Opinion Change. New Haven, Conn.: Yale University Press. *127–8, 130.*

Hovland, C.I. and Sherif, M. (1952). Judgmental phenomena and scales of attitude measurement: item displacement in Thurstone Scales. *Journal of Abnormal and Social Psychology*, 47, 822–32. *6–9, 12.*

Hunt, W.A. and Matarazzo, J.D. (1973). Three years later. Recent developments in the experimental modification of smoking behavior. *Journal of Abnormal Psychology*, 81, 107–14. *118.*

Insko, C.A. (1984). Balance theory, the Jordan paradigm, and the Wiest tetrahedron. In L. Berkowitz (ed.). *Advances in Experimental Social Psychology*, vol. 18. New York: Academic Press. *22.*

Jaffé, J.H. (1977). Tobacco use as a mental disorder: The re-discovery of a medical problem. In Jarvik, M.E. et al. (eds). *Research on Smoking Behavior*. NIDA Research Monograph 17. Rockville, MD: DHEW. *108.*

Jaffé, J.H. (1980). Drug addiction and drug abuse. In A.G. Gilman, L.S. Goodman and A. Gilman (eds). *Goodman and Gilman's: The Pharmacological Basis of Therapeutics*. 6th edn. New York: Macmillan. *112.*

Janis, I.L. (1967). Effects of fear-arousal on attitude change: recent developments in theory and experimental research. In L. Berkowitz (ed.). *Advances in Experimental Social Psychology*, vol. 3. New York: Academic Press. *128.*

Janis, I.L. (1972). *Victims of Groupthink*. Boston, Mass.: Houghton Mifflin. *101–2.*

Janis, I.L. (1982). *Groupthink*. 2nd edn. Boston, Mass.: Houghton Mifflin. *101–3.*

Janis, I.L. and Feshbach, S. (1953). Effects of fear-arousing communications. *Journal of Abnormal and Social Psychology*, 48, 78–92. *128–30.*

Janis, I.L. and Mann, L. (1977). *Decision Making: A Psychological Analysis of Conflict, Choice, and Commitment*. New York: Free Press. *33, 98, 100–1, 128, 170–1.*

Jaspars, J.M.F., Hewstone, M. and Fincham, F.D. (1983). Attribution theory and research: the state of the art. In J.M.F. Jaspars, F.D. Fincham and M. Hewstone (eds). *Attribution Theory and Research: Conceptual, Developmental and Social Dimensions*. London: Academic Press. *56.*

Jellinek, E.M. (1960). *The Disease Concept of Alcoholism*. Highland Park, NJ: Hillhouse Press. *107.*

Johnson, S.B., Pollak, T., Silverstein, J.H., Rosenbloom, A.L., Spillar, R., McCallum, M. and Harkavy, J. (1982). Cognitive and behavioral knowledge about insulin dependent diabetes among children and parents. *Pediatrics*, 69, 708–13. *135.*

Jones, E.E. and Davis, K.E. (1965). From acts to dispositions: the attribution process in person perception. In: L. Berkowitz (ed.). *Advances in Experimental Social Psychology*, vol. 2. New York: Academic Press. *46–9, 51–2.*

Jones, E.E. and Harris, V.A. (1967). The attribution of attitudes. *Journal of Experimental Social Psychology*, 3, 1–24. *50.*

Jones, E.E. and McGillis, D. (1976). Correspondent inferences and the attribution cube: a comparative reappraisal. In J.H. Harvey, W.J. Ickes and R.F. Kidd (eds). *New Directions in Attribution Research*, vol. 1. Hillsdale, N.J.: Erlbaum. *46–7, 50.*

Jones, E.E. and Nisbett, R.E. (1971). The actor and the observer: divergent perceptions of the causes of behavior. In E.E. Jones, D.E. Kanouse, H.H. Kelley, R.E. Nisbett, S. Valins and B. Weiner (eds). *Attribution: Perceiving the Cause of Behavior*. Morristown, N.J.: General Learning Press. *60.*

Jones, R.A., Linder, D.E., Kiesler, C., Zanna, M. and Brehm, J.W. (1968). Internal states or external stimuli: Observers' attitude judgments and the dissonance theory-self-persuasion controversy. *Journal of Experimental Social Psychology*, 4, 247–69. *37.*

Kahneman, D., Slovic, P. and Tversky, A. (eds) (1982). *Judgment under Uncertainty: Heuristics and Biases*. Cambridge: Cambridge University Press. *79, 89.*

Kahneman, D. and Tversky, A. (1972). Subjective probability: a judgment of representativeness. *Cognitive Psychology*, 3, 430–54. *76, 92.*

Kahneman, D. and Tversky, A. (1973). On the psychology of prediction. *Psychological Review*, 80, 237–51. *93, 145.*

Kahneman, D. and Tversky, A. (1979). Prospect theory: an analysis of decision under risk. *Econometrica*, 47, 263–91. *80–8.*

Kahneman, D. and Tversky, A. (1984). Choices, values, and frames. *American Psychologist*, 39, 341–50. *76.*

Kasperson, R.E. (1985). Rethinking the siting of hazardous waste facilities. Paper presented at the Conference on transport, Storage and Disposal of Hazardous Materials. IIASA, Vienna, Austria, July. *174, 175.*

Kassin, S.M. and Hochreich, D.J. (1977). Instructional set: a neglected variable in attribution research? *Personality and Social Psychology Bulletin*, 3, 620–3. *66.*

Kelley, H.H. (1967). Attribution in social psychology. In D.L. Vine (ed.). *Nebraska Symposium on Motivation*. Lincoln, Neb.: University of Nebraska Press. *46–7, 52–6.*

Kelley, H.H. (1972). *Causal Schemata and the Attribution Process*. Morristown, N.J.: General Learning Press. *46–7, 54–5.*

Kelley, H.H. (1973). The process of causal attribution. *American Psychologist*, 28, 107–28. *46–7, 54–5.*

Kelley, H.H. and Michela, J.L. (1980). Attribution theory and research. *Annual Review of Psychology*, 31, 457–501. *74, 121.*

Kenrick, D.T., Reich, J.W. and Cialdini, R.B. (1976). Justification and compensation: Rosier skies for the devalued victim. *Journal of Personality and Social Psychology*, 34, 654–7. *106.*

Kiesler, C.A., Nisbett, R.E. and Zanna, M.P. (1969). On inferring one's beliefs from one's behavior. *Journal of Personality and Social Psychology*, 11, 321–7. *37.*

Kothandapani, V. (1971). Validation of feeling, belief, and intention to act as three components of attitude and their contribution to prediction of contraceptive behavior. *Journal of Personality and Social Psychology*, 19, 321–33. *23.*

Kristiansen, C.M. (1985). Value correlates of preventive health behavior. *Journal of Personality and Social Psychology*, 49, 748–58. *106.*

Krosnick, J.A. and Judd, C.M. (1982). Transitions in social influence at adolescence: who induces cigarette smoking? *Developmental Psychology*, 18, 359–68. *115.*

Kunreuther, H., Linnerooth, J. and Vaupel, J.W. (1984). A decision-process perspective on risk and policy analysis. *Management Science*, 30, 475–85. *175.*

Langer, E.J. (1978). Rethinking the role of thought in social interaction. In J.H. Harvey, W.J. Ickes and R.F. Kidd (eds). *New Directions in Attribution Research*, vol. 2. Hillsdale, N.J.: Erlbaum. *18.*

Lepper, M. (1973). Dissonance, self-perception and honesty in children. *Journal of Personality and Social Psychology*, 25, 65–74. *66.*

Lerner, M.J. (1980). *The Belief in a Just World: A Fundamental Delusion.* New York: Plenum. *106.*

Leventhal, H. (1980). Toward a comprehensive theory of emotion. In L. Berkowitz (ed.). *Advances in Experimental Social Psychology*, vol. 13. New York: Academic Press. *117.*

Leventhal, H. (1984). A perceptual-motor theory of emotion. In L. Berkowitz (ed.). *Advances in Experimental Social Psychology*, vol. 17. New York: Academic Press. *117.*

Lewinsohn, P.M., Steinmetz, J.L., Larson, D.W. and Franklin, J. (1981). Depression related cognitions: antecedent or consequence? *Journal of Abnormal Psychology*, 90, 213–19. *71.*

Ley, P. (1972). Comprehension, memory and the success of communications with the patient. *Journal of the Institute of Health Education*, 10, 23–9. *133.*

Ley, P. (1982). Giving information to patients. In J.R. Eiser (ed.). *Social Psychology and Behavioral Medicine.* Chichester: Wiley. *132, 135.*

Lichtenstein, S. and Slovic, P. (1971). Reversal of preferences between bids and choices in gambling decisions. *Journal of Experimental Psychology*, 89, 46–55. *79.*

Lichtenstein, S., Fischhoff, B. and Philips, L.D. (1977). Calibration of probabilities: the state of the art. In H. Jungermann and G. de Zeeuw (eds). *Decision Making and Change in Human Affairs*. Amsterdam: D. Reidel. *79*.

Lichtenstein, S., Slovic, P. and Zinc, D. (1969). Effect of instruction in expected value on optimality of gambling decisions. *Journal of Experimental Psychology*, 79, 236–40. *79*.

Lichtenstein, S., Slovic, P., Fischhoff, B., Layman, M. and Combs, B. (1978). Judged frequency of lethal events. *Journal of Experimental Psychology: Human Learning and Memory*, 4, 551–78. *90, 30*.

Likert, R. (1932). A technique for the measurement of attitudes. *Archives of Psychology*, 22, no. 140. *5–6*.

Lindell, M.K. and Earle, T.C. (1983). How close is close enough? Public perceptions of the risks of industrial facilities. *Risk Analysis*, 3, 245–53. *174*.

Linder, D.E., Cooper, J. and Jones, E.E. (1967). Decision freedom as a determinant of the role of incentive magnitude in attitude change. *Journal of Personality and Social Psychology*, 6, 245–54. *35*.

Locker, D. and Dunt, D. (1978). Theoretical and methodological issues in sociological studies of consumer satisfaction with medical care. *Social Science and Medicine*, 12, 283–92. *133*.

Lynn, D.B., Glaser, H.H. and Harrison, G.S. (1962). Comprehensive medical care for handicapped children: III. Concepts of illness in children with rheumatic fever. *American Journal of Diseases of Children*. CIII. 42–50. *138*.

McArthur, L.Z. (1972). The how and what of why: some determinants and consequences of causal attribution. *Journal of Personality and Social Psychology*, 22, 171–93. *55–6, 61*.

McArthur, L.Z. (1976). The lesser influence of consensus than distinctiveness information on causal attributions. a test of the person-thing hypothesis. *Journal of Personality and Social Psychology*, 33, 733–42. *55*.

McAuliffe, W.E. and Gordon, R.A. (1980). Reinforcement and the combination of effects: summary of a theory of opiate addiction. In D.J. Lettieri, M. Sayers and H.W. Pearson (eds). *Theories on Drug Abuse*. NIDA Research Monograph 30. Washington, DC: US Government Printing Office. *112*.

McFarland, C. and Ross, M. (1982). The impact of causal attributions on affective reactions to success and failure. *Journal of Personality and Social Psychology*, 43, 937–46. *58*.

McKennell, A.C. and Thomas, R.K. (1967). *Adults' and Adolescents' Smoking Habits and Attitudes*. Government Social Survey, London: HMSO. *119, 121*.

Manstead, A.S.R., Proffitt, C. and Smart, J.L. (1983). Predicting and

197

understanding mothers' infant-feeding intentions and behavior: Testing the theory of reasoned action. *Journal of Personality and Social Psychology*, 44, 657–71. *26.*

Marks, G. and Miller, N. (1987). Ten years of research on the false consensus effect: an empirical and theoretical view. *Psychological Bulletin*, 102, 72–90. *165.*

Markus, H. and Zajonc, R.B. (1985). The cognitive perspective in social psychology. In G. Lindzey and E. Aronson (eds). *Handbook of Social Psychology*, vol. 1. New York: Random House. *58, 65.*

Marsh, A. (1984). Smoking: habit or choice? *Population Trends* (HMSO), 36, 14–20. *117.*

Marsh, A. and Matheson, J. (1983). *Smoking Attitudes and Behaviour* (Government Social Survey). London: HMSO. *124.*

Martin, A.J., Landau, L.I. and Phelan, P.D. (1982). Asthma from childhood at age 21: the patient and his disease. *British Medical Journal*, 284, 380–2. *135.*

Mausner, B. and Platt, E.S. (1971). *Smoking: A Behavioral Analysis*. New York: Pergamon. *119.*

Melamed, B.C. and Siegel, L.J. (1975). Reduction of anxiety in children facing hospitalization and surgery by use of filmed modeling. *Journal of Consulting and Clinical Psychology*, 43, 511–21. *139.*

Mendel, D. (1984). *Proper Doctoring*. Heidelberg: Springer-Verlag. *132–3, 149.*

Milgram, S. (1974). *Obedience to Authority*. London: Tavistock. *61.*

Miller, D.T. and Norman, S.A. (1975). Actor-observer differences in perceptions of effective control. *Journal of Personality and Social Psychology*, 31, 503–15, *61.*

Miller, D.T. and Porter, C.A. (1980). Effects of temporal perspective on the attribution process. *Journal of Personality and Social Psychology*, 40, 532–41. *61.*

Miller, D.T. and Ross, M. (1975). Self-serving biases in the attribution of causality: fact or fiction? *Psychological Bulletin*, 82, 213–25. *58.*

Miller, F.D., Smith, E.R. and Uhleman, J. (1981). Measurement and interpretation of situational and dispositional attributions. *Journal of Experimental Social Psychology*, 17, 80–95. *66.*

Miller, G.A. (1956). The magical number seven, plus or minus two: some limits on our capacity for processing information. *Psychological Review*, 63, 81–97. *79.*

Monk, A.F. and Eiser, J.R. (1980). A simple, bias-free method for scoring attitude scale responses. *British Journal of Social and Clinical Psychology*, 19, 17–22. *6.*

Mullen, B. (1983). Egocentric biases in estimates of consensus. *Journal of Social Psychology*, 121, 31–8. *59.*

Mullen, B., Atkins, J.L., Champion, D.S., Edwards, C., Hardy, D.,

Story, J.E. and Vanderklok, M. (1985). The false consensus effect: A meta-analysis of 115 hypothesis tests. *Journal of Experimental Social Psychology*, 21, 262–83. *60*.

Myers, D.G. and Lamm, H. (1977). The polarizing effect of group discussion. In T.L. Janis (ed.). *Current Trends in Psychology: Readings from the American Scientist*. Los Altos, Calif.: Kaufmann. *84*.

Nealy, S.M., Melber, B.D. and Rankin, W.L. (1983). *Public Opinion and Nuclear Energy*. Lexington M.A.: Lexington. *152–3, 173*.

Newcomb, T.M. (1968). Interpersonal balance. In: R.P. Abelson, E. Aronson, W.J. McGuire, T.M. Newcomb, M.J. Rosenberg and P.H. Tannenbaum (eds). *Theories of Cognitive Consistency: A Source Book*. Chicago: Rand-McNally. *21*.

Newcomb, T.M. (1981). Heiderian balance as a group phenomenon. *Journal of Personality and Social Psychology*, 40, 862–7. *21*.

Newell, A. and Simon, H.A. (1972). *Human Problem-solving*. Englewood Cliffs, N.J.: Prentice-Hall. *89*.

Nisbett, R.E., Caputo, P., Legant, P. and Marecek, J. (1973). Behavior as seen by the actor and as seen by the observer. *Journal of Personality and Social Psychology*, 27, 154–65. *61*.

Nisbett, R.E. and Ross, L. (1980). *Human Inference: Strategies and Shortcomings of Social Judgment*. Englewood Cliffs, N.J.: Prentice-Hall. *52, 56, 65, 91, 130*.

Novack, D.H., Plumer, R., Smith, R.L., Ochitil, H., Morrow, G.R. and Bennett, J.M. (1979). Changes in physicians' attitudes towards telling the cancer patient. *Journal of the American Medical Association*, 241, 897–900. *134*.

Nowell-Smith, P.H. (1956). *Ethics*. Harmondsworth: Penguin. *18*.

Nuttin, J.M., Jr. (1975). *The Illusion of Attitude Change: Towards a Response Contagion Theory of Persuasion*. London: Academic Press. *40*.

O'Hare, M., Bacow, L. and Sanderson, D. (1983). *Facility Siting and Public Opposition*. New York: Van Nostrand. *174–5*.

Oken, D. (1961). What to tell cancer patients: A study of medical attitudes. *Journal of the American Medical Association*, 175, 1120–8. *134*.

Orvis, B.R., Cunningham, J.D. and Kelley, H.H. (1975). A closer examination of causal inferences: the roles of consensus, distinctiveness and consistency information. *Journal of Personality and Social Psychology*, 32, 605–16. *55*.

Osgood, C.E. and Tannenbaum, P.H. (1955). The principle of congruity in the prediction of attitude change. *Psychological Review*, 62, 42–55. *21*.

Oskamp, S. (1965). Overconfidence in case-study judgments. *Journal of Consulting Psychology*, 29, 261–5. *146*.

Ostrom, T.M. (1969). The relationship between the affective, behavioral and cognitive components of attitude. *Journal of Experimental Social Psychology*, 5, 12–30. *23*.

Otway, H.J., Maurer, D. and Thomas, K. (1978). Nuclear power: the question of public acceptance. *Futures*, 10, 109–18. *155–6*.

Pagel, M.D. and Davidson, A.R. (1984). A comparison of three social-psychological models of attitude and behavioral plan: prediction of contraceptive behavior. *Journal of Personality and Social Psychology*, 47, 517–33. *26*.

Pantell, R.H., Stewart, T.J., Dias, J.K., Wells, P. and Ross, A.W. (1982). Physician communication with children and parents. *Pediatrics*, 70, 396–402. *135*.

Parsons, T. (1951). *The Social System*. Chicago: Free Press. *105*.

Payne, J.W. (1982). Contingent decision behavior. *Psychological Bulletin*, 92, 382–402. *80*.

Pendleton, D. and Bochner, S. (1980). The communication of medical information in general practice consultations as a function of patients' social class. *Social Science and Medicine*, 14A, 669–73. *134*.

Pendleton, D. and Hasler, J. (eds) (1983). *Doctor–Patient Communication*. London: Academic Press. *132*.

Perrin, E.C. and Perrin, J.M. (1983). Clinicians' assessments of children's understanding of illness. *American Journal of Diseases of Children*, 137, 874–8. *136*.

Peterson, C., Schwartz, S.M. and Seligman, M.E.P. (1981). Self-blame and depressive symptoms. *Journal of Personality and Social Psychology*, 41, 253–9. *71*.

Peterson, L. and Ridley-Johnson, R. (1984). Pediatric hospital response to survey of prehospital preparation for children. *Journal of Pediatric Psychology*, 5, 1–7. *139*.

Petty, R.E. and Cacioppo, J.T. (1979). Issue-involvement can increase or decrease persuasion by enhancing message-relevant cognitive responses. *Journal of Personality and Social Psychology*, 37, 1915–26. *17*.

Petty, R.E. and Cacioppo, J.T. (1985). The elaboration likelihood model of persuasion. In L. Berkowitz (ed.). *Advances in Experimental Social Psychology*, vol. 19. New York: Academic Press. *17–18, 21, 127, 130*.

Piaget, J. (1930). *The Child's Conception of Physical Causality*. London: Routledge & Kegan Paul. *137*.

Piliavin, J.A., Piliavin, I.M., Loewenton, E.P., McCauley, C. and Hammond, P. (1969). On observers' reproductions of dissonance effects: the right answers for the wrong reasons? *Journal of Personality and Social Psychology*, 13, 98–106. *37*.

Pless, I.B. and Douglas, J.W.B. (1971). Chronic illness in childhood:

1. Epidemiological and clinical observations. *Pediatrics*, 47, 405–14. *135*.

Portney, K.E. (1983). Citizen attitudes toward hazardous waste facility siting: public opinion in five Massachusetts communities. Medford, M.A.: Tufts University, Centre for Citizenship Public Affairs. *175*.

Quattrone, G.A. (1982). Overattribution and unit formation: when behavior engulfs the person. *Journal of Personality and Social Psychology*, 42, 593–607. *65*.

Ramsey, F.P. (1926). Truth and probability. In F.P. Ramsey (1931), *The Foundations of Mathematics and other Logical Essays*. London: Kegan Paul. *77*.

Raven, B.H. (1974). The comparative analysis of power and power preference. In J.T. Tedeschi (ed.). *Perspectives on Social Power*. Chicago Ill.: Aldine-Atherton. *140*.

Raven, B.H. and Haley, R.W. (1982). Social influence and compliance of hospital nurses with infection control policies. In J.R. Eiser (ed.). *Social Psychology and Behavioral Medicine*. Chichester: Wiley. *139–40*.

Regan, D.R. and Totten, J. (1975). Empathy and attribution: turning observers into actors. *Journal of Personality and Social Psychology*, 32, 850–6. *63*.

Reisenzein, R. (1983). The Schachter theory of emotion: two decades later. *Psychological Bulletin*, 94, 239–64. *117*.

Robins, L.N., Davis, D.H. and Goodwin, D.W. (1974). Drug use by U.S. Army enlisted men in Vietnam. A follow-up on their return home. *American Journal of Epidemiology*, 99, 235–49. *111*.

Robins, L.N., Helzer, J.E. and Davis, D.H. (1975). Narcotic use in Southeast Asia and afterwards. *Archives of General Psychiatry*, 32, 955–61. *111*.

Robinson, D. (1972). The alcohologist's addiction: some implications of having lost control over the disease concept of alcoholism. *Quarterly Journal of Studies on Alcohol*, 33, 1028–42. *120*.

Rokeach, M. (1979). *Understanding Human Values: Individual and Societal*. New York: Free Press. *106*.

Romer, D. (1983). Effects of own attitude on polarization of judgment. *Journal of Personality and Social Psychology*, 44, 273–84. *12–13*.

Rosenberg, M.J. and Abelson, R.P. (1960). An analysis of cognitive balancing. In M.J. Rosenberg, C.I. Hovland, W.J. McGuire, R.P. Abelson and J.W. Brehn (eds). *Attitude Organization and Change: An Analysis of Consistency Among Attitude Components*. New Haven, Conn.: Yale University Press. *22*.

Rosenberg, M.J. and Hovland, C.I. (1960). Cognitive, affective and behavioral components of attitudes. In M.J. Rosenberg, C.I. Hovland, W.J. McGuire, R.P. Abelson and J.W. Brehm (eds). *Atti-*

tude Organization and Change: An Analysis of Consistency Among Attitude Components. New Haven, Conn.: Yale University Press, 1–14. *23–4.*

Ross, L. (1977). The intuitive psychologist and his shortcomings: distortions in the attribution process. In L. Berkowitz (ed.). *Advances in Experimental Social Psychology*, vol. 10. New York: Academic Press. *59, 64, 163.*

Ross, L., Greene, D. and House, P. (1977). The 'false consensus effect': an egocentric bias in social perception and attribution processes. *Journal of Experimental Social Psychology*, 13, 279–301. *59, 163.*

Ross, M. and Fletcher, G.J.O. (1985). Attribution and social perception. In G. Lindzey and E. Aronson (eds). *Handbook of Social Psychology*, vol. 2. New York: Random House. *52.*

Rotter, J.B. (1966). Generalized expectancies for internal versus external control of reinforcement. *Psychological Monographs*, 80 (1, Whole No.609). *67.*

Russell, M.A.H. (1971). Cigarette smoking: natural history of a dependence disorder. *British Journal of Medical Psychology*, 44, 1–16. *108.*

Russell, M.A.H. (1974). The smoking habit and its classification. *Practitioner*, 212, 791–800. *113.*

Russell, M.A.H. (1976). Tobacco smoking and nicotine dependence. In R.J. Gibbins et al. (eds). *Research Advances in Alcohol and Drug Problems*, vol. 3. New York: Wiley. *113.*

Russell, M.A.H., Peto, J. and Patel, U.A. (1974). The classification of smoking by factorial structure of motives. *Journal of the Royal Statistical Society*: Series A. (General), 137, 313–46. *114.*

Schachter, S. (1978). Pharmacological and psychological determinants of smoking. *Annals of Internal Medicine*, 88, 104–14. *113, 117.*

Schachter, S. (1982). Recidivism and self-cure of smoking and obesity. *American Psychologist*, 37, 436–44. *118.*

Schachter, S. and Singer, J.E. (1962). Cognitive, social and physiological determinants of emotional state. *Psychological Review*, 69, 379–99. *117.*

Schlegel, R.P., Crawford, C.A. and Sanborn, M.D. (1977). Correspondence and mediational properties of the Fishbein model: An application to adolescent alcohol use. *Journal of Experimental Social Psychology*, 13, 421–30. *32.*

Schlenker, B.R. (1982). Translating actions into attitudes: an identity-analytic approach to the explanation of social conduct. In L. Berkowitz (ed.). *Advances in Experimental Social Psychology*, vol. 15. New York: Academic Press, 194–247. *38.*

Schwartz, S. and Griffin, T. (1986). *Medical Thinking: The Psychology of Medical Judgment and Decision Making.* New York: Springer-Verlag. *143, 146, 148.*

Seligman, M.E.P. (1972). Learned helplessness. *Annual Review of Medicine*, 23, 407–12. *70*.

Seligman, M.E.P. (1975). *Helplessness*. San Francisco: Freeman. *70*.

Seligman, M.E.P., Abramson, L.Y., Semmel, A. and von Baeyer, C. (1979). Depressive attributional style. *Journal of Abnormal and Social Psychology*, 88, 242–7. *71*.

Seligman, M.E.P. and Maier, S.F. (1967). Failure to escape traumatic shock. *Journal of Experimental Psychology*, 74, 1–9. *70*.

Sellitz, C., Edrich, H. and Cook, S.W. (1965). Ratings of favorableness about a social group as an indication of attitude toward the group. *Journal of Personality and Social Psychology*, 2, 408–15. *7, 12*.

Sherif, M. and Hovland, C.I. (1961). *Social Judgment: Assimilation and Contrast Effects in Communication and Attitude Change*. New Haven, Conn.: Yale University Press. *7, 10–3*.

Sherman, S.J., Cialdini, R.B., Schwartzman, D.F. and Reynolds, K. (1985). Imagining can heighten or lower the perceived likelihood of contracting a disease: the mediating effect of ease of imagery. *Personality and Social Psychology Bulletin*, 11, 118–27. *131*.

Sherman, S.J., Presson, C.C. and Chassin, L. (1984). Mechanisms underlying the false consensus effect: the special role of threats to the self. *Personality and Social Psychology Bulletin*, 10, 127–38. *59*.

Sherr, L. (1987). An evaluation of the UK government health education campaign on AIDS. *Psychology and Health*, 1, 61–72. *132*.

Siegel, S. (1977). Morphine tolerance acquisition as an associative process. *Journal of Experimental Psychology: Animal Behavior Processes*, 3, 1–13. *111–12*.

Simon, H.A. (1955). A behavioral model of rational choice. *Quarterly Journal of Economics*, 69, 99–118. *76, 88–9*.

Simon, H.A. (1957). *Models of Man: Social and Rational*. New York: Wiley. *79, 88–9*.

Slovic, P. (1974). Hypothesis testing in the learning of positive and negative linear functions. *Organizational Behavior and Human Performance*, 11, 368–76. *79*.

Slovic, P., Fischhoff, B. and Lichtenstein, S. (1979). Rating the risks. *Environment*, 21, 14–20, 36–9. *91*.

Snyder, M.L. and Jones, E.E. (1974). Attitude attribution when behavior is constrained. *Journal of Experimental Social Psychology*, 10, 585–600. *51*.

Solomon, R.L. (1980). The opponent-process theory of acquired motivation: The cost of pleasure and the benefits of pain. *American Psychologist*, 35, 691–712. *109, 112*.

Spears, R., van der Pligt, J. and Eiser, J.R. (1986). Generalizing the illusory correlation effect in social perception. *Journal of Personality and Social Psychology*, 51, 1127–34. *56, 96*.

Stevens, D.P., Staff, R.N. and Mackay, I.R. (1977). What happens when hospitalized patients see their records? *Annals of Internal Medicine*, 86, 474–7. *135*.

Stevens, L. and Jones, E.E. (1976). Defensive attribution and the Kelley cube. *Journal of Personality and Social Psychology*, 34, 809–20. *56*.

Storms, M.D. (1973). Video tape and the attribution process: reversing actors' and observers' point of view. *Journal of Personality and Social Psychology*, 27, 165–75. *62–3*.

Streufert, S. and Streufert, S.C. (1978). *Behavior in the Complex Environment*. Washington, D.C.: Winston. *22*.

Sundstrom, E., DeVault, R. and Peele, E. (1981). Acceptance of a nuclear power plant: applications of the expectancy value model. In A. Baum and J.E. Singer (eds). *Advances in Environmental Psychology*, vol. 3. Hillsdale, N.J.: Erlbaum. *79*.

Sutton, S.R. (1982). Fear-arousing communications: A critical examination of theory and research. In J.R. Eiser (ed.). *Social Psychology and Behavioral Medicine*. Chichester: Wiley. *129*.

Sutton, S.R. and Eiser, J.R. (1984). The effect of fear-arousing communications on cigarette smoking: An expectancy-value approach. *Journal of Behavioral Medicine*, 7, 13–33. *124*.

Sutton, S.R., Marsh, A. and Matheson, J. (1987). Explaining smokers' decisions to stop: Test of an expectancy-value approach. *Social Behaviour*, 2, 35–49. *124, 130*.

Swets, J.A. (1973). The receiver operating characteristic in psychology. *Science*, 182, 990–1000. *142*.

Tajfel, H. (1959). Quantitative judgement in social perception. *British Journal of Psychology*, 50, 16–29. *10*.

Tajfel, H. (ed.) (1978). *Differentiation between Social Groups: Studies in the social psychology of intergroup relations*. London: Academic Press. *115*.

Tajfel, H. and Wilkes, A.L. (1963). Classification and quantitative judgement. *British Journal of Psychology*, 54, 101–14. *10*.

Tarpy, R.M. (1982). *Principles of Animal Learning and Motivation*. Glenview, Ill.: Scott, Foresman. *42*.

Taylor, S.E. and Fiske, S.T. (1978). Salience attention and attribution: top of the head phenomena. In L. Berkowitz (ed.). *Advances in Experimental Social Psychology*, vol. 11. New York: Academic Press. *63, 157*.

Taylor, S.E. and Koivumani, J.H. (1976). The perception of self and others; acquaintanceship, affect and actor-observer differences. *Journal of Personality and Social Psychology*, 33, 403–8. *61*.

Taylor, S.E., Lichtman, R.R. and Wood, J.V. (1984). Attributions, beliefs about control and adjustment to breast cancer. *Journal of Personality and Social Psychology*, 46, 489–502. *71*.

Teasdale, J.D. (1973). Conditioned abstinence in narcotic addicts. *International Journal of the Addictions*, 8, 273–92. *112*.

Tedeschi, J.T. and Rosenfeld, P. (1981). Impression management theory and the forced compliance situation. In J.T. Tedeschi (ed.). *Impression Management Theory and Social Psychological Research*. New York: Academic Press. *38*.

Tedeschi, J.T., Schlenker, B.R. and Bonoma, T.V. (1971). Cognitive dissonance: private ratiocination or public spectacle? *American Psychologist*, 26, 685–95. *38*.

Tetlock, P.E. and Manstead, A.S.R. (1985). Impression management versus intrapsychic explanations in social psychology: a useful dichotomy? *Psychological Review*, 92, 59–77. *38*.

Thurstone, L.L. (1928). Attitudes can be measured. *American Journal of Sociology*, 33, 529–54. *4*.

Tillman, W.S. and Carver, C.S. (1980). Actors' and observers' attributions for success and failure: a comparative test of predictions from Kelley's cube, self-serving bias, and positivity bias formulations. *Journal of Experimental Social Psychology*, 16, 18–32. *56*.

Turner, J.C. (1982). Towards a cognitive redefinition of the social group. In H. Tajfel (ed.). *Social Identity and Intergroup Relations*. Cambridge: Cambridge University Press. *116*.

Tversky, A. and Kahneman, D. (1973). Availability: a heuristic for judging frequency and probability. *Cognitive Psychology*, 5, 207–32. *90, 130*.

Tversky, A. and Kahneman, D. (1974). Judgment under uncertainty: heuristics and biases. *Science*, 185, 1127–31. *76, 92, 95*.

Tversky, A. and Kahneman, D. (1981). The framing of decisions and the psychology of choice. *Science*, 211, 453–8. *86–7*.

Tversky, A. and Kahneman, D. (1982). Judgments of and by representativeness. In D. Kahneman, P. Slovic and A. Tversky (eds). *Judgment under Uncertainty: Heuristics and Biases*. Cambridge: Cambridge University Press. *94*.

Tversky, A. and Kahneman, D. (1983). Extensional vs. intuitive reasoning: the conjunction fallacy in probability judgment. *Psychological Review*, 90, 293–315. *94*.

Upshaw, H.S. (1962). Own attitude as an anchor in equal-appearing intervals. *Journal of Abnormal and Social Psychology*, 64, 85–96. *7, 8*.

Upshaw, H.S. (1965). The effect of variable perspectives on judgments of opinion statements for Thurstone scales: Equal-appearing intervals. *Journal of Personality and Social Psychology*, 2, 60–9. *7, 8*.

Upshaw, H.S. and Ostrom, T.M. (1984). Psychological perspective in attitude research. In J.R. Eiser (ed.). *Attitudinal Judgment*. New York: Springer-Verlag. *8*.

van der Pligt, J. (1984). Attributions, false consensus, and valence: two field studies. *Journal of Personality and Social Psychology*, 46, 57–68. *59*.

van der Pligt, J. (1985). Public attitudes to nuclear energy: salience and anxiety. *Journal of Environmental Psychology*, 5, 87–97. *169*.

van der Pligt, J. and Eiser, J. R. (1980). Negativity and descriptive extremity in impression formation. *European Journal of Social Psychology*, 10, 415–19. *14*.

van der Pligt, J. and Eiser, J.R. (1983). Actors' and observers' attributions, self-serving bias and positivity bias. *European Journal of Social Psychology*, 13, 95–104. *61, 66*.

van der Pligt, J. and Eiser, J.R. (1984). Dimensional salience, judgment and attitudes. In J.R. Eiser (ed.). *Attitudinal Judgment*. New York: Springer-Verlag. *14, 29*.

van der Pligt, J., Eiser, J.R. and Spears, R. (1986). Construction of a nuclear power station in one's locality: Attitudes and salience. *Basic and Applied Social Psychology*, 7, 1–15. *152, 160, 167*.

van der Pligt, J., Eiser, J.R. and Spears, R. (1987). Comparative judgments and preferences: The influence of the number of response alternatives. *British Journal of Social Psychology*, 26, 269–80. *95*.

van der Pligt, J., Ester, P. and van der Linden, J. (1983). Attitude extremity, consensus and diagnosticity. *European Journal of Social Psychology*, 13, 437–9. *59*.

van der Pligt, J., van der Linden, J. and Ester, P. (1982). Attitudes to nuclear energy: beliefs, values and false consensus. *Journal of Environmental Psychology*, 2, 221–31. *156, 160–6*.

van der Pligt, J. and van Dijk, J.A. (1979). Polarization of judgment and preference for judgmental labels. *European Journal of Social Psychology*, 9, 233–42. *14*.

Verplanken, B. (1987). Beliefs, attitudes and intentions towards nuclear energy before and after Chernobyl in a longitudinal within-subjects design. Unpublished manuscript. *153*.

Vlek, C.A.J. and Stallen, P.J.M. (1981). Risk perception in the small and in the large. *Organizational Behavior and Human Performance*, 28, 235–71. *154*.

Weiner, B. (1979). A theory of motivation for some classroom experiences. *Journal of Educational Psychology*, 71, 3–25. *67–9, 121*.

Weiner, B. (1985a). An attributional theory of achievement motivation and emotion. *Psychological Review*, 92, 548–73. *70, 121–3*.

Weiner, B. (1985b). 'Spontaneous' causal thinking. *Psychological Bulletin*, 97, 74–84. *72, 121*.

Weiner, B. (1986). *An Attributional Theory of Motivation and Emotion*. New York: Springer-Verlag. *70*.

Weiner, B. and Kukla, A. (1970). An attributional analysis of achievement motivation. *Journal of Personality and Social Psychology*, 15, 1–20. *68, 121*.

Weiner, B., Frieze, I.H., Kukla, A., Reed, L., Rest, S. and Rosenbaum, R.M. (1971). *Perceiving the Causes of Success and Failure*. Morristown, N.J.: General Learning Press. *68–9*.

Whitt, J.K., Dykstra, W. and Taylor, C.A. (1979). Children's conceptions of illness and cognitive development. *Clinical Pediatrics*, 18, 327–39. *136–7*.

Wicker, A.W. (1969). Attitudes versus actions: the relationship of overt and behavioral responses to attitude objects. *Journal of Social Issues*, 25, 41–78. *22, 26*.

Wolpe, J., Groves, G.A. and Fischer, S. (1980). Treatment of narcotic addiction by inhibition of craving: contending with a cherished habit. *Comprehensive Psychiatry*, 21, 308–16. *112*.

Wong, P.T.P. and Weiner, B. (1981). When people ask 'why' questions, and the heuristics of attributional search. *Journal of Personality and Social Psychology*, 40, 650–63. *72*.

Woo, T.O. and Castore, C.H. (1980). Expectancy-value and selective exposure determinants of attitudes toward a nuclear power plant. *Journal of Applied Social Psychology*, 10, 224–34. *156, 169*.

Zanna, M.P. and Cooper, J. (1974). Dissonance and the pill: An attribution approach to studying the arousal properties of dissonance. *Journal of Personality and Social Psychology*, 29, 703–9. *39*.

Zavalloni, M. and Cook, S.W. (1965). Influence of judges' attitudes on ratings of favorableness of statements about a social group. *Journal of Personality and Social Psychology*, 1, 43–54. *7, 11*.

Zuckerman, M. (1978). Use of consensus information in prediction of behavior. *Journal of Experimental Social Psychology*, 14, 163–71. *55*.

Zuckerman, M. (1979). Attribution of success and failure revisited, or: the motivational bias is alive and well in attribution theory. *Journal of Personality*, 47, 245–87. *57*.

Zuckerman, M., Mann, R.W. and Bernieri, F.J. (1982). Determinants of consensus estimates: attribution, salience and representativeness. *Journal of Personality and Social Psychology*, 42, 839–52. *59*.

Subject index